ISIS

BATTLING THE MENACE

Mango Media
Miami
in collaboration with
The Independent

Independent Print Limited

Published by Mango Media, Inc.
www.mango.bz

This is a work of non-fiction adapted from articles and content by journalists of The Independent and published with permission.

Front Cover Image: alexskopje/Shutterstock.com
Back Cover Image: Rena Schild/Shutterstock.com

ISIS *Battling the Menace*

ISBN: 978-1-63353-435-3

" ISIS can only be crushed in Iraq if they are also defeated in Syria."

– Patrick Cockburn, January 2016, *The Independent*

Table of Contents

FOREWORD

On 29 June 2014, the first day of Ramadan, the leaders of a Sunni army operating on the Syria-Iraq border proclaimed an 'Islamic State' under the rule of Abu Bakr al-Baghdadi, its new 'caliph'. For many, this was the first we had heard of the Islamic State of Iraq and al-Sham (Isis), or the Islamic State of Iraq and the Levant (Isil); but its forces, fanaticism and cruelty were to become all too familiar.

Sunday, 22 December 2013

ABU BAKR AL BAGHDADI

Who was the most successful leader in the Middle East in 2013? It is a hoary tradition of newspapers and magazines to produce end-of-year league tables listing the successful and the unsuccessful.

The results are often anodyne or quirky, but in the Middle East over the past 12 months such an approach has the advantage of cutting through the complexities of half a dozen distinct but interrelated crises by focusing on winners and losers.

In this year of turmoil, a shortlist is not so difficult to draw up, because so many leaders were in more trouble at the end of the year than they were at the beginning. The Turkish Prime Minister, Recep Tayyip Erdogan, for instance, would have been an easy winner in previous years for his undoubted success in ending the era of military coups and for presiding over unprecedented economic prosperity.

But in the past few days he has watched the sons of his most powerful ministers being arrested amid accusations of corruption while his maladroit intervention in the Syrian civil war blasted Turkey's hopes of becoming a regional power. Hubris brought on by three election victories probably explains why Mr Erdogan has lost his touch.

Another contender to top the list of successful leaders in the region in previous years would have been Israeli Prime Minister Benjamin Netanyahu. Always an under-rated politician internationally, he has been highly successful in manipulating the threat of war to get what he wants while being careful not to fire a shot. His threats to bomb Iranian nuclear facilities, always discounted as a well-sustained bluff by this column, led to severe sanctions against Iran and diverted attention from the Palestinians. For all Mr Netanyahu's denunciations of the interim deal between the US and its allies and Iran, he has not lost much, even if his influence on American policy is diminished. The most astute and experienced politician in the Middle East is probably the Kurdish leader Massoud Barzani, President of the Kurdistan Regional Government (KRG) and head of the Kurdistan Democratic Party, who has pursued Kurdish self-determination, so far within the context of Iraq, through victory and defeat. His has been an extraordinary career, with abrupt reversals, such as total defeat in 1990 being followed by sudden triumph when the Kurds took advantage of Saddam Hussein's debacle in Kuwait to seize back their heartlands in Iraq. The KRG is now one of the few places on earth enjoying a genuine economic boom, thanks to the discovery of oil and gas. Mr Barzani has balanced between the US, Iran, Turkey and the Iraqi central government in Baghdad without becoming the pawn or the victim of any of them.

Given the hostility between Turks and Kurds, one of the most remarkable sights of the year was Mr Barzani in full Kurdish uniform standing on a platform with Mr Erdogan in Dyabakir, effectively the Kurdish capital in Turkey, in November and speaking of Kurdish-Turkish brotherhood.

Kurdish nationalism is close to winning a degree of autonomy not far from self-determination in Iraq, Turkey and Syria. Unlike other successful leaders, Mr Barzani has a certain modesty and realism that keeps him from overplaying his hand when times are good.

Mr Barzani has had a particularly good year but his outstanding abilities are scarcely news. Less calculable are the achievements of Hassan Rouhani, who won the Iranian presidential election in June on a platform of greater civil rights, an improved economy and a rapprochement with the West. Almost anybody would look good compared with his predecessor, President Mahmoud Ahmadinejad, but Mr Rouhani's visit to the US was successful and was followed by the interim deal with the P5+1 (the permanent members of the UN Security Council plus Germany) on the Iranian nuclear programme signed in Geneva on 24 November.

But the deal leaves Mr Rouhani vulnerable because Iran froze and, to some extent, rolled back its nuclear programme in return for very minor concessions on sanctions - perhaps worth as little as $6 billion - which will make no economic difference to Iran. It may be that the US is now talking so tough to placate Congress and Israel, but if it turns out that Iranian negotiators reached a one-sided agreement that will bring few political or economic benefits to Iran, then the future prospects for Mr Rouhani do not look so bright. It may also be that his domestic opponents - in the Islamic Revolutionary Guard Corps (IRGC) and elsewhere - are holding back because they are convinced that the meagerness of his achievements will become apparent. President Obama publicly put the chances for a final agreement at 50:50. The US may believe that, if sanctions have brought Iran so far, further pressure will eliminate forever its capacity to produce a nuclear device. At this stage the prospects for long-term agreement do not look so good.

But there is one leader in the Middle East who can look back on the achievements of the past year with unmitigated satisfaction. He leads an organisation that was supposedly on its way to extinction or irrelevance three years ago, but today it is an ever more powerful force in the vast triangle of territory in Iraq and Syria between Mosul, Baghdad and the Mediterranean coast.

Unfortunately, the most successful leader in the Middle East this year is surely Abu Bakr al-Baghdadi, also known as Abu D'ua, the leader of al-Qa'ida in Iraq (AQI), which changed its name this year to Isis and claims to be the sole al-Qa'ida affiliate in Syria as well as Iraq. The US says al-Baghdadi is based in Syria and is offering $10 million to anyone who can kill or capture him.

One of the most extraordinary developments in the Middle East is that 12 years after 9/11 and six years after "the surge" in Iraq was supposed to have crushed AQI, it is back in business. It is taking over its old haunts in northern and central Iraq and is launching attacks on Shia civilians that have killed 9,000 people so far this year. Yesterday it killed a general commanding a division in an ambush in Anbar province.

Al-Qa'ida has benefited from the Iraqi government failing to conciliate the Sunni Arab protest movement that began a year ago, with the result that it is mutating into armed resistance. In July, a carefully planned Isis attack on Abu Ghraib prison in Baghdad freed 500 prisoners, many of them al-Qa'ida veterans.

Even more spectacular has been the rise of Isis in Syria, where it is the most effective single military group aside from the Syrian Army. It has taken control of Raqqa, the one Syrian provincial capital held by the rebels, and has started killing off leaders of the Western-backed Free Syrian Army (FSA) that do not come over to its side. Jessica D Lewis, in a study published by the Institute for the Study of War, writes: "AQI [al-Qa'ida in Iraq] in 2013 is an extremely vigorous, resilient and capable organisation that can operate from Basra to coastal Syria." The resurgence of al-Qa'ida is already a crucial factor in promoting horrific sectarian conflicts in both Iraq and Syria.

INTRODUCTION

Flag of Al-Qa'ida

Monday, 17 March 2014

JIHADI RESURGENCE

It is now 12-and-a-half years since the September 11 attacks that put al-Qa'ida firmly on the map of global terrorism.

The US has spent billions of dollars on its 'war on terror' to counter the threat and succeeded in killing Osama bin Laden three years ago. And yet al-Qa'ida-type groups are arguably stronger than ever now, especially in Syria and Iraq where they control an area the size of Britain, but also in Libya, Lebanon, Egypt and beyond.

Al-Qa'ida-type organisations, with beliefs and methods of operating similar to those who carried out the 9/11 attacks, have become a lethally powerful force from the Tigris to the Mediterranean in the past three years. Since the start of 2014, they have held Fallujah, 40 miles west of Baghdad, much of the upper Euphrates valley, and exert increasing control over the Sunni heartlands of northern Iraq. In Syria, their fighters occupy villages and towns from the outskirts of Damascus to the border with Turkey, including the oilfields in the north-east of the country. Overall, they are now the most powerful military force in an area the size of Britain.

The spectacular resurgence of al-Qa'ida and its offshoots has happened despite the huge expansion of American and British intelligence services and their budgets after 9/11. Since then, the US, closely followed by Britain, has fought wars in Afghanistan and Iraq, and adopted procedures formerly associated with police states, such as imprisonment without trial, rendition, torture and domestic espionage. Governments justify this as necessary to wage the "war on terror", claiming that the rights of individual citizens must be sacrificed to secure the safety of all.

Despite these controversial security measures, the movements against which they are aimed have not only not been defeated but have grown stronger. At the time of 9/11, al-Qa'ida was a very small organisation, but in 2014 al-Qa'ida-type groups are numerous and powerful. In other words, the "war on terror", the waging of which determined the politics of so much of the world since 2001, has demonstrably failed.

How this failure happened is perhaps the most extraordinary development of the 21st century. Politicians were happy to use the threat of al-Qa'ida to persuade people that their civil liberties should be restricted and state power expanded, but they spent surprisingly little time calculating the most effective practical means to combat the movement. They have been able to get away with this by giving a misleading definition of al-Qa'ida, which varied according to what was politically convenient at the time.

Jihadi groups ideologically identical to al-Qa'ida are relabelled as moderate if their actions are deemed supportive of US policy aims. In Syria, the US is backing a plan by Saudi Arabia to build up a "Southern Front" based in Jordan against the Assad government in Damascus, but also hostile to al-Qa'ida-type rebels in the north and east. The powerful but supposedly "moderate" Yarmouk Brigade, which is reportedly to receive anti-aircraft missiles from Saudi Arabia, will be the leading element in this new formation. But numerous videos show that the Yarmouk Brigade has frequently fought in collaboration with Jabhat al-Nusra (JAN), the official al-Qa'ida affiliate. Since it is likely that, in the midst of battle, these two groups will share their munitions, Washington will be permitting advanced weaponry to be handed over to its deadliest enemy.

This episode helps explain why al-Qa'ida and its offshoots have been able to survive and flourish.

The "war on terror" has failed because it did not target the jihadi movement as a whole and, above all, was not aimed at Saudi Arabia and Pakistan, the two countries that had fostered jihadism as a creed and a movement. The US did not do so because they were important American allies whom it did not want to offend.

Saudi Arabia is an enormous market for American arms, and the Saudis have cultivated and, on occasion bought up, influential members of the American political establishment.

A measure of the seriousness of the present situation is that, in recent weeks, Saudi Arabia has for the first time been urgently seeking to stop jihadi fighters, whom it previously allowed to join the war in Syria, from returning home and turning their weapons against the rulers of the Saudi kingdom. This is an abrupt reversal of previous Saudi policy, which tolerated or privately encouraged Saudi citizens going to Syria to take part in a holy war to overthrow President Bashar al-Assad and combat Shia Muslims on behalf of Sunni Islam.

In recent weeks, Saudi Arabia has called on all foreign fighters to leave Syria, and King Abdullah has decreed it a crime for Saudis to fight in foreign conflicts. The Saudi intelligence chief, Prince Bandar bin Sultan, who had been in charge of organising, funding and supplying jihadi groups fighting in Syria, has been unexpectedly removed from overseeing Saudi policy towards Syria, and replaced by a prince who has led a security clampdown against al-Qa'ida inside Saudi Arabia.

The US is increasingly fearful that support for the Syrian rebels by the West and the Sunni monarchies of the Gulf has created a similar situation to that in Afghanistan in the 1980s, when indiscriminate backing for insurgents ultimately produced al-Qa'ida, the Taliban and jihadi warlords. The US Under-Secretary for Terrorism and Financial Intelligence, David Cohen, warned this month that "terrorist" movements, such as JAN and Isis, were not only destabilising Syria but "these well-funded and well-equipped groups may soon turn their attention to attacks outside of Syria, particularly as scores of newly radicalised and freshly trained foreign recruits return from Syria to their home countries". The number of foreign fighters that Mr Cohen gives is a significant underestimate, since the head of US intelligence, James Clapper, estimates foreign fighters in Syria to number about 7,000, mostly from the Arab world, but also from countries such as Chechnya, France and Britain.

Al-Qa'ida has always been a convenient enemy. In Iraq, in 2003 and 2004, as armed Iraqi opposition to the American and British-led occupation mounted, US spokesmen attributed most attacks to al-Qa'ida, though many were carried out by nationalist and Baathist groups.

According to a poll by the Pew Group, this persuaded 57 per cent of US voters before the Iraq invasion to believe that there was a connection between Saddam Hussein and those responsible for 9/11, despite a complete absence of evidence for this. In Iraq itself, indeed the whole Muslim world, these accusations benefited al-Qa'ida by exaggerating its role in the resistance to the US and British occupation.

Precisely the opposite PR tactics were employed by Western governments in 2011 in Libya, where they played down any similarity between al-Qa'ida and the Nato-backed rebels fighting to overthrow the Libyan leader, Muammar Gaddafi. This was done by describing as dangerous only those jihadis who had a direct operational link to the al-Qa'ida "core" of Osama bin Laden. The falsity of the pretence that the anti-Gaddafi jihadis in Libya were less threatening than those in contact with al-Qa'ida was forcefully, if tragically, exposed when US ambassador Chris Stevens was killed by jihadi fighters in Benghazi in September 2012. These were the same fighters lauded by governments and media for their role in the anti-Gaddafi uprising.

Al-Qa'ida is an idea rather than an organisation, and this has long been so. For a five-year period after 1996, it did have cadres, resources and camps in Afghanistan, but these were eliminated after the overthrow of the Taliban in 2001. Subsequently, al-Qa'ida's name was a rallying cry, a set of Islamic beliefs such as the creation of an Islamic state, the imposition of sharia, a return to Islamic customs, the subjugation of women and waging holy war against other Muslims, notably the Shia, as heretics worthy of death. At the centre of this doctrine for making war is an emphasis on self-sacrifice and martyrdom as a symbol of religious faith and commitment. This has turned out to be a way of using untrained but fanatical believers to devastating effect as suicide bombers.

It has always been in the interests of the US and other governments that al-Qa'ida should be viewed as having a command-and-control structure like a mini-Pentagon, or the Mafia in America as shown in the Godfather films. This is a comforting image for the public because organised groups, however demonic, can be tracked down and eliminated through imprisonment or death. More alarming is the reality of a movement whose adherents are self-recruited and may spring up anywhere. Osama bin Laden's gathering of militants, which he did not call al-Qa'ida until after 9/11, was just one of many jihadi groups 12 years ago. But today its ideas and methods are predominant among jihadis because of the prestige and publicity it gained through the destruction of the twin towers, the war in Iraq and its demonisation by Washington as the source of all anti-American evil. These days, there is a decreasing difference in the beliefs of jihadis, regardless of whether or not they are formally linked to al-Qa'ida central, now headed by Ayman al-Zawahiri. An observer in southern Turkey discussing 9/11 with a range of Syrian jihadi rebels earlier this year found that "with-out exception they all expressed enthusiasm for the 9/11 attacks and hoped the same thing would happen in Europe as well as the US".

Unsurprisingly, governments prefer the fantasy picture of al-Qa'ida because it enables them to claim a series of victories by killing its better-known members and allies. Often, those eliminated are given quasi-military ranks, such as "head of operations", to enhance the significance of their demise. The culmination of this most publicised but largely irrelevant aspect of the "war on terror" was the killing of Bin Laden in Abbottabad in Pakistan in 2011. This enabled President Obama to grandstand before the American public as the man who had presided over the hunting down of al-Qa'ida's leader. In practice, his death had no impact on al-Qa'ida-type jihadi groups, whose greatest expansion has been since 2011.

The resurgence of these jihadis is most striking on the ground in Iraq and Syria, but is evident in Afghanistan, Libya, Somalia and, in recent months, Lebanon and Egypt. In Iraq, it was a final humiliation for the US, after losing 4,500 soldiers, that al-Qa'ida's black flag should once again fly in Fallujah, captured with much selfcongratulatory rhetoric by US Marines in 2004. Aside from Fallujah, Isis, the premier jihadi movement in the country, has rapidly expanded its influence in all parts of Sunni Iraq in the past three years. It levies local taxes and protection money in Mosul, Iraq's third largest city, estimated to bring in $8 million (£4.8 million) a month. It has been able to capitalise on two factors: the Sunni revolt in Syria and the alienation of the Iraqi Sunni by a Shia-led government. Peaceful protests by Sunni started in December 2012, but a lack of concessions by Prime Minister Nouri al-Maliki and a massacre at a peace camp at Hawijah last April is transmuting peaceful protest into armed resistance.

Last summer, Isis freed hundreds of its leaders and experienced militants in a spectacular raid on Abu Ghraib prison. Its stepped-up bombing campaign killed 9,500 people, mostly Shia civilians, in the course of last year, the heaviest casualties since 2008. But there is a crucial difference between then and now. Even at the previous peak of its influence in 2004-06, AQI did not enjoy as strong a position in the Sunni armed opposition as it does today.

In Syria, Isis was the original founder in early 2012 of JAN, sending it money, arms and experienced fighters. A year later, it tried to reassert its authority over JAN by folding it into a broader organisation covering both Syria and Iraq. The two are now involved in a complicated intra-jihadi civil war that began at the start of the year, pitting Isis, notorious for its cruelty and determination to monopolise power, against the other jihadi groups. The more secular FSA, once designated along with its political wing by the West as the next rulers of Syria, has collapsed and been marginalised.

The armed opposition is now dominated by jihadis who wish to establish an Islamic state, accept foreign fighters, and have a vicious record of massacring Syria's minorities, notably the Alawites and the Christians. The Islamic Front, for instance, a newly established and powerful alliance of opposition brigades backed by Turkey and Qatar, is fighting Isis. But that does not mean that it is not complicit in sectarian killings, and it insists on strict imposition of sharia, including the public flogging of those who do not attend Friday prayers. The Syrian jihadis rule most of north-east Syria aside from that part of it held by the Kurds. The government clings to a few outposts in this vast area, but does not have the forces to recapture it.

The decisions that enabled al-Qa'ida to avoid elimination, and later to expand, were made in the hours immediately after 9/11. Almost every significant element in the project to crash planes into the twin towers and other iconic American buildings led back to Saudi Arabia. Bin laden was a member of the Saudi elite, whose father had been a close associate of the Saudi monarch. Of the 19 hijackers on 9/11, 15 were Saudi nationals. Citing a CIA report of 2002, the official 9/11 report says that al-Qa'ida relied for its financing on "a variety of donors and fundraisers, primarily in the Gulf countries and particularly in Saudi Arabia". The report's investigators repeatedly found their access limited or denied when seeking information in Saudi Arabia. Yet President George W Bush never considered holding the Saudis in any way responsible for what had happened. The exit of senior Saudis, including Bin Laden relatives, from the US was facilitated by the government in the days after 9/11. Most significantly, 28 pages of the 9/11 Commission Report about the relationship between the attackers and Saudi Arabia was cut and never published - despite a promise by President Obama to do so - on the grounds of national security.

Nothing much changed in Saudi Arabia until recent months. In 2009, eight years after 9/11, a cable from the US Secretary of State, Hillary Clinton, revealed by WikiLeaks, complains that "donors in Saudi Arabia constitute the most significant source of funding to Sunni terrorist groups worldwide".

Moreover, the US and the west Europeans showed themselves indifferent to Saudi preachers, their message spread to millions by satellite TV, YouTube and Twitter, calling for the killing of Shia as heretics. These calls came as al-Qa'ida bombs were slaughtering people in Shia neighbourhoods in Iraq. A sub-headline in another State Department cable in the same year reads: "Saudi Arabia: Anti-Shi'ism As Foreign Policy?" Five years later, Saudi-supported groups have a record of extreme sectarianism against non-Sunni Muslims.

Pakistan, or rather Pakistani military intelligence in the shape of the Inter-Services Intelligence (ISI), was the other parent of al-Qa'ida, the Taliban and jihadi movements in general. When the Taliban was disintegrating under the weight of US bombing in 2001, its forces in northern Afghanistan were trapped by anti-Taliban forces. Before they surrendered, hundreds of ISI members, military trainers and advisers were hastily evacuated by air. Despite the clearest evidence of ISI's sponsorship of the Taliban and jihadis in general, Washington refused to confront Pakistan, and thereby opened the way for the resurgence of the Taliban after 2003, which neither the US nor Nato has been able to reverse.

Al-Qa'ida, the Taliban and other jihadi groups are the offspring of America's strange alliance with Saudi Arabia, a theocratic absolute monarchy, and Pakistani military intelligence. If this alliance had not existed, then 9/11 would not have happened. And because the US, with Britain never far behind, refused to break with these two Sunni powers, jihadism survived and prospered after 9/11.

Following a brief retreat, it took advantage of the turmoil created by wars in Iraq and Afghanistan and, later, by the Arab uprisings of 2011, to expand explosively. Twelve years after the "war on terror" was launched it has visibly failed and al-Qa'ida-type jihadis, once confined to a few camps in Afghanistan, today rule whole provinces in the heart of the Middle East.

SPRING 2014: CALIPHATE

Black Flag of Jihad

POINT THE FINGER AT SAUDI ARABIA

It is a chilling five-minute film made by Isis, showing its fighters stopping three large trucks on what looks like the main highway linking Syria and Iraq. A burly bearded gunman takes the ID cards of the drivers who stand nervously in front of him.

"You are all Shia," he says threateningly.

"No, we are Sunni from Homs," says one of the drivers in a low, hopeless tone of voice. "May Allah give you victory."

"We just want to live," pleads another driver. "We are here because we want to earn a living." The Isis man puts them through a test to see if they are Sunni. "How many times do you kneel for the dawn prayer?" he asks. Their answers vary between three and five.

"What are the Alawites doing with the honour of Syria?" rhetorically asks the gunman who by this stage has been joined by other fighters. "They are raping women and killing Muslims. From your talk you are polytheists." The three drivers are taken to the side road and there is gunfire as they are murdered.

The armed opposition in Syria and Iraq is today dominated by Salafi jihadists, fundamentalist Islamic fighters committed to holy war. Those killing non-Sunni drivers on the Damascus-Baghdad road are an all too typical example of this. Western governments may not care very much how many Shia die in Syria, Iraq or Pakistan, but they can see that Sunni movements with beliefs similar to the al-Qa'ida of Osama bin Laden, today have a base in Iraq and Syria far larger than anything they enjoyed in Afghanistan before 9/11 when they were subordinate to the Taliban.

The pretence that the Western-backed and supposedly secular FSA was leading the fight to overthrow President Bashar al-Assad finally evaporated last December as jihadists overran their supply depots and killed their commanders.

In the past six months there have been signs of real anger in Washington at actions by Saudi Arabia and the Sunni monarchies of the Gulf in supplying and financing jihadi warlords in Syria who are now so powerful. US Secretary of State John Kerry privately criticised Prince Bandar bin Sultan, head of Saudi intelligence since 2012 and former Saudi ambassador in Washington, who had been masterminding the campaign to overthrow the Assad government.

He struck back by denouncing President Obama for not intervening militarily in Syria when chemical weapons were used against civilians.

Last month, it was revealed that Prince Bandar, while remaining intelligence chief, was no longer in charge of Saudi policy in Syria. He has been replaced by interior minister Mohammed bin Nayef, who gets on with the US and is chiefly known for his campaign against al-Qa'ida in the Arabian Peninsula (AQAP).

Prince Miteb bin Abdullah, son of the Saudi King Abdullah and head of the Saudi National Guard, will also play a role in formulating a new Syrian policy. Saudi Arabia's differences with some of the other Gulf monarchies are becoming more explicit, with the Saudis, Bahrain and the United Arab Emirates withdrawing their ambassadors from Qatar this month. This was primarily because of Qatar's backing for the Muslim Brotherhood in Egypt, but also for its funding and supplying of out-of-control jihadi groups in Syria. Saudi Arabia took over from Qatar as the main funder of the Syrian rebels last summer. But Saudi involvement is much deeper and more long term than this, with more fighters coming from Saudi Arabia than from any other country.

Saudi preachers call vehemently for armed intervention against Assad, either by individual volunteers or by states. The beliefs of Wahhabism, the puritanical literalist Saudi version of Islam, are not much different from those of al-Qa'ida or other Salafi jihadist groups in Syria, Iraq, Afghanistan, Pakistan, Egypt and Libya.

The Saudis have always ideologically opposed Shi'ism as a heresy, much as Roman Catholics in Reformation Europe detested and sought to eliminate Protestantism. This hostility goes back to the alliance between the Wahhabis and the House of Saud dating from the 18th century. But the key date for the development of the jihadist movements as political players is 1979, with the Soviet invasion of Afghanistan and the Iranian revolution, when Ayatollah Khomeini turned Iran into a Shia theocracy.

During the 1980s, an alliance was born between Saudi Arabia, Pakistan (or more properly the Pakistani army) and the US which has proved extraordinarily durable. It has been one of the main supports of American predominance in the region, but also provided a seed plot for jihadist movements of which Osama Bin Laden's al-Qa'ida was originally only one strain.

The shock of 9/11 provided a Pearl Harbour moment in the US when public revulsion and fear could be manipulated to implement a pre-existing neo-conservative agenda by targeting Saddam Hussein and invading Iraq. A reason for waterboarding al-Qa'ida suspects was to extract confessions implicating Iraq rather than Saudi Arabia.

The 9/11 Commission report identified Saudi Arabia as the main source of al-Qa'ida financing. But six years after the attack - at the height of US-al-Qa'ida military conflict in Iraq in 2007 - Stuart Levey, the Under-Secretary of the US Treasury in charge of monitoring and impeding terror financing, told ABC News that, when it came to al-Qa'ida, "if I could somehow snap my fingers and cut off the funding from one country, it would be Saudi Arabia." He added that not one person identified by the US or the UN as funding terrorism had been prosecuted by the Saudis.

Despite this high-level frustration at the Saudis for not cooperating, nothing much had improved a couple of years later. US Secretary of State Hillary Clinton wrote in December 2009 in a cable released by Wikileaks: "Saudi Arabia remains a critical financial support base for al-Qa'ida, the Taliban, LeT [Lashkar-e-Taiba in Pakistan] and other terrorist groups." She complained that in so far as Saudi Arabia did act against al-Qa'ida, it was as a domestic threat and not against its activities abroad.

The US Under-Secretary for Terrorism and Financial Intelligence, David Cohen, last week praised Saudi Arabia for progress in stamping out al-Qa'ida funding sources within its own borders, but said that other jihadist groups could access donors in the kingdom.

Saudi Arabia is not alone among the Gulf monarchies in supporting jihadists. Mr Cohen says sourly that "our ally Kuwait has become the epicentre for fundraising for terrorist groups in Syria". He complains particularly of the appointment of Nayef al-Ajmi as both Minister of Justice and Minister of Islamic Endowments (Awqaf) and Islamic Affairs. He says: "Al-Ajmi has a history of promoting jihad in Syria. In fact, his image has been featured on fundraising posters for a prominent al-Nusra Front financier." He adds that the Awqaf ministry has recently announced that fundraisers can now collect donations for the Syrian people at Kuwait mosques, opening the door wide to jihadist fundraisers.

A further point coming across strongly in leaked American diplomatic traffic is the extent to which the Saudis gave priority to confronting the Shia. Here the paranoia runs deep: take Pakistan, Saudi Arabia's most important Muslim ally, of which a senior Saudi diplomat said that "we are not observers in Pakistan, we are participants". Pre-9/11, only Saudi Arabia, Pakistan and the United Arab Emirates (UAE) had given official recognition to the Taliban as the government of Afghanistan.

There is something hysterical and exaggerated about Saudi fear of Shia expansionism, since the Shia are only powerful in the handful of countries where they are in the majority or are a strong minority. Of 57 Muslim countries, just four have a Shia majority.

Nevertheless, the Saudis were highly suspicious of Pakistani President Asif Ali Zardari and made clear they would have much preferred a military dictatorship in Pakistan. The reason for the dislike was sectarian, according to UAE foreign minister Sheikh Abdullah bin Zayed who told the Americans that "Saudi Arabia suspects that Zardari is Shia, this creating Saudi concern of a Shia triangle in the region between Iran, the Maliki government in Iraq, and Pakistan under Zardari".

Sectarian hostility to the Shia as heretics is combined with fear and loathing of Iran. King Abdullah continuously urged America to attack Iran and "cut off the head of the snake". Rolling back the influence of the Shia majority in Iraq was another priority.

Here was another reason why so many Saudis sympathised with the actions of jihadists in Iraq against the government.

The takeover of Iraq by a Shia government - the first in the Arab world since Saladin overthrew the Fatimid dynasty in Egypt in 1171 - had caused serious alarm in Riyadh and other Sunni capitals, whose rulers wanted to reverse this historic defeat. The Iraqi government noticed with alarm in 2009 that when a Saudi imam issued a fatwa calling on Shia to be killed that Sunni governments in the region were "suspiciously silent" when it came to condemning his statement. The Arab uprisings of 2011 exacerbated sectarianism, not least in Saudi Arabia which is always highly conscious of its Shia minority in the Eastern Province. In March, 1,500 Saudi troops provided back up for the al-Khalifa royal family in Bahrain as they crushed pro-democracy protests by the Shia majority on the island, the openly sectarian nature of the clampdown underlined when Shia shrines were bulldozed.

In Syria, the Saudis believed that the Syrian government would be swiftly overwhelmed like that of Muammar Gaddafi. They underestimated its staying power and the support it was getting from Russia, Iran and Hezbollah in Lebanon. But Saudi involvement, along with that of Qatar and Turkey, de-emphasised secular democratic change as the ideology of the uprising, which then turned into a Sunni bid for power in which the Salafi jihadist brigades were the cutting edge of the revolt. Predictably, the Alawites and other minorities feel they have no choice but to fight to the death.

Many nonsensical conspiracy theories have evolved, peddling the idea that the US government was somehow complicit in the 9/11 attacks. The very absurdity of these theories has diverted attention from the fact that in one sense there was a conspiracy, but it was quite open and never a secret.

The price of the triple alliance between the US, Saudi Arabia and Pakistan was the jihadi movement. So far, this is anti-Shia before it is anti-Western, but, as the Isis gunmen on the Damascus-Baghdad road showed, any non-Sunni is at risk.

HIJACKED BY JIHADISTS

Just after the sarin poison gas attacks on rebel-held districts of Damascus in August last year, I appeared on an American television programme with Razan Zaitouneh, a human rights lawyer and founder of the Violations Documentation Centre, who was speaking via Skype from the opposition stronghold of Douma in East Damascus.

She gave a compelling, passionate, wholly believable account of what had happened. "I have never seen so much death in my whole life," she said, describing people breaking down the doors of houses to find everybody inside dead. Doctors in the few medical centres wept as they vainly tried to treat gas victims with the few medicines they had. Bodies were being tipped, 15 to 20 at a time, into mass graves. She contemptuously dismissed any idea that the rebels might be behind the use of sarin, asking: "Do you think we are crazy people that we would kill our own children?"

Ms Zaitouneh, 36, had been defending political prisoners for a dozen years and was the sort of credible advocate that won the Syrian opposition so much international support in its first years. But on 8 December, gunmen burst into her office in Douma and kidnapped her, along with her husband, Wael Hamada, and two civil rights activists, Samira al-Khalili, a lawyer, and Nazem al-Hamadi, a poet. None of the four has been heard from since. The group suspected of being behind the kidnapping is the Saudi-backed Army of Islam, although it denies being involved. Ms al-Khalili's husband, Yassin al-Hajj Saleh, told the online publication al-Monitor: "Razan and Samira were part of a national inclusive secular movement and this led them to collide with the Islamist factions, who are inclined towards despotism."

The kidnapping and disappearance of Ms Zaitouneh and the others have many parallels elsewhere in Syria, where Islamists have killed civil activists or forced them to flee. Usually, this has happened when the activists have criticised them for killings, torture, imprisonment or other crime. All revolutions have notoriously devoured their earliest and most humane advocates, but few have done so with the speed and ferocity of Syria's.

Instead of modernising Syrian society in a progressive and democratic manner, the Salafi-jihadists want a return to the norms of early Islam and are prepared to fight a holy war to achieve this.

Why has the Syrian uprising, whose early supporters demanded that tyranny should be replaced by a secular, non-sectarian, law-bound and democratic state, so totally failed to achieve these aims? Syria has descended into a nightmarish sectarian civil war as the government bombs its own cities as if they were enemy territory and the armed opposition is dominated by Salafi-jihadist fighters who slaughter Alawites and Christians simply because of their religion. Syrians have to choose between a violent dictatorship in which power is monopolised by the presidency and brutish security services, and an opposition that shoots children in the face for minor blasphemy and sends pictures of decapitated soldiers to their parents.

Syria is now like Lebanon during the 15-year-long civil war between 1975 and 1990. I was recently in Homs, once a city known for its vibrant diversity but now full of "ghost neighbourhoods" where all the buildings are abandoned, smashed by shellfire or bombs. Walls still standing are so full of small holes from machinegun fire that they look as if giant woodworms have been eating into the concrete.

Syria is a land of checkpoints, blockades and sieges, in conducting which the government seals off, bombards but does not storm rebel-held enclaves unless they control important supply routes. This strategy is working but at a snail's pace, and it will leave much of Syria in ruins.

Aleppo, once the largest city in the country, is mostly depopulated. Government forces are advancing but are overstretched and cannot reconquer northern and eastern Syria unless Turkey shuts its 500-mile-long border. Government success strengthens the jihadists because they have a hard core of fighters who will never surrender. So, as the Syrian army advances behind a barrage of barrel bombs in Aleppo, its troops are mostly fighting the official al-Qa'ida affiliate Jabhat al-Nusra and the Salafist Ahrar al-Sham, backed by Qatar and Turkey.

The degenerate state of the Syrian revolution stems from the country's deep political, religious and economic divisions before 2011 and the way in which these have since been exploited and exacerbated by foreign intervention. The first protests happened when they did because of the uprisings in Tunisia, Egypt, Libya, Yemen and Bahrain. They spread so rapidly because of over-reaction by state security forces firing on peaceful demonstrators, thereby enraging whole communities and provoking armed resistance. The government insists that protests were not as peaceful as they looked and from an early stage their forces came under armed attack. There is some truth in this, but if the opposition's aim was to trap the government into a counter-productive punitive response, it succeeded beyond its dreams.

Syria was always a less coherent society than it looked to outside observers, and its divisions were not just along religious lines. In July 2011, the Brussels-based International Crisis Group (ICG) wrote in a report: "The Syrian authorities claim they are fighting a foreign-sponsored, Islamist conspiracy, when for most part they have been waging war against their original social constituency. When it first came to power, the Assad regime embodied the neglected countryside, its peasants and exploited underclass. Today's ruling elite has forgotten its roots."

In the four years of drought before 2011, the United Nations noted that up to three million Syrian farmers had been pushed into "extreme poverty" and fled the countryside to squat in shanty towns on the outskirts of the cities. Middle-class salaries could not keep up with inflation. Cheap imports, often from Turkey, forced small manufacturers out of business and helped to pauperise the urban working class. The state was in contact with whole areas of life in Syria solely through corrupt and predatory security services. The ICG conceded that there was "an Islamist undercurrent to the uprising" but it was not the main motivation for the peaceful protests that were mutating into military conflict.

Compare this analysis of the situation in the summer of 2011 with that two and a half years later. By late 2013, the war was stalemated and the armed opposition was dominated by the Isis, the former official al-Qa'ida affiliate now displaced by Jabhat al-Nusra.

Ideologically, there was not much difference between them and Ahrar al-Sham or the Army of Islam, which also a theocratic Sunni state under Sharia law. Pilloried in the West for their sectarian ferocity, these jihadists were often welcomed by local people for restoring law and order after the looting and banditry of the Western-backed FSA, the loose umbrella group to which at one time 1,200 rebel bands owed nominal allegiance. In Afghanistan in the 1990s the iron rule of the Taliban had at first been welcomed by many for the same reason.

The degree to which the armed opposition at the end of 2013 was under the thumb of foreign backers is well illustrated by the confessions of Saddam al-Jamal, a brigade leader in the Ahfad al-Rasoul Brigade and the former FSA commander in eastern Syria.

A fascinating interview with Jamal, conducted by Isis and translated by the Brown Moses blog, was recorded after he had defected to Isis and appears to be reliable, ignoring his self-serving denunciations of the un-Islamic actions of his former FSA associates. He speaks as if it was matter of course that his own group, al-Ahfad, was funded by one or other of the Gulf monarchies: "At the beginning of the Syrian revolution, the file was handled by Qatar. After a while, they switched to Saudi Arabia."

Jamal says meetings of the FSA military council were invariably attended by representatives of the Saudi, UAE, Jordanian and Qatari intelligence services, as well as intelligence officers from the US, Britain and France.

At one such meeting, apparently in Ankara, Jamal says the Saudi Deputy Defence Minister, Prince Salman bin Sultan, the brother of Saudi intelligence chief Bandar bin Sultan, addressed them all and asked Syrian leaders of the armed opposition "who have plans to attack Assad positions to present their needs for arms, ammo and money". The impression given is of a movement wholly controlled by Arab and Western intelligence agencies.

The civil war between jihadist groups that started with a coordinated attack on Isis positions on 3 January is damaging the standing of all of them. Foreign fighters who came to Syria to fight Assad and the Shia find they are being told to kill Sunni jihadists with exactly the same ideological views as themselves. The Islamic State sent a suicide bomber who killed Abdullah Muhammad al-Muhaysani, the official al-Qa'ida representative in Syria, and also a leader of Ahrar al-Sham (evidence of how al-Qa'ida has links at different levels to jihadi organisations with which it is not formally associated).

Returning jihadists are finding the way home is not easy, since governments in, for example, Saudi Arabia or Tunisia, which may have welcomed their departure as a way of exporting dangerous fanatics, are now appalled by the idea of battle-hardened Salafists coming back. An activist in Raqqa, seeking to speed the departure of Tunisian volunteers, showed them a video of bikini-clad women on Tunisian beaches and suggested that their puritanical presence was needed back home to prevent such loose practices.

It is a measure of Syria's descent into apocalyptic violence that the official representative of al-Qa'ida, Jabhat al-Nusra, should be deemed more moderate than Isis. The latter may be on the retreat but this could be tactical and it has a vast territory in eastern Syria and western Iraq into to which to retreat and plan a counterattack. In any case, Jabhat al-Nusra has always sought mediation with Isis and does not want a fight to the finish. The jihadist civil war has made life easier for the government militarily, since its enemies are busy killing each other, but it does not have the resources to eliminate them.

Crucial to making peace is bringing an end to the proxy war between Saudi Arabia and Iran which is intertwined with the vicious conflict between Shia and Sunni. Russia and the US need to be at one in ending the war, as they briefly seemed to be at the end of last year. Syrians gloomily say the outcome of their civil war is no longer in Syrian hands, but in those of the US, Russia, Saudi Arabia, Iran, Turkey and their various allies. Peace, if it ever comes, will come in stages and with many false starts such as the failure of the Geneva II peace talks.

SYRIA'S POWER STRUGGLE WHO CONTROLS WHAT

KEY

● Isis and other al-Qa'ida-type organisations ● Other opposition forces
◐ Syrian armed forces ◐ Kurdish forces

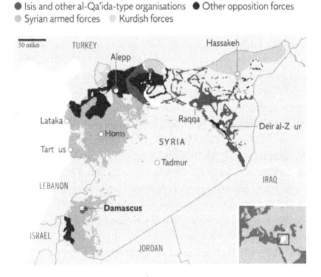

Friday, 21 March 2014

"HALF OF JIHAD IS MEDIA"

Since 9/11, the US National Security Agency (NSA) and Britain's GCHQ have justified their mass interception of their citizens' private communications by claiming that this helps them to identify "terrorists". At the same time, the US Treasury has made great efforts to detect and block financial donations to al-Qa'ida-type movements across the world. But, given the spectacular expansion of such groups over the past 12 and a half years, the efforts by these institutions are demonstrably failing.

A reason for this failure is that, in seeking to disrupt the secret infrastructure of jihadists, security services neglect the public support systems of the movements which are as important as their covert backing.

"Half of Jihad is Media" is one slogan posted on a jihadist website, which, taking media in its broadest sense, is wholly correct. The ideas, actions and aims of fundamentalist Sunni jihadists are broadcast daily through satellite television stations, YouTube, Twitter, Facebook. As long as these powerful means of propagandising exist, groups similar to al-Qa'ida will never go short of money or recruits.

Much of what is disseminated is hate-propaganda against Shia and, more occasionally, against Christians, Sufis and Jews. It calls for support for jihad in Syria, Iraq, Yemen and anywhere else holy war is being waged: a recent posting shows a romantic looking suicide bomber who was "martyred" carrying out an attack on an Egyptian police station in Sinai.

Looking at a selection of online posters and photos, what is striking is not only their violence and sectarianism but also the professionalism with which they are produced. The jihadists may yearn for a return to the norms of early Islam, but their skills in using modern communications and the internet are well ahead of most political movements in the world.

On the other hand, the content, as opposed to the technical production, is frequently violent and crudely sectarian, as in three typical pictures transmitted recently from Iraq. The first shows two men in uniform, their hands tied behind their backs, lying dead on what looks like a cement floor. Blood flows from their heads as if they have been shot or their throats cut. The caption reads: "Shia have no medicine but the sword - Anbar victories."

The second picture shows two armed men beside two bodies, identified by the caption as members of the anti al-Qa'ida Sunni Awakening movement in Iraq's Salah ad-Din province. The third shows a group of Iraqi soldiers holding a regimental banner, but the words on it have been changed to make them offensive to Sunni: "God curse Omar and Abu Bakr" (two early Sunni leaders).

More sophisticated are appeals for money for jihadi fighters by Sunni clergy and politicians, one raising $2,500 (£1,500) for every fighter sent to Syria and claiming to send 12,000 fighters to the country. One picture shows seven shelves, as if in a shop, but when you look closely you see that each shelf carries a different type of grenade. The caption reads: "Anbar's mujahedeen pharmacy for Shia."

It is not just Twitter and Facebook accounts that are used but two television stations, Safa and Wesal, based in Egypt but reportedly financed from Saudi Arabia and Kuwait, with journalists and commentators who are vocally hostile to the Shia. Wesal TV broadcasts in five languages: Arabic, Farsi, Kurdish, Indonesian and Hausa.

Hate preachers, likewise, have enormous followings on YouTube. For instance, Sheikh Mohammad al-Zughbi in Egypt calls God to protect Egypt from "the criminal traitors and the criminal Shia," as well as from the Jews and Crusaders. Another sermon entitled "Oh Syria, the victory is coming," says President Bashar al-Assad is "seeking help from these Persians, the Shia, the traitors, the Shia criminals."

These rants could be dismissed as being addressed to a small, fanatical audience, but the numbers of viewers show them to be immensely popular. Muhammad Ali Haji, of the Centre for Academic Shia Studies, points out that "the 3.9 million Saudi Facebook users use it much more than in the US or UK".

The internet has allowed jihadist fighters to establish an intimate link with their financial and political supporters because they can post pictures and films of their exploits.

Observers of rebels in Syria notice that they spend much of their time on the internet, from which they get their vision of what is happening (the same is true of pro-government civilians). Film of atrocities by the other side are a driving force for sectarian and political hatred, although some of these are fabricated.

A foreign journalist in a Syrian refugee camp in southeast Turkey noticed children watching a video of what was claimed to be Alawites cutting off the heads of Sunni prisoners with a chainsaw. He recognised the film as in fact coming from Mexico, where a drug lord had decapitated some of his rivals and posted a film of it to intimidate others.

There is additional evidence about the impact of satellite television and jihadist websites from prisoners taken in Iraq. While, like all prisoners they are likely to say what their captors want them to say, their accounts in interviews on Iraqi television ring true. Waleed bin Muhammad al-Hadi al-Masmoudi from Tunisia, the third-largest supplier of foreign jihadists to Syria, said he was a driver in his home country. In taking his decision to come to Iraq to fight, he said, "I was deeply influenced by al-Jazeera TV channel". Together with 13 other volunteers from Saudi Arabia, Jordan and Yemen, he had no difficulty in making his way to Fallujah.

Abdullah Azam Salih al-Qahtani, a former Saudi officer, said: "Arabic media and jihadist websites convinced me to come."

An interesting point that emerges from these interviews is the degree to which the war is self-generating, because veteran fighters had all lost brothers and other relatives. An Iraqi car mechanic, Sinan Abd Himood Nisaif al-Janabi, said he was deeply affected when "the Americans, who lost some of their soldiers in an explosion, killed my brother".

How far will the flood of Salafi-jihadist propaganda, most of which emanates from or is paid for by Saudi Arabia and the Sunni monarchies of the Gulf, be restrained by the recent Saudi turn against the jihadists? This change of policy has so far involved decrees against Saudis fighting in other countries. The Saudi official who was most associated with using jihadists to overthrow Assad, the intelligence chief Prince Bandar bin Sultan, has been removed from control of Syrian policy.

Ominously for the Saudi state, jihadist social media has begun to attack the Saudi royal family. There is a picture of King Abdullah giving a medal to President George W Bush, captioned: "Medal for invading two Islamic countries."

Another more menacing photo on a Twitter account is taken in the back of a pickup truck. It shows armed and masked fighters and the caption reads: "With God's will we'll enter the Arabia Peninsula like this. Today the Levant and tomorrow al-Qurayat and Arrar [two cities in northern Saudi Arabia]."

But the propaganda tap cannot be switched off so abruptly because the jihadist cause has too many genuine adherents in Saudi Arabia and other Sunni states. Saudi second thoughts have come too late because jihadist movements such as Isis and Jabhat al-Nusra are well-established and have their own revenues. Isis has a tax system in Sunni parts of Iraq and both movements have control of oil wells in north-east Syria.

A deep-seated problem is that the Wahhabi variant of Islam, the creed which is at the heart of the Saudi state, is not so different from the ideology of al-Qa'ida-type groups. Both wholly reject other types of Islamic worship as well as non-Muslim beliefs.

Shia leaders are doubtful that the Saudi about-turn on its support for the jihadists is happening at a deep enough level. Yousif al-Khoei, who heads the Centre for Academic Shia Studies, says: "The recent Saudi fatwas delegitimising suicide killings is a positive step, but the Saudis need a serious attempt to reform their educational system which currently demonises Shias, Sufis, Christians, Jews and other sects and religions. They need to stop the preaching of hate from so many satellite stations, and not allow a free ride for their preachers of hate on the social media."

The Saudi educational and judicial system recognises only Wahhabism, the puritanical and literalist version of Islam as interpreted by Abdul Wahab in the 18th century. Its most rigorous adherents regard Shia and Sufis as non-believers and polytheists. Those worshipping at shrines or praying at the graves of holy men are denounced as apostates or "takfiri", against whom it is legitimate to use violence.

Shia cite a number of fatwas targeting them as non-Muslims, such as one that declares: "To call for closeness between Shia and Sunni is similar to closeness between Islam and Christianity."

Christian churches are considered places of idolatry and polytheism because of pictures of Jesus and his mother and the use of the cross, all of which shows that Christians do not worship a single God. This is not a view confined to Saudi Arabia: in Bahrain, 71 Sunni clerics demanded that the government withdraw its permission for a Christian church to be built. When the al-Khalifa royal family crushed pro-democracy protests by the Shia majority in Bahrain in 2011, the first act of the security forces was to destroy several dozen mosques, shrines and graves of Shia holy men, on the grounds that they had not received the correct building permits.

There is no doubt that well-financed Wahhabi propaganda has contributed to the deepening and increasingly violent struggle between Sunni and Shia. A study published last year by the directorate-general for external policies of the European Parliament is called "The involvement of Salafism/Wahhabism in the support and supply of arms to rebel groups around the world". It begins by saying: "Saudi Arabia has been a major source of financing to rebel and terrorist organisations since the 1980s." It adds that Saudi Arabia has given $10bn (£6bn) to promote the Wahhabi agenda and predicts that the "number of indoctrinated jihadi fighters" will increase.

So far the jihadists have largely targeted Shia or related sects in Syria, Iraq, Yemen and Pakistan, where they are numerous, and in Egypt, Libya and Tunisia where they are a small minority. But violent hostility to Shia does not mean that the Salafi-jihadists approve of Sunni or Western states. If there is another Palestinian uprising, or some such event creating pan-Islamic anger, then the West is likely to be targeted once again. All the ingredients for a repeat of 9/11 are slipping into place, the difference today being that al-Qa'ida-type organisations are now far more powerful.

Sunday, 13 April 2014

THE RAT LINE

The US's Secretary of State John Kerry and its UN ambassador, Samantha Power have been pushing for more assistance to be given to the Syrian rebels. This is despite strong evidence that the Syrian armed opposition are, more than ever, dominated by jihadi fighters similar in their beliefs and methods to al-Qa'ida. The recent attack by rebel forces around Latakia, northern Syria, which initially had a measure of success, was led by Chechen and Moroccan jihadis.

America has done its best to keep secret its role in supplying the Syrian armed opposition, operating through proxies and front companies. It is this which makes Seymour Hersh's article "The Red Line and The Rat Line: Obama, Erdogan and the Syrian rebels" published last week in the London Review of Books, so interesting.

Attention has focussed on whether the Syrian jihadi group, Jabhat al-Nusra, aided by Turkish intelligence, could have been behind the sarin gas attacks in Damascus last 21 August, in an attempt to provoke the US into full-scale military intervention to overthrow President Bashar al-Assad. "We now know it was a covert action planned by [Turkish Prime Minister Recep Tayyip] Erdogan's people to push Obama over the red line," a former senior US intelligence officer is quoted as saying.

Critics vehemently respond that all the evidence points to the Syrian government launching the chemical attack and that even with Turkish assistance, Jabhat al-Nusra did not have the capacity to use sarin.

A second and little-regarded theme of Hersh's article is what the CIA called the rat line, the supply chain for the Syrian rebels overseen by the US in covert cooperation with Turkey, Saudi Arabia and Qatar. The information about this comes from a highly classified and hitherto secret annex to the report by the US Senate Intelligence Committee on the attack by Libyan militiamen on the US consulate in Benghazi on 11 September 2012 in which US ambassador Christopher Stevens was killed. The annex deals with an operation in which the CIA, in cooperation with MI6, arranged the dispatch of arms from Mu'ammer Gaddafi's arsenals to Turkey and then across the 500-mile long Turkish southern frontier with Syria. The annex refers to an agreement reached in early 2012 between Obama and Erdogan with Turkey, Saudi Arabia and Qatar supplying funding. Front companies, purporting to be Australian, were set up, employing former US soldiers who were in charge of obtaining and transporting the weapons. According to Hersh, the MI6 presence enabled the CIA to avoid reporting the operation to Congress, as required by law, since it could be presented as a liaison mission.

The US involvement in the rat line ended unhappily when its consulate was stormed by Libyan militiamen. The US diplomatic presence in Benghazi had been dwarfed by that of the CIA and, when US personnel were airlifted out of the city in the aftermath of the attack, only seven were reportedly from the State Department and 23 were CIA officers. The disaster in Benghazi, which soon ballooned into a political battle between Republicans and Democrats in Washington, severely loosened US control of what arms were going to which rebel movements in Syria.

This happened at the moment when Assad's forces were starting to gain the upper hand and al-Qa'ida type groups were becoming the cutting edge of the rebel military.

The failure of the rebels to win in 2012 left their foreign backers with a problem. At the time of the fall of Gaddafi they had all become overconfident, demanding the removal of Assad when he still held all Syria's 14 provincial capitals. "They were too far up the tree to get down," according to one observer. To accept anything other than the departure of Assad would have looked like a humiliating defeat.

Saudi Arabia and Qatar went on supplying money while Sunni states turned a blind eye to the recruitment of jihadis and to preachers stirring up sectarian hatred against the Shia. But for Turkey the situation was worse. Efforts to project its power were faltering and all its chosen proxies - from Egypt to Iraq - were in trouble. It was evident that al-Qa'ida-type fighters, including Jahat al-Nusra, Isis and Ahrar al-Sham were highly dependent on Turkish border crossings for supplies, recruits and the ability to reach safety. The heaviest intra-rebel battles were for control of these crossings. Turkey's military intelligence (MIT), and the paramilitary Gendarmerie played a growing role in directing and training jihadis and Jabhat al-Nusra in particular.

The Hersh article alleges that the MIT went further and instructed Jabhat al-Nusra on how to stage a sarin gas attack in Damascus that would cross Obama's red line and lead to the US launching an all-out air attack. Vehement arguments rage over whether this happened. That a senior US intelligence officer is quoted by America's leading investigative journalist as believing that it did, is already damaging Turkey.

Part of the US intelligence community is deeply suspicious of Erdogan's actions in Syria. It may also be starting to strike home in the US and Europe that aid to the armed rebellion in Syria means destabilising Iraq. When Isis brings suicide bombers from across the Turkish border into Syria it can as easily direct them to Baghdad as Aleppo. The Pentagon is much more cautious than the State Department about the risks of putting greater military pressure on Assad, seeing it as the first step in a military entanglement along the lines of Iraq and Afghanistan. The chairman of the Joint Chiefs of Staff, General Martin Dempsey and Defence Secretary Chuck Hagel are the main opponents of a greater US military role. Both sides in the US have agreed to a programme under which 600 Syrian rebels would be trained every month and jihadis would be weeded out. A problem here is that the secular moderate faction of committed Syrian opposition fighters does not really exist. As always, there is a dispute over what weapons should be supplied, with the rebels, Saudis and Qataris insisting that portable antiaircraft missiles would make all the difference. This is largely fantasy, the main problem being that the rebel military forces are fragmented into hundreds of war bands.

It is curious that the US military has been so much quicker to learn the lessons of Iraq, Afghanistan and Libya than civilians like Kerry and Power. The killing of Ambassador Stevens shows what happens when the US gets even peripherally involved in a violent, messy crisis like Syria where it does not control many of the players or much of the field.

Meanwhile, a telling argument against Turkey having orchestrated the sarin gas attacks in Damascus is that to do so would have required a level of competence out of keeping with its shambolic interventions in Syria over the past three years.

Monday, 21 April 2014

IRAQ ON THE BRINK OF CIVIL WAR

A wave of suicide bombings carried out by foreign volunteers entering Iraq from Syria is killing some 1,000 civilians a month, bringing the country back to the brink of civil war. Many of the bombers are likely to have entered Syria across the 500-mile border with Turkey in the expectation that they would be giving their lives to overthrow Syrian President Bashar al-Assad and his government.

The foreign jihadists are brought to Iraq by Isis, which in recent weeks has started to publicise on its Twitter feed the national origins of the bombers. According to a study by Bill Roggio, of the Long War Journal website, of 26 Isis bombers in one much-fought over Iraqi province, Diyala, north-east of Baghdad, no less than 24 were foreigners whose noms de guerre indicate that the majority came from North Africa, with 10 from Tunisia, five from Saudi Arabia, two each from Libya and Egypt, and one each from Denmark, Chechnya, Iran and Tajikistan.

Isis, which is seeking to establish an Islamic state in Iraq and Syria, does not recognise the border between the two countries. The bombers carried out their missions between September 2012 and to-day, but there has been a sharp escalation in bombings, usually aimed at killing as many Shia as possible, over the past year, with 9,571 ci-vilians killed in 2013 and 3,630 killed so far in 2014.

The Iraqi government has for the first time become more open about which foreign states it holds responsible for supporting foreign jihadists fighting on its territory. In an interview last month with France 24 television, the Prime Minister, Nouri al-Maliki, directly ac-cused Saudi Arabia and Qatar of being "primarily responsible for the sectarian, terrorist and security crisis in Iraq". He said allegations that his government was marginalising the Sunni Arab community were made by "sectarians with ties to foreign agendas, with Saudi and Qa-tari incitement".

Isis should have little problem transporting suicide bombers from Syria because it controls much of the northeast of the country, but their transit through Turkey in large numbers would require at least the passive consent of the Turkish forces. The Syrian govern-ment now controls almost all of its border with Lebanon, while Iraq's other neighbours - Jordan, Saudi Arabia, Kuwait and Iran - tightly con-trol their frontiers.

The Danish suicide bomber was identified by Isis as Abu Khattab al Dinmarki but, as with the other foreign jihadists, his real name was not revealed and his face was blurred in a picture. Isis is eager to pub-licise its pan-Islamic support, and two other of its units have also given details of their foreign volunteer bombers.

Isis has increased spectacularly in strength in Iraq over the past year. In March it staged a parade of vehicles, some of them military Humvees taken from security forces, in Fallujah.

The Iraqi government has recently evacuated the notorious Abu Ghraib prison, just west of the capital, which Isis stormed last sum-mer, freeing hundreds of its militants. Iraqi government forces have not launched a counter-attack to retake Fallujah despite Isis filming the execution of 20 of its soldiers captured there.

Some 380,000 people have fled Anbar and other provinces to es-cape the surge in fighting, according to the UN High Commission for Refugees.

Sunday, 4 May 2014

PLEDGING ANOTHER 9/11

It is only a matter of time before jihadis in al-Qa'ida type groups that have taken over much of eastern Syria and western Iraq have a violent impact on the world outside these two countries. The road is open wide to new attacks along the lines of 9/11 and 7/7, and it may be too late to close it.

Those who doubt that these are the jihadis' long-term intentions should have a look at a chilling but fascinating video posted recently by Isis, formerly AQI. It shows a group of foreign fighters burning their passports to emphasise their permanent commitment to jihad. Many of the passports thrown into the flames have grassgreen covers and are Saudi; others are dark blue and must be Jordanian. Some of the fighters show their faces while others are masked. As each one destroys his passport, sometimes tearing it in half before throwing it into the fire, he makes a declaration of faith and a promise to fight against the ruler of the country from which he comes.

A Canadian makes a short speech in English before switching to Arabic, saying: "It is a message to Canada, to all American powers. We are coming and we will destroy you." A Jordanian says: "I say to the tyrant of Jordan: we are the descendants of Abu Musab al-Zarqawi [the Jordanian founder of AQI killed by US aircraft in 2006] and we are coming to kill you." A Saudi, an Egyptian and a Chechen make similar threats.

The film is professionally made, and was probably shot somewhere in northern or eastern Syria. It is worth looking at carefully, and keeping in mind that these are not an isolated band hiding in desert wastes or mountain caves. Isis and Jabhat al-Nusra, the official affiliate of al-Qa'ida, now control, or can easily operate in, a great swathe of territory from the Tigris to the Mediterranean, and from the Jordanian border to southern Turkey. Threats, such as those made by the group burning their passports, are creating something near panic among Iraq's neighbours, who were slow to take on board last year that Syrian armed opposition had come to be dominated by al-Qa'ida or its clones. A report by ICG, "The Rising Cost of Turkey's Syrian Quagmire", published last week, cites a Turkish official saying: "The armed al-Qa'ida element will be a problem for the Turks. As a secular country, we do not fit with their ideology. What happens if they can't get what they want in Syria? They will blame Turkey and attack it." Bear in mind that the thousands of foreign jihadis who have poured into Syria and Iraq mostly got there by crossing the 510-milelong Turkish-Syrian border. The head of an influential Turkish think tank is quoted by ICG as saying that "When Turkey starts arresting them [jihadis], which it will do, we know what will happen. There will be bombs all over Turkey."

Jordan is also showing signs of extreme nervousness over support being given to the Syrian armed opposition, just across its border in southern Syria. American, Saudi and Jordanian intelligence have been working on creating a "southern front" around Daraa, the southern city where the Syrian revolt began, a front supposedly made up of moderate, secular fighters, who are both anti-Assad and anti-jihadi. This is deceptive, since an important force in such operations would be Jabhat al-Nusra which, on this front, is reportedly acting in coordination with a Jordanian, Saudi and US intelligence joint operations room in Amman.

But the Jordanians have got cold feet over the idea of a southern offensive launched from their territory. They are no longer as confident as they were in 2011 and 2012 that President Assad is bound to lose. They worry about an estimated 2,000 Jordanian jihadis in Syria, and what happens when they return to Jordan. There was a mysterious Jordanian airforce attack destroying vehicles entering Jordan from Syria on 16 April in which the Syrian government denied any involvement. The Jordanians also forbade an opposition offensive at Daraa timed to coincide with a rebel assault in Aleppo.

Even the US State Department's annual report on terrorism, issued last week, has noted that al-Qa'ida type groups are getting stronger. Its image of al-Qa'ida in the past has been along the lines of a bureaucratic entity somewhat similar to the State Department itself. It therefore takes heart from the belief that because of organisational and leadership losses "AQ's core leadership has been degraded, limiting its ability to conduct attacks." The word "core" is useful here since it can mean either "a central command" or simply "at the centre of". In practice, al-Qa'ida since 2001 has primarily been an ideology and a method of operating, not a cohesive organisation. The State Department has finally noted this, speaking of "the rise of increasingly aggressive and autonomous AQ affiliates and like-minded groups".

In reality, the situation is worse than the State Department admits, since over the last year Isis has taken over much of Sunni Iraq. It levies taxes in cities such as Mosul and Tikrit and has substantial control in Fallujah and along the Euphrates valley, through western Iraq and eastern Syria up to the Turkish border. It has captured the Fallujah dam on the Euphrates, and can flood or deny water to areas further south; at Baiji on the Tigris, north of Baghdad, it has blown up an oil pipeline, polluting the river which had been used, after treatment, to supply drinking water to Baghdad. On the western outskirts of Baghdad at Abu Ghraib, Isis has held a military parade and the famous prison was hastily evacuated. A comforting theory explaining the surge in Isis's strength in Iraq is that Prime Minister Nouri al-Maliki exaggerated its power to frighten Shia voters before last Wednesday's parliamentary election. He thereby diverted attention from his administration's appalling record of corruption and incompetence by focusing on the danger of a Sunni counter-revolution. The outcome of the election will show if this strategy had worked.

Unfortunately, all the signs are that the political and military incapacity of the Iraqi government is all too real. Its armed forces are said in Baghdad to have suffered 5,000 casualties including 1,000 dead in fighting in Anbar province in the last four months. Whole battalions are reported to have melted away because the men were not being paid, or they have not received supplies of food and ammunition. According to one report, even the job of army divisional commander can be bought for $1 million with the assumption that whoever takes the job can show a profit by making $50,000 a month through protection money and levies on vehicles passing checkpoints. After the election the government may try to repeat the US strategy of successfully using the Sunni tribes against al-Qa'ida groups such as Isis. The difficulty is that for the moment Sunni communities hate the Iraqi army and security forces more than they do al-Qa'ida.

Monday, 9 June 2014

BATTLE TO ESTABLISH ISLAMIC STATE ACROSS IRAQ AND SYRIA

Islamic fundamentalists have opened new fronts in their battle to establish an Islamic state across Iraq and Syria as they launch attacks in cities which were previously under the control of the Baghdad government.

A multi-pronged assault across central and northern Iraq in the past four days shows that Isis has taken over from the al-Qa'ida organisation founded by Osama bin Laden as the most powerful and effective extreme jihadi group in the world.

Isis now controls or can operate with impunity in a great stretch of territory in western Iraq and eastern Syria, making it militarily the most successful jihadi movement ever.

Led since 2010 by Abu Bakr al-Baghdadi, also known as Abu Dua, it has proved itself even more violent and sectarian than what US officials call the "core" al-Qa'ida, led by Ayman al-Zawahiri, who is based in Pakistan. Isis is highly fanatical, killing Shia Muslims and Christians whenever possible, as well as militarily efficient and under tight direction by top leaders.

In Iraq in the past four days, it has fought its way into the northern capital of Mosul, sent a column of its fighters into the central city of Samarra and taken over Iraq's largest university at Ramadi, in the west of the country. In addition, it launched devastating bombings targeting Shia civilians in Baghdad that killed at least 52 people.

The creation of a sort of proto-Caliphate by extreme jihadis in northern Syria and Iraq is provoking fears in surrounding countries such as Jordan, Saudi Arabia and Turkey that they will become targets of battle-hardened Sunni fighters.

The well-coordinated attacks appear designed to keep the Iraqi security forces off balance, uncertain where the next attack will come. They started on Thursday when Isis fighters in trucks with heavy machine guns stormed into the city of Samarra, which is mostly Sunni but contains the golden-domed al-Askari shrine sacred to Shia. Destruction of this shrine by al-Qa'ida bombers in 2006 led to wholesale massacres of Sunni by Shia.

The Isis tactic is to make a surprise attack, inflict maximum casualties and spread fear before withdrawing without suffering heavy losses. On Friday, they attacked in Mosul, where their power is already strong enough to tax local businesses, from family groceries to mobile phone and construction companies. Some 200 people were killed in the fighting, according to local hospitals, though the government gives a figure of 59 dead, 21 of them policemen and 38 insurgents.

This assault was followed by an early-morning attack on Saturday on the University of Anbar at Ramadi that has 10,000 students. Ahmed al-Mehamdi, a student who was taken hostage, told a news agency that he was woken up by the sound of shots, looked out the window and saw armed men dressed in black running across the campus. They entered his dormitory, said they belonged to Isis, told everybody to stay in their rooms but took others away.

One leader told female students: "We will teach you a lesson you'll never forget." They turned the science building into their headquarters, but may later have retreated. On the same day, seven bombs exploded in an hour in Baghdad, killing at least 52 people.

Isis specialises in using militarily untrained foreign volunteers as suicide bombers either moving on foot wearing suicide vests, or driving vehicles packed with explosives. Often more than one suicide bomber is used, as happened yesterday when a vehicle exploded at the headquarters of a Kurdish party, the Patriotic Union of Kurdistan in the town of Jalawla in the divided and much fought-over province of Diyala, northeast of Baghdad. In the confusion caused by the blast, a second bomber on foot slipped into the office and blew himself up, killing some 18 people, including a senior police officer.

The swift rise of Isis since Abu Bakr al-Baghdadi became its leader has come because the uprising of the Sunni in Syria in 2011 led the Iraqi Sunni to protest about their political and economic marginalisation since the fall of Saddam Hussein. Peaceful demonstrations from the end of 2012 won few concessions, with Iraq's Shia-dominated government convinced that the protesters wanted not reform but a revolution returning their community to power. The five or six million Iraqi Sunni became more alienated and sympathetic towards armed action by Isis.

Isis launched a well-planned campaign last year including a successful assault on Abu Ghraib prison last summer to free leaders and experienced fighters. This January, they took over Fallujah, 40 miles west of Baghdad, and have held it ever since in the face of artillery and air attack. The military sophistication of Isis in Iraq is much greater than al-Qa'ida, the organisation out of which it grew, which reached the peak of its success in 2006-07 before the Americans turned many of the Sunni tribes against it.

Isis has the great advantage of being able to operate on both sides of the Syrian-Iraq border, though in Syria it is engaged in an intra-jihadi civil war with Jabhat al-Nusra, Ahrar al-Sham and other groups. But Isis controls Raqqa, the only provincial capital taken by the opposition, and much of eastern Syria outside enclaves held by the Kurds close to the Turkish border.

ISLAMIC STATE THE BATTLEGROUND

Territory influenced by the Islamic State of Iraq and the Levant (ISIS)

Isis is today a little more circumspect in killing all who work for the government including rubbish collectors, something that alienated the Sunni population previously. But horrifically violent, though professionally made propaganda videos show Isis forcing families with sons in the Iraqi army to dig their own graves before they are shot. The message is that their enemies can expect no mercy.

The violence continued yesterday as at least 18 people were killed in two explosions at the headquarters of a Kurdish political party in Iraq's ethnically mixed province of Diyala. Isis claimed responsibility.

Most of the victims of Sunday's attack were members of the Kurdish security forces who were guarding the office of the Patriotic Union of Kurdistan (PUK) party in the town of Jalawla.

The explosions were the latest in a show of strength by militants who in recent days have overrun parts of two major cities, occupied a university campus in western Iraq and set off a dozen car bombs in Baghdad.

Jalawla lies in disputed territory, and is one of several towns where Iraqi troops and Kurdish Peshmerga regional guards have previously faced off, asserting their claims over the area. Both are a target for Sunni Islamist insurgents.

Wednesday, 11 June 2014

WARLORD WHO HAS PROFITED FROM CHAOS

In the space of a year he has become the most powerful jihadi leader in the world and on Monday night his forces captured Mosul, the northern capital of Iraq. Abu Bakr al-Baghdadi, also known as Abu Dua, the leader of Isis, has suddenly emerged as a figure who is shaping the future of Iraq, Syria and the wider Middle East.

He begins to appear from the shadows in the summer of 2010, when he became leader of AQI after its former leaders were killed by US and Iraqi troops.

AQI was at a low point as the Sunni rebellion, in which it had once played a leading role, was collapsing. It was revived by the revolt of the Sunni in Syria in 2011 and, over the next three years, by a series of carefully planned campaigns in both Iraq and Syria.

How far Abu Bakr is directly responsible for the military strategy and tactics of Isis (formerly AQI) is uncertain: former Iraqi army and intelligence officers from the Saddam era are said to play a crucial role, but are under Abu Bakr's overall leadership.

There are disputes over his career, depending on whether the source is Isis itself, or US or Iraqi intelligence, but the overall picture is fairly clear. He was born in Samarra, a largely Sunni city north of Baghdad, in 1971 and is well educated. With black hair and brown eyes, a picture of Abu Bakr taken when he was a prisoner of the Americans in Bocca Camp, in southern Iraq, between 2005 and 2009, makes him look like any Iraqi man in his thirties.

His real name is believed to be Awwad Ibrahim Ali al-Badri al-Samarrai, and he has degrees in Islamic studies from the Islamic University of Baghdad. He may have been an Islamic militant under

Saddam as a preacher in Diyala province north-east of Baghdad where, after the US invasion of 2003, he had his own armed group.

Insurgent movements have a strong motive for giving out misleading information about their command structure and leadership, but it appears Abu Bakr spent five years as a prisoner of the Americans.

After the old AQI leadership was killed in April 2010, Abu Bakr took over and AQI became increasingly well organised, even issuing detailed annual reports over the past two years, itemising its operations in each Iraqi province. Recalling the fate of his predecessors as AQI leader, he insisted on extreme secrecy, so few people knew where he was and AQI prisoners say they have either never met him or, when they did, he was wearing a mask.

Taking advantage of the Syrian civil war, Abu Bakr sent experienced fighters and funds to Syria to set up Jabhat al-Nusra as al-Qa'ida's affiliate in Syria.

He split from it last year, but remains in control of a great swathe of territory in northern Syria and Iraq. Against fragmented and dysfunctional opposition, he is moving fast towards establishing himself as the emir of a new Islamic state.

Wednesday, 11 June 2014

ANARCHY IN IRAQ

Islamic militants have captured Iraq's northern capital, Mosul, in a devastating defeat for the Iraqi government, whose forces fled the city discarding weapons and uniforms.

The victory by the Isis is likely to transform the politics of the Middle East as foreign powers realise that an al-Qa'ida-type group has gained control over a large part of northern Iraq and northern Syria. The US said it supported a "strong, coordinated response to push back against this aggression".

An Iraqi army colonel admitted: "We have lost Mosul this morning. Army and police forces left their positions and Isis terrorists are in full control. It's a total collapse of the security forces."

As well as police stations, army bases and the airport, the insurgents have captured two prisons and freed 1,200 prisoners, many of them Isis fighters. Roads out of Mosul are choked with refugees heading for what they hope is safety in Kurdish held territory.

A university lecturer from a well-known family in Mosul told *The Independent*: "Mosul has fallen completely into the hands of the terrorists. Everyone is fleeing. It's after midnight here. We are also packing up to leave home, but we have no idea where to go."

In Baghdad the Prime Minister, Nouri al-Maliki, has asked parliament to declare a state of emergency and called on the international community to support Iraq in its fight against "terrorism".

But in the streets of the capital, where the population is mostly Shia, there is growing panic and fear that Isis forces may take the Sunni city of Tikrit, which they are approaching, and then move on to Baghdad.

One woman in Baghdad, who did not want to give her name, said: "People are buying up food and may not come to work tomorrow because they think the situation is going to get worse."

She added that her relatives in Mosul who had been living in the western part of the city, which is bisected by the Tigris River, have moved to the eastern side that contains large Kurdish districts and is defended by well-trained and resolute Kurdish Peshmerga troops. She said: "People in Mosul have seen government forces run away so they think the government will use aircraft to bomb Mosul indiscriminately."

Mosul is a majority Sunni Arab city and traditionally the home of many families that joined the Iraqi army under Saddam Hussein. His defence minister was normally somebody from the area. Ever since the US-led invasion in 2003, control of the city by Baghdad has been unstable. In 2004 it was stormed by Sunni insurgents who captured most of it and held it for three days until they retreated after the US military appealed to the Kurds to send Peshmerga units from Dohuk inside the KRG.

Could this happen again? Many of the refugees fleeing towards the KRG and the Kurdish capital, Arbil, are Sunni Arabs but they are likely to be joined by members of small sects and ethnic groups such as the Yazidis and Shabak, whom Isis might kill.

The Kurds lay claim to large parts of Nineveh province though not to Mosul itself. The Isis success shows that the local Sunni political leadership has little influence since the governor Atheel Nujaifi only narrowly escaped from his provincial headquarters before Isis captured it. His brother Osama, the Speaker of parliament, called on

Massoud Barzani, President of the KRG, to send Peshmerga to recapture Mosul from "terrorists".

What will the Iraqi government do now? It could counter-attack and in theory it has 900,000 soldiers under arms. But the Iraqi army is more of a patronage system to provide jobs rather than a trained military force.

Though Isis took Falluja, 40 miles west of Baghdad, in January the government has shelled it and dropped barrel bombs but has failed to retake it. Soldiers in Anbar province, where much of the fighting has been concentrated, complain that money for their food and fuel is embezzled by officers and many have deserted.

Even so, the failure of the Iraqi armed forces to fight in Mosul is very striking. "We can't beat them," one officer told a news agency. "They're trained in street fighting and we're not. We need a whole army to drive them out of Mosul. They're like ghosts; they appear to hit and disappear within seconds." Two army officers claim that the security forces were ordered out of the city after the fall of the Ghizlani base which had contained 200 prisoners in a high-security prison. A further 1,000 inmates escaped from a prison called Badush, west of the city. The army and police set fire to fuel dumps and ammunition depots as they retreated, but there is no doubt that the insurgents will have captured large quantities of weapons.

Saturday, 14 June 2014

IRAN MOVING TO STOP ISIS

Iran is moving to stop Isis from capturing Baghdad and the provinces immediately to the north of the capital. The IRGC is taking a central role in planning and strategy in Baghdad in the wake of the disintegration of the Iraqi army in the country's north, an Iraqi source has told *The Independent*.

With the Iraqi army command completely discredited by recent defeats, the aim of the IRGC is to create a new and more effective fighting force by putting together trustworthy elements of the old army and the Shia militias. According to the source, the aim of the new force would be to give priority "to stabilising the front and rolling it back at least into Samarra and the contested areas of Diyala". The Iraqi army has 14 divisions, of which four were involved in last week's debacle, but there is no sign of the remaining units rallying and staging a counter-attack.

Militants driving pickups with machine guns in the back have captured two towns, Jalula and Sadiyah, in the mixed Sunni-Shia-Kurdish Diyala province. Both have been the scene of bloody sectarian fighting in the past and Sadiyah is only 60 miles from Baghdad. Iraqi soldiers abandoned their positions without offering any resistance after being given an ultimatum that they must hand over their weapons if they wanted to leave unharmed.

The Iranian President, Hassan Rouhani, told the Iraqi Prime Minister, Nouri al-Maliki, by phone that "Iran will apply all its efforts on the international and regional levels to confront terrorism."

Iraq, with its long common border with Iran and a 60 per cent Shia majority, is Iran's most important ally, more important even than Syria. The Iranians are horrified by the sudden military collapse of their ally and the prospect of a viscerally anti-Shia quasi-independent Sunni state emerging in northern and western Iraq and eastern Syria. This would create problems for Iran in Syria where it has been struggling with some success to stabilise the rule of President Bashar al-Assad.

The leading Shia clerics in Iraq are likewise anxious about the future of Iraq as the first Arab state to be ruled by Shia since the days of Saladin (in the 12th century). The senior cleric, Sheikh Abdul-Mahdi al-Karbaklai, who normally represents the Grand Ayatollah Ali al-Sistani, the most revered Shia spiritual leader in Iraq, said at Friday prayers "that citizens who can carry weapons and fight the terrorists in defence of their country, its people and its holy sites should volunteer and join the security forces".

The US, Britain and their allies such as Saudi Arabia and the Sunni monarchies of the Gulf might object to further Iranian involvement in Iraq. On the other hand, Washington's only effective alternative policy would be air strikes, but even these may not be enough to put down what is turning into a general uprising of the Sunni community in Iraq, which is five or six million strong and mainly concentrated in the north and west.

It is becoming clear that Isis is not the only Sunni militant group involved in the Sunni insurgents' multipronged offensive that was carefully coordinated. Among those engaged are the Jaish

Naqshbandi, led by Saddam Hussein's former deputy Izzat Ibrahim al-Douri, former members of the Baath party, the Mukhbarat security services and the Special Republican Guard. It is these groups, rather than Isis, which captured Tikrit.

Mr Maliki has blamed "a conspiracy" for the army failing to fight and, though he produced no evidence, it is possible senior Sunni officers in the Iraqi army were involved in a plot. Some 80 per cent of the senior officers in Saddam Hussein's army are estimated to have been Sunni and Mosul was famous as the home of many of them. Saddam traditionally picked his defence minister from Mosul.

Isis fighters are the shock troops of the Sunni offensive but are also part of a broad anti-government coalition, the unity of which may be difficult to maintain if Isis gives full range to its bigoted anti-Shia ideology and starts destroying their mosques, churches and other religious monuments. Some leaflets circulating in Mosul insist that women should not leave the house unless absolutely necessary.

The victories of Isis over superior forces in such a short space of time will greatly increase its prestige and its appeal to the Sunni not only in Iraq but in the rest of the Muslim world. It has also captured military equipment including at least two helicopters. Government forces have made some air attacks - such as one against a mosque in Tikrit yesterday - but not enough to prevent the advance of Isis, whose commanders are eager not to give their enemy time to reorganise. Intoxicated by unexpected success the Isis fighters will be difficult to stop.

For the moment, the government in Baghdad appears paralysed, Mr Maliki having failed to assemble a quorum in parliament to give him emergency powers. But even if such powers had been secured it is not clear how far they would enable him to tackle his main problem, which is that security forces are refusing to fight.

Monday, 16 June 2014

ISIS MASSACRES IRAQI SOLDERS

Iraq is close to all-out sectarian war as Isis massacres dozens of Iraqi soldiers in revenge for the loss of one of its commanders, and government supporters in Baghdad warn that the spread of fighting to the capital could provoke mass killings of the Sunni minority there.

One unverified statement from Isis militants on Twitter says that it has executed 1,700 prisoners. Pictures show killings at half a dozen places. Isis has posted pictures that appear to show prisoners being loaded onto flatbed trucks by masked gunmen and later forced to lie face down in a shallow ditch with their arms tied behind their backs.

Final pictures show the blood-covered bodies of captive soldiers, probably Shia, who make up much of the rank-and-file of the Iraqi army. Captions say the massacre was in revenge for the death of an Isis commander, Abdul-Rahman al-Beilawy, whose killing was reported just before Isis's surprise offensive last week that swept through northern Iraq, capturing the Sunni strongholds of Mosul and Tikrit.

Shia militiamen are pouring out of Baghdad to establish a new battle line 60 or 70 miles north of the capital. Demography is beginning to count against Isis as its fighters enter mixed provinces such as Diyala, where there are Shia and Kurds as well as Sunni.

In Mosul, from where 500,000 refugees first fled, the Sunni are returning to the city. Isis ordered traders to cut the price of fuel and foodstuffs, but religious and ethnic minorities are too terrified of Isis to go home. "People in Baghdad are frightened about what the coming days will bring," said one resident, but added that they were "used to being frightened by coming events".

Baghdadis have been stocking up on food and fuel in case the capital is besieged. There is no sound of shooting in the city, though searches at checkpoints are more intense than previously and three out of four of the entrances to the Green Zone are closed.

Isis may be the shock troops in the fighting but their swift military success and the disintegration of four Iraqi army divisions have provoked a general Sunni uprising. At least seven or eight militant Sunni factions are involved, many led by former Baathists and officers from Saddam Hussein's security services. But the most important factor working in favour of Isis is the sense among Iraq's five or six million Sunni that the end of their oppression is at hand.

"The Shia in Iraq see what is happening not as the Sunni reacting justifiably against the government oppressing them but as an attempt to re-establish the old Sunni-dominated type government," said one observer in the capital. On both the Shia and Sunni sides the factors are accumulating for a full-scale bloody sectarian confrontation.

The surge of young Shia men into militias was touched off by the appeal of Grand Ayatollah Ali al-Sistani, the revered Shia cleric, for people to join militias. "The street is boiling," said the observer.

Some 1,000 volunteers have left the holy city of Kerbala for Samarra which is on the front line, being the site of the al-Askari mosque, one of the holiest Shia shrines in a city where the majority is Sunni.

Asaib Ahl al-Haq, a Shia militia force close to the Iranians, is said to have recaptured the town of Muqdadiyah in Diyala and Dulu'iyah further west towards Samarra.

A problem in Iraq is that the country's sectarian divisions are at their worst in areas where there are mixed populations: the country could not be partitioned without a great deal of bloodshed, as occurred in India at the time of independence.

The Sunni-Shia civil war of 2006-07 was centred on Baghdad and eliminated most mixed neighbourhoods, leaving those Sunni who had not already fled holding out in enclaves mostly in the west of the capital.

A cadre of advisers from the IRGC is believed to be putting together a new military force drawn from the army and militias. The regular army command has been discredited by the spectacular failure of the last 10 days.

The involvement of Shia militia fighters at the front increases the likelihood of mass killings of Sunni. This had started to happen even before the present offensive in Diyala province and at Iskandariya, south-east of Baghdad, where militants were said to be building car and truck bombs and where the Shia militiamen are said by witnesses to have adopted a "scorched-earth policy".

Iraq has effectively broken up as the Kurds take advantage of the collapse of the regular army in the north to take over Kirkuk, northern Diyala and the Nineveh plateau.

The Kurds have long claimed these territories, saying they had been ethnically cleansed from there under Saddam Hussein. Many of these areas are rich in oil.

The government in Baghdad, though vowing to return to Mosul, has a weakened hand to play. Its military assets have turned out to be much less effective than even its most severe critics imagined.

If there is going to be a counter-attack it will have to come soon but there is no sign of it yet.

Isis has taken some of the tanks, artillery and other heavy equipment to Syria which might indicate that it doesn't want to use it in Iraq.

But as a military force, it has recently depended on quick probing attacks and forays using guerrilla tactics, so its need for heavy weaponry may not be high.

Sunday, 22 June 2014

ISIS FIGHTERS LOOK FOR WIVES

The Iraqi army and Isis are battling for control of Iraq's largest refinery outside Baiji north of Baghdad, with each side holding part of the complex. But in the town of Baiji itself, a few miles away, which is completely under the control of Isis, residents say they are most frightened by Isis militants going door to door asking about the numbers of married and unmarried women in the house.

"I told them that there were only two women in the house and both were married," said Abu Lahid. "They said that many of their mujahedin [fighters] were unmarried and wanted a wife. They insisted on coming into my house to look at the women's ID cards [which in Iraq show marital status]."

Isis says its men have been ordered not to bother local people if they are Sunni, but in many places they are imposing their puritanical social norms in the towns they have captured. In Mosul people were at first jubilant that Isis had removed the checkpoints that for years had made movement in the city very slow.

Merchants and farmers were ordered to reduce the prices of their goods. But tolerance and moderation on the part of Isis is intermittent and may be temporary. In one case in Mosul a woman was reportedly whipped, along with her husband, because she was only wearing a headscarf rather than the niqqab cloak covering the whole body. In some captured towns fanatical Isis militants start imposing rules about women's clothing, watching TV in coffee shops and cigarette smoking almost before the fighting is ended.

The restraint, or lack of it, shown by Isis has important political implications. When AQI, the forerunner of Isis, insisted on local women marrying their fighters during the Sunni-Shia civil war between 2004 and 2008, they alienated much of the Sunni community. They killed even minor government employees.

"I would rather have my door kicked in by American soldiers than by al-Qa'ida because, with the Americans, I would stand a better chance of staying alive," a young Sunni man in Baghdad said at the time. Such feelings enabled the Americans to create Sahwa, an anti al-Qa'ida force among the Sunni. Isis could isolate itself again through its brutality and bigotry, though its leaders show signs of recognising where they went wrong last time. Its fighters act as the shock troops of what has turned into a general Sunni uprising, but it is only one part, albeit the most important, of a loose alliance of seven or eight militant Sunni groups that could easily break apart.

For now, it is held together by a common sense of grievance and hatred against Nouri al-Maliki, the Prime Minister, and his government whom it sees as persecuting and marginalising the Sunni community. The departure of Mr Maliki will remove part of the glue holding together the Isis-led Sunni alliance.

Some strains between the Sunni rebel factions are already evident: When the Naqshabandi Army, of which Saddam Hussein's former deputy Izzat al-Douri is titular head, put up posters of Saddam in Mosul, Isis gave them 24 hours to take them down or face the consequences. The Naqshabandi Army did not want a confrontation and complied.

Government television channels try to push the idea that the Sunni coalition is already in disarray, but this is probably premature. In most Sunni towns captured by the insurgents, people say they are more frightened by the return of vengeful government forces than they are by the presence of Isis.

For the moment, the battle lines have steadied north of Baghdad after the blitzkrieg advance of Isis and its allies. The fighting for Baiji refinery has been swaying backwards and forwards for the past five days. Further south, Isis holds Tikrit, though a resident said "many people are fleeing to Erbil and Sulaimaniyah in Kurdistan because they think that if the Iraqi Army returns, it will shoot everybody indiscriminately". In Sunni areas Isis is still mopping up resistance: yesterday its fighters captured al-Qaim close to the border with Syria after a fight in which 30 government soldiers were killed.

One aspect of Isis's success receives too little attention. Its prestige has been enhanced across the Sunni world, especially among young Sunni men in bordering countries.

For a decade television in Sunni states has dwelt on the oppression of the Iraqi Sunni and it is undeniable that it was Isis forces that broke Baghdad's dominance over its Sunni minority. Isis successes may already be having an impact in Syria, where its fighters have overrun the headquarters of the Western-backed FSA in Deir Ezzor province in the north-east of the country.

In the mainly Shia city of Baghdad, there is terror of Isis breaking through and conducting a general massacre. It is noticeable that Isis has not activated its cells in Sunni enclaves and there have, by Baghdad standards, been few bombs. It may be that Isis is over-stretched, but it could be waiting for its fighters advancing from the north to get closer to the capital before activating its cells inside the city.

Sunni and Shia in the capital are both worried for a further reason. The government has handed over security in many parts of Baghdad to militiamen who have been setting up their own checkpoints. Some belong to Asa'ib Ahl al-Haq, a splinter group from the Shia cleric Muqtada al-Sadr's movements, who are well armed and wear black. There are other militias such as Ketaeb Hezbollah, no relation to the Lebanese movement of that name, who wear a green uniform like the army. Both these militias carry more authority than regular soldiers and the police, many of the latter melting away and staying at home.

Baghdadis consider these militias as semi-criminal groups quite capable of kidnapping likely targets for ransom at their checkpoints. Asa'ib Ahl al-Haq is seen as being under the influence of Mr Maliki and the Iranians but its men act generally in their own interests.

The strength of the militias was on display yesterday in Sadr City, the stronghold of the movement led by Mr Sadr. Twenty thousand armed men were paraded with heavy weapons such as machine guns, multiple rocket launchers and missiles as well as assault rifles. Mr Sadr has pledged that these militia will only act in defence of the Shia shrines in Samarra, Baghdad, Karbala and Najaf, but the state's inability to defend these holy sites illustrates how far its authority has withered in the past two weeks.

The military situation remains fluid. "My bet is that the government will not be able to retake Mosul, but Isis will not be able to keep it longterm," said an Iraqi political analyst who did not want to be named. He argued that Mosul was a traditional and nationalist city and not a particularly religious one, so Isis will ultimately be evicted by its people.

That may be so, but Isis has proved by its ferocity that it is difficult to dislodge once in power. In its Syrian capital at Raqqa on the Euphrates it publicly crucified young men who had started an armed resistance movement to oppose it.

Monday, 23 June 2014

THE BARBARIANS ARE AT THE GATE

Iran's spiritual leader Ayatollah Ali Khamenei has warned against US intervention in Iraq, but US officials suspect that Iran wants to use its cooperation in political changes in Baghdad to extract concessions in negotiations on Iran's nuclear programme. *The Independent* has learned that US officials have told Iraqi leaders that the Iranians are linking their agreement to the departure of Iraqi Prime Minister Nouri al-Maliki, seen as being under Iranian influence, to greater flexibility by the US in talks on the level of uranium enrichment permitted to Iran.

"The main dispute in Iraq is between those who want Iraq to join the US camp and those who seek an independent Iraq," said Khamenei, in words that could be interpreted as supporting the political status quo here. He added: "The US aims to bring its own blind followers to power."

The next few weeks are likely to prove decisive in determining the future political leadership of Iraq as Maliki, Prime Minister since 2006, seeks a third term in office despite recent disasters that have seen him lose control of the north and west of his country.

Speaking during a trip to Cairo yesterday, the US Secretary of State, John Kerry, said America wanted the Iraqi people to find a leader that represented all the country's communities and is "prepared to be inclusive and share power".

There is no sign of the offensive by Isis, which has turned into a general Sunni revolt, coming to an end. Isis has ceased to make spectacular gains north of Baghdad, but is mopping up towns previously under government control in the giant western Sunni province of Anbar.

There were reports yesterday that Isis had taken two key border crossings: al-Waleed and Turaibil on the Syrian and Jordanian borders respectively. In the last few days Isis and Sunni tribal forces have also taken al-Qaim on the border with Syria; Rutba, a truck-stop town on the main highway to Jordan; Rawah and Anah on the Euphrates. This brings the armed opposition close to the dam at Haditha which the Iraqi army says it has sent an extra 2,000 troops to defend. Sunni rebels control dams on the upper reaches of the Euphrates, which gives them the capacity to flood or deprive of water the Shia heartlands in the southern half of the Mesopotamian plain. The mood in the Iraqi capital continues to be panicky. There were trucks leaving the city piled high with the belongings of people seeking safety elsewhere. There is a big traffic jam outside the passport office as people look for travel documents. Prices in the markets have shot up because Baghdad receives much of its food supplies from Turkey and the north and Isis has cut the roads.

Probably untrue government propaganda on television creates a vacuum of information rapidly filled by rumours. The latest is that there will be a government offensive aimed at retaking Salahudin province starting on 29 June.

Residents of Isis-held towns and cities like Baiji and Tikrit fear a government counteroffensive may use tactics similar to those employed by the Syrian armed forces and launch an indiscriminate bombardment against Sunni population centres.

Iraq has effectively broken up and some people are on the wrong side of the line. One family in Baghdad recently got a message by phone from their son Najim, 22, who is in a unit of the Iraqi army which has fallen back from Mosul city to villages outside. Najim said he was literally starving and needed money to buy food from village stores. His family sent him about £100.

Iraq has not only been at war but its three main fragments - Sunni, Shia and Kurdish - are at war with each other or think they might be at any minute. The government and predominantly Shia forces are engaged in a full-scale conflict with Isis and the five or six million-strong Sunni Arab community who make up a fifth of the population.

The Kurds have taken advantage of the crisis to take territory disputed with the Arabs. But the Kurds are only intermittently at war with Isis, which wants to concentrate its forces against the Baghdad government. As a result, in a city like Baquba, the capital of the Shia-Sunni-Kurdish Diyala province, different parts of the city are held by Isis, the Iraqi army and the Kurdish Peshmerga (soldiers).

Iraqis see themselves as being the playthings of foreign powers and, particularly, of the US and Iran. Washington and Tehran have a complex record of open confrontation combined with intermittent and covert cooperation in Iraq. Both countries wanted to get rid of Saddam Hussein and were glad when he went. Both supported the Shia-Kurdish government that replaced him and opposed the Sunni revolt between 2004 and 2008. But the US and Iran have also competed to be the predominant influence in Iraq with unfortunate results for the country.

Maliki is a product of this strange relationship. He was appointed by the US in 2006 but was also a man who Iran could get on with. After the 2010 election he served a second term as Prime Minister because of his acceptability to Washington and Tehran.

At election time, Maliki has been prepared to play the sectarian card as the communal chief of the Shia faced by a Sunni counter-revolution. Discrimination and persecution alienated the Sunni community but until 2011 there was nothing much they could do about it. However, it is always dangerous to humble any of Iraq's communities because they will wait for their moment to strike back.

The Sunni of Iraq found the balance of power in the region turning in their favour after the revolt of the Sunni in Syria from 2011. Saudi Arabia, Kuwait, Qatar and Turkey were prepared to give financial and military aid to the Syrian rebels and this reignited the rebellion in Iraq. Isis, as its name implies, straddles the border and has created a sort of proto-Caliphate from the Tigris River to the outskirts of Aleppo.

Washington and Tehran are horrified by this new development but are finding it difficult to cooperate to stop it. Since the US supports the Syrian opposition and the Syrian opposition is dominated by Isis and al-Qa'ida groups, the Iranians wonder if the US might not be complicit in the Isis blitzkrieg that destabilised Maliki and his Shia-dominated pro-Iranian government.

In reality, the differences between the US and Iran in Iraq, Syria and over Iran's nuclear programme crossinfect each other so negotiations on the topics are bound to be inter-related. But cooperation with Iran remains politically toxic in the US. When Mohammad Naha-vandian, chief of staff to Iran's President, Hassan Rouhani, suggested last week that nuclear talks and the Iraqi crisis were connected, the State Department rejected any linkage.

Probably, in the long term the US and Iran could work out some semi-secret accommodation on Iraq. The problem is that a high de-gree of cooperation is needed immediately because the barbarians, in the shape of Isis, are at the gates of Baghdad.

Cooperation is needed to see Maliki depart as Prime Minister when the Iraqi parliament meets and the installation of a new and ef-fective Iraqi government. Khamenei is suggesting this would be a pro-Iranian prime minister being replaced by a pro-American one and this should therefore be resisted by Iran.

In practice, any new Iraqi leader will have to get on with Ameri-cans and Iranians. Whatever happens Maliki will have to go after the humiliating defeats of the last fortnight.

"The Iranians argue that the first priority is to defend Baghdad and later deal with the leadership question," says one Iraqi observer who did not want his name published. Another priority is to prevent Iraq being engulfed in a sectarian civil war much like that in Syria. Maliki is demonstrably not the man to stop this happening, but the longer he stays the more it becomes inevitable. It may already be too late.

Tuesday, 24 June 2014

US PLEDGES 'INTENSE' SUPPORT IN WAR AGAINST ISIS

John Kerry pledged "intense and sustained" support for Iraq yes-terday while urging its leaders to save their country from breaking up along sectarian lines by bringing it together.

The US Secretary of State sounded upbeat after his 90-minute meeting in Baghdad with Prime Minister Nouri al-Maliki, despite Isis, making huge gains across the giant, overwhelmingly Sunni province of Anbar, without much resistance. The Iraqi army abandoned the border with Jordan, where Sunni tribes took over the Turaibal cross-ing on a road built by Saddam Hussein as a crucial supply route during the Iran-Iraq war. "The support will be intense and sustained and, if Iraq's leaders take the necessary steps to bring the country together, it will be effective," Mr Kerry declared.

President Barack Obama and Mr Kerry have called for an inclusive government with Sunnis as well as Shia and Kurds getting a share of power. They have implied that Mr Maliki cannot stay in power if such a government is to be created, but it may already be too late for a power-sharing solution since Sunni tribes have already displaced the government as the main authority in provinces where they are the majority.

Tribes are negotiating to hand over Turaibal to Isis, which captured the two main border crossings to Syria over the weekend. A tribal leader said he was mediating with Isis in a "bid to spare blood and make things safer for the employees of the crossing. We are receiving positive messages."

The Jordanian army says its troops have been put in a state of alert in recent days along the 112-mile border with Iraq, to ward off "any potential or perceived security threats" in this sparsely populated desert area. The Iraqi army said troops had redeployed from cities in Anbar for "tactical reasons".

SUMMER 2014: THE WEST RESPONDS

Boeing F/A-18F Superhornet

Tuesday, 1 July 2014

CAN THE CALIPH ATTRACT MORE JIHADIS TO THE CAUSE?

As Abu Bakr al- Baghdadi, the leader of Isis, declares himself the caliph of a new Islamic state larger in size than Great Britain, people in Baghdad wait for a fresh assault on the capital by his fighters, who have already captured much of northern Iraq.

The move by Abu Bakr and Isis, which wants to be known as simply the Islamic State, has the power to convulse many of the 57 countries that follow the Islamic faith. The group's spokesman, Abu Mohamed al-Adnani, said: "The legality of all emirates, groups, states and organisations becomes null by the expansion of the caliph's authority and the arrival of its troops to their areas."

It is not that all Islamic radicals will rise up to follow the new caliph, but his message will attract many followers and will force other jihadi groups to choose if they are going to follow the new leader. "Listen to your caliph and obey him. Support your state, which grows every day," Abu Mohamed said. For Iraq the declaration of a new caliphate, to replace the one abolished 90 years ago by Mustafa Kemal Ataturk in Turkey in 1924, is a declaration of war, because the Islamic State is viscerally anti-Shia - who make up 60 per cent of Iraq's population and who it regards as heretics and apostates worthy of death. Its propaganda films show Shia truck drivers being questioned about how Sunni pray and, if they fail the test, they are shot in the head.

For people in Baghdad, a city of seven million people, the majority Shia, the expansion of the newly declared Islamic State is a terrifying prospect. The government counteroffensive towards Tikrit, 80 miles to the north, has stalled or been repulsed. As yet there has been no uprising by the Sunni enclaves in Baghdad or a renewed suicide bombing campaign in the capital, but Baghdadis think it could happen at any moment.

In a wide-ranging interview on security questions with *The Independent* in Baghdad, Safa Hussein al-Sheikh, Iraq's Deputy National Security Adviser, said: "Many people think there will be synchronised attacks inside and outside [Baghdad]." He said Isis had the capability to do more, and to try to repeat what it achieved in Mosul, which it captured on 10 June, adding that there were some reports of insurgents seeking to slip into Baghdad along with genuine refugees from the north. "Some days ago there were weapons discovered in one of the mosques in the al-Amariya area," he said.

Mr Sheikh said one scenario was that there would be an assault from outside Baghdad accompanied by many attacks inside the city "to affect psychologically the security forces defending Baghdad from the outside." But, at the end of the day, he did not believe that Isis "has a chance in Baghdad. They can do disruption but they can't do any victory." Aside from the regular army, the capital is now packed with tens of thousands of Shia militiamen summoned by a fatwa from Grand Ayatollah Ali al- Sistani.

Many Sunni leaders inside and outside Iraq have criticised or derided Abu Bakr's declaration of a new caliphate, but it will have a deep appeal for millions of young Sunni men for whom the political and economic status quo promises nothing but joblessness and poverty.

Mr Sheikh said the establishment of the caliphate would increase "the recruitment of jihadis" into Isis. "They will get more recruits from abroad." One piece of evidence for this is the celebrations and waving of the black Isis flag in the strongly Sunni and tribal town of Maan in Jordan, far from any Isis strongholds.

The Islamic State has a large territory from which to draw recruits and money. In the past, the Iraqi security forces found that when AQI took over an area, it could recruit between five and 10 times the original attack force. If it had used 100 men then it could expect to recruit 500 or 1,000 fighters. These may not be shock troops, and many would have joined to protect their families, but the numbers fighting for Isis have grown rapidly.

As the Iraqi Sunni, which number about five or six million, find they have joined a new state, the country as a whole is about to get a new leader. It is now considered that there is no chance of Nouri al-Maliki retaining the job he has held since 2006.

Although his coalition of parties did well in the parliamentary election of 30 April, he has been discredited by the loss of Mosul and the collapse of the army in northern Iraq. He was acting as Defence Minister, Interior Minister and supreme commander of the army, so it is impossible for him to avoid personal responsibility for the debacle.

The call of Grand Ayatollah Sistani, who makes a point of not involving himself in politics, last Friday for new leadership is regarded as decisive in ending Mr Maliki's rule, which has been characterised by all embracing corruption as politicians and officials syphoned off billions of dollars into shell companies abroad. Some $7 billion was spent on Baghdad's sewer system but when rains fell last year the streets flooded because the sewers had never been built.

Corruption was also at the heart of the rapid disintegration of the 350,000-strong armed forces when Isis attacked. Commanders drew the salaries for "ghost battalions" that didn't exist, receiving money to feed a battalion of 600 men when in fact there were only 200.

Despite the vast expenditure on the army, said to total $41.6 billion in the past three years, units were sent to the front short of ammunition with only four magazines for each assault rifle. Isis produced chilling videos showing the ease with which its snipers could wound and kill soldiers.

Mr Sheikh said one of the problems for the Iraqi security forces has been that AQI, which preceded Isis, had consisted of "small terrorist groups that could be combated by police work". But after 2011 Isis units began to gain military experience in Syria that was superior to the Iraqi armed forces'. This enabled Isis to hold on to Fallujah, 40 miles west of Baghdad, which it captured with local allies in January.

Iraqi officials say the morale of the army has improved since the humiliating loss of Mosul, almost without a fight. It has been strengthened by militias such as Asaib Ahl al- Haq and the followers of the Shia nationalist cleric Muqtada al- Sadr that have been deployed for the first time around Fallujah. Some of these militiamen have been fighting against jihadis in Syria over the past three years and have military experience.

Iraqis as a whole are either bemused or cynical about the US, Britain and Sunni Arab states such as Saudi Arabia, Qatar, Jordan and Turkey claiming to support moderate Sunni rebels in Syria but not jihadis. Officials are dubious that such moderate rebels really exist.

In any case, Mr Sheikh says that once weapons are supplied to militia forces in Syria or elsewhere they invariably find their way into the hands of extremists. He cites as an example Iranian weapons supplied to Shia militias in Iraq after 2004 that ended up in the hands of al-Qa'ida, which was killing Shia, because they were sold or went to middlemen working for both sides.

Isis is not the only armed opponent of the Baghdad government, although it is the most effective one. The Iraqi state has also been hit in the past three weeks by the Kurdish takeover of long-disputed territories in the north including Kirkuk, which are now held by Peshmerga. Baghdad officials note suspiciously that a mainly Kurdish regular army division did not fight for Mosul, but add that to be fair this was also true of mainly Sunni and Shia divisions as well.

The regime and its foreign allies hope that a new government in Baghdad will be able to offer the Sunni community in Iraq a big enough share in power for Isis's "fight only for victory" strategy to become increasingly unattractive. Mr Maliki would no longer be in office as a hate figure uniting the Sunni against Baghdad.

Life is already becoming miserable in Isis-held Mosul, with no money in the banks to pay people their pensions or salaries. Isis has not conducted any mass killings in the city but has made people nervous by collecting the names of all those who once worked for the government. In Tikrit the 200,000 population has largely fled because of lack of electricity and water, and fear of indiscriminate bombing.

But it will be difficult and dangerous for Sunni military groups and organisations which allied themselves to Isis to get rid of men who believe they are establishing the new caliphate and believe that God and history are on their side. The Islamic State of its new caliph, Abu Bakr al- Baghdadi, has many enemies but it will not go down easily.

Wednesday, 16 July 2014

ISIS MARCHES FURTHER INTO SYRIA

Isis fighters have captured much of eastern Syria in the past few days while international attention has been focused on the Israeli bombardment of Gaza. Using tanks and artillery seized in Iraq, it has taken almost all of oil-rich Deir Ezzor province and is battling to crush the resistance of the Syrian Kurds.

Isis is establishing dominance over the opposition to Syria's President, Bashar al-Assad, as other rebel groups flee or pledge allegiance to the caliphate declared by the Isis leader, Abu Bakr al-Baghdadi, after the capture of Mosul on 10 June. On Monday, the jihadists took over the rebel-held half of Deir Ezzor on the Euphrates river, raising their black flag over the city and executing the rebel commander from Jabhat al-Nusra, the al-Qa'ida affiliate that was previously in control.

The recent Isis advances in Syria, following victories in Iraq last month, are altering the balance of power in the whole region. The opposition military forces not aligned with the Syrian government or Isis are being squeezed out of existence, making obsolete the US, British, Saudi and Turkish policy of backing groups hostile to both Assad and Isis.

Isis is seeking to capture the Syrian Kurdish enclave at Kobani, or Ayn al-Arab, where some 500,000 Kurds are concentrated, many of them refugees from other parts of northern Syria. "Isis have about 5,000 fighters which have been attacking us for the past 13 days using tanks and rockets and American Humvees captured in Iraq," Idris Naasan, a political activist in Kobani, told *The Independent* by telephone. "The fighting is very heavy and we have lost three villages we are trying to regain."

He said the normal population of Kobani region was 200,000 but this number is swollen by refugees from the border area and from Aleppo. Causing particular concern is the fate of 400 Kurdish hostages taken by Isis, including 133 schoolchildren aged between 13 and 14. Mr Idris said negotiations with Isis to exchange them for Isis prisoners "took place three days ago but fell through because Isis tried to take more hostages".

Maria Calivis, the Unicef regional director for Middle East and Northern Africa, said in a statement at the start of the month that all of the children, with the exception of four who escaped, were still captive. "It has been over four weeks since the children were abducted as they returned to their home town of Ayn al-Arab [Kobani], after taking their junior high school final exams in Aleppo," she said.

There is no eyewitness information about the children but a report in the al-Quds al-Arabi newspaper said some of those abducted by Isis may have been tortured. It added that they were being held in two schools and that families living nearby said they could not sleep because of the sound of children crying and screaming as they were tortured. They said they heard three shots from the direction of one of the schools, leading them to fear that children may have been killed.

The Kurdish enclave under attack at Kobani is one of several regions which are home to Syria's 2.5 million strong Kurdish minority, most of whom live in the north and north-east of the country. The fate of Kobani has become a national cause for Kurds, particularly in Turkey just across the border. A statement from the Kurdish Democratic Union Party, whose "people's protection units" are doing most of the fighting to defend the enclave, says "all the Kurds should head towards Kobani and participate in the resistance". Mr Idris accuses the Turkish government of giving "logistical aid intelligence information to Isis". Other Kurdish sources say this is unlikely, though they concede that Turkey has helped Isis and Jabhat al-Nusra in the past.

The other main thrust of the Isis offensive in eastern Syria has been towards Deir Ezzor, where it has defeated the Jabhat al- Nusra and Ahrar al-Sham groups. They say they are out-gunned and out-numbered by Isis, which by one estimate has 10,000 fighters in Syria. Its morale is high, it is well financed through plundering banks and through the capture of oil wells in north-east Syria. Isis has been successful in winning the allegiance of tribes, which are strong in Deir Ezzor and Raqqa provinces, by allocating to them oil production from different wells that can be sold on the black market.

Isis has been engaged in a "civil war within the civil war" since the start of the year in which it battled the rest of the Syrian armed opposition, jihadi and non-jihadi. Up to 7,000 fighters may have been killed in this fighting. Isis, which has always been well-led militarily, withdrew from Idlib province, Aleppo city and northern Aleppo province earlier in the year, a retreat misinterpreted as a sign of weakness by other rebel groups, but apparently a tactically astute manoeuvre to concentrate its forces.

Fresh from success in Iraq, Isis is now counter-attacking strongly and, having taken Deir Ezzor, may seek to move back into Aleppo city from its base at al-Bab in east Aleppo province. Meanwhile, government forces in Aleppo city have been advancing against weakening rebel resistance and may soon have isolated the rebel-held districts. The Syrian army and Isis may then confront each other as the only important players left in the civil war.

The Syrian opposition has always claimed that Isis and Syrian government forces have had a sort of de facto ceasefire and hinted at undercover links. This was mostly propaganda, though regurgitated in Washington, London and Paris, but it is true that since Isis helped to take Minnigh air base north of Aleppo last summer, it has mainly fought other rebel groups. When President Assad and al-Baghdadi do confront each other, the West and its allies will have to decide if they will go on trying to weaken the Syrian government.

Monday, 21 July 2014

TIME RUNS OUT FOR CHRISTIAN IRAQ

The last Christians in northern Iraq are fleeing from places where their communities have lived for almost 2,000 years, as a deadline passed for them to either convert to Islam, pay a special tax or be killed.

Isis issued a decree last week offering Christians the three options accompanied by the ominous threat that, if they did not comply by midday on 19 July, "then there is nothing to give them but the sword".

It is the greatest mass flight of Christians in the Middle East since the Armenian massacres and the expulsion of Christians from Turkey during and after the First World War.

Isis, which now rules an area larger than Great Britain, has already eliminated many of the ancient Christian communities of eastern Syria, where those who had not escaped were given a similar choice between conversion, payment of a special tax or death.

Christians leaving Mosul - which was captured by Isis on 10 June - in order to seek refuge in Iraqi Kurdistan are being stripped of all their possessions.

A Christian man said: "The Islamic State [Isis] stopped my relatives at a checkpoint when they were fleeing and when they found out they were Christians, they took everything they were carrying, including their mobile phones. They left them only with the clothes they were wearing."

Mosul is one of the most ancient centres of Christianity and on the east bank of the Tigris river that flows through the city is a mosque housing the tomb of the Biblical figure of Jonah. This is now in danger of being destroyed by Isis, whose puritan and iconoclastic version of Islam is opposed to the worship of tombs, shrines, statues and pictures.

Tens of thousands of Shabak and Shia Turkmen, demonised as polytheists have fled their homes following raids by Isis gunmen.

The persecution of Christians, of whom there were over one million in Iraq before the US and British invasion of 2003, was slower to develop.

But a report by Human Rights Watch (HRW) says that from 14 July a number of homes in Mosul were painted with the letter "N" for Nasrani (the Arabic word for Christian). Others were painted with the letter "R" for Rafidah, a word commonly used by Sunni to describe Shia.

Mosul previously had a great diversity of Muslim and Christian communities, all of which are vulnerable. The Christians are mostly

Assyrians, known as the Church of the East, or Chaldeans, an Eastern rite of the Catholic Church.

The Yazidis are linked to the Kurds and have a 4,000-year old religion that centres on the Peacock Angel.

The Shabak, also ethnically connected to the Kurds, are mostly Shia, though some are Sunni, while the Turkmen are majority Sunni with a Shia minority.

Christians were ordered by Isis to attend a meeting with them on 16 July, but they refused to go and a decree was issued the following day offering the three options of conversion, payment of jizia or special tax by non-Muslims or expulsion on pain of death.

The decree had the black logo of Isis and was issued by "Caliph Ibrahim", who is otherwise known as Abu Bakr al-Baghdadi, the group's leader. But even before the decree was issued, the report says that money was demanded from Christians: one merchant with a mobilephone shop was asked to pay between $200 (£117) and $250 a month.

Two Christian nuns and three orphans were kidnapped for 15 days when they stopped at a petrol station. Christian churches in Mosul have been progressively occupied and despoiled.

Chaldean Archbishop Nona told HRW that four cars had come to his archdiocese compound: "Each car carried three gunmen, most of them with masks. They broke open the doors and took some small statues from inside the property and broke them outside. They took control of the premises and placed their black banners on the roof and entrance.

"They told neighbours, 'this is our property, don't touch it'."

Isis's treatment of the Shia, or any Muslims they do not believe are orthodox Sunni, has been even more brutal than that of the Christians.

A statue of the Virgin Mary was destroyed, but so were 13 Shia mosques and shrines. Some 28 Yazidi border guards were held captive for ransom for 25 days, repeatedly beaten with guns and sticks and denounced as "infidels".

HRW says that "between 13 June and 10 July, Isis rounded up at least 83 Shia Shabak men from villages on the eastern outskirts of Mosul. Seven of the men were later found dead and the rest remain missing".

Isis raiding parties have been plundering Shia villages, seizing men whose names are on lists, as well as driving off sheep and cattle and telling people to leave.

One man said that Isis told people in one village that the Shia "'shouldn't be living here, leave by Friday'. Before they left they tried to make people chant 'Islamic State! Islamic State'."

Isis may not be liked by the Sunni population, though there is not much they can do about it for the moment. But there is also deep fear about what government forces would do if they recaptured Mosul.

One woman says that Mosul University has been bombed, adding that she dreads the time when the army of Iraqi Prime Minister Nouri al-Maliki "will reach us in Mosul, killing its people or turning them into refugees".

The Sunni majority has not been targeted by Isis, whose members, a source living in the city said, are mostly non-Iraqis. He added that people "sense that the locals (Baathists, ex-army and tribes) are biding their time.

"There is no sympathy for Isis. The shops have been told to get rid of 'unsuitable merchandise' (eg women's wear, sportswear, etc) and they are complying'."

The draconian measures are coming from foreign fighters from Libya, Algeria, Afghanistan, Pakistan, etc. Their language is barely intelligible, so here is no attempt to communicate. Money is very tight, so it seems it is going into buying arms.

Friday, 1 August 2014

ISIS WINNING ITS WAR ON TWO FRONTS

In the early hours of 24 July a Saudi volunteer belonging to Isis drove a car packed with explosives towards the perimeter wall of a base manned by 300 soldiers of the 17th Division of the Syrian army near the city of Raqqa in north-east Syria.

As the Saudi raced at high speed towards the wall he was given covering fire by a barrage of artillery shells and rockets, but he did not quite make it. His car was hit by Syrian army fire and blew up with an explosion that shook buildings miles away in Raqqa city. The plan had been for 40 Isis fighters to burst through a breach in the perimeter wall made by the suicide bomber. A further 600 Isis fighters were to follow up the first assault, if it made headway.

A second Saudi suicide bomber in a truck drove towards the base, but his explosives also detonated prematurely when hit by Syrian fire. Even so, the Syrian army detachment appears to have been too small to defend the base and 50 of them were ambushed and killed as they pulled back. A Twitter account linked to Isis later showed horrific pictures of the heads of decapitated soldiers stuck on the spikes of what looks like a gate.

It turned out that the assault on the 17th Division was not even Isis's main assault which was directed against Regiment 121, a major Syrian army stronghold outside Hasakah City in north-east Syria. The regimental commander General Mozid Salama was reported killed and pictures posted by Isis show captured T-55 tanks, artillery pieces and multiple rocket launchers.

Omar al-Shishani, a Chechen rebel commander, issued a statement saying the battle had gone on for three days, during which there were "dense missile, air, artillery, tank, machine gun and sniper fire on small mujahedin assault groups". He added that 50 guns, including a 120mm artillery piece, and two tanks had been captured by his forces.

The fighting was among the most severe between the Syrian army and the armed opposition for a year. It put an end to a conspiracy theory that President Bashar al-Assad's army and Isis secretly collaborated and never fought each other. The victories of Isis, which has taken over much of eastern Syria in the last three weeks, have established its position as the dominant force among the Syrian rebels. It has driven the al-Qa'ida affiliate Jabhat al-Nusra out of the oil province of Deir Ezzor and other groups are disintegrating as their fighters defect to Isis, attracted by its astonishing victories in Syria and Iraq since the fall of Mosul on 10 June.

There is no sign that Isis is running out of steam in either the Syrian or Iraqi parts of the caliphate declared by Abu Bakr al-Baghdadi on 29 June. In both countries its fighting force is growing in numbers and effectiveness, if not in popularity. In Mosul its blowing up of the Sunni mosque above the Tomb of Jonah, as well as the destruction of at least 30 other Sunni and Shia shrines, has dismayed local inhabitants.

"Believe me the destruction of the ancient mosques and the persecution of the Mosul Christians have left everyone here helpless," writes a Sunni woman living in Mosul. "We are very angry and bitter."

But the anger is mixed with helplessness and there is no sign of a counter-revolution by the Iraqi Sunni against Isis which is becoming militarily more powerful by the day. Arabic television stations like al-Arabiya and Al Jazeera, see hopeful signs of Isis being displaced by the Sunni tribes, neo-Baathists and ex-army officers as happened in 2006 during the American occupation. But this time around Isis is expecting a stab in the back and has taken counter measures by demanding that all swear allegiance to the caliphate and arresting those it suspects of disloyalty.

Its run of victories makes Isis difficult to displace and there is no sign of these ending. It is increasing its stranglehold on Baghdad and a government counter-attack to recapture Tikrit failed dismally. Shia volunteers who answered a call from Grand Ayatollah Ali al-Sistani to help the army are streaming home disillusioned and complaining that they suffered heavy losses when they fought and were left without food, arms and ammunition. Nouri al-Maliki, whose administration is considered responsible for recent disasters, is still Prime Minister. For many Shia he is the beleaguered leader of their community whom they see as betrayed by the Kurds who expanded their quasi-independent zone by 40 per cent after the fall of Mosul.

Isis has seized most of the wholly Sunni parts of Iraq outside Baghdad, where there are large Sunni enclaves, and south of the capital where there are strategically placed Sunni towns. Advances into mixed or purely Shia districts will mean harder fighting and heavy casualties. Isis, which so far has made few military mistakes, may feel it is easier to take ground in Syria, particularly north of Aleppo from which it made a tactical withdrawal earlier in the year. It may want to eliminate or bring under its sway other rebel groups so, as in Iraq, there is no opposition military force around which its enemies can rally.

Isis has been lucky in that its advances in eastern Syria have taken place as international attention is absorbed by events in Ukraine and Gaza. The Shia political leadership has taken refuge in wishful thinking that the Sunni community is open to a powersharing deal and regional autonomy. In fact, there is no evidence that Isis or its Baathist allies want to end a war that so far they are winning. Isis might not be able to storm Baghdad by a direct assault but it could reduce it to mayhem by bombs or by blockading it. "If the fall of northern Iraq was the first act of this tragedy, then I suspect there is a second act still to come," said one Iraqi observer.

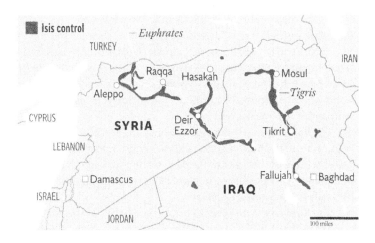

Saturday, 9 August 2014

OBAMA SENDS BOMBERS INTO IRAQ

The US has sent aircraft to bomb fighters of Isis in a desperate attempt to stop their advance on the Kurdish capital, Erbil. Two F-18 jets dropped 500lb laserguided bombs on mobile artillery firing in support of advancing Isis forces that are half an hour's drive from the city.

The US intervention comes after the surprise defeat of Kurdish Peshmerga forces by Isis, which has captured a quarter of Iraq and a third of Syria in the past two months.

Britain said it would provide technical assistance to the US, but last night refused to rule out joining air strikes in future if the bloodshed worsened.

The American air strikes, at 1.45pm local time, were authorised by President Barack Obama to protect Christians and to avert "a potential act of genocide" against tens of thousands of Yazidis, an ancient sect denounced by Isis as "polytheists". Many Yazidis have taken refuge on a mountain top in Sinjar to escape massacre and are receiving relief supplies dropped by US aircraft.

The Isis offensive has shown the Peshmerga, the fighting forces of the KRG, to be weaker than expected. They have offered little effective resistance in Sinjar and have failed to protect Christian towns in Nineveh province, of which Mosul is the capital. In a humiliating series of reverses they have retreated back to Kalak, a town on the Greater Zaab river which is the last defensible position on the road to Erbil.

The US will have to do more than launch limited air strikes if Isis is to be stopped. Since the self-styled "Islamic State" captured Mosul on 10 June it has taken most of northern and western Iraq and last month scored a series of victories in eastern Syria against the Syrian army and Syrian rebel groups.

The Kurds have lost the Mosul dam on the Tigris river, enabling Isis to control the flow of water and electricity from a hydroelectric power station. Isis could blow the dam, sending a 65-foot-high wall of water down the Tigris Valley, but is unlikely to do so because territory it already holds would be affected.

The Kurds did not expect to be targeted by Isis at this time, believing that it was fully engaged in Syria and further south against the Iraqi army.

The Peshmerga were overextended after the KRG had expanded its territory by 40 per cent via an opportunistic land-grab following the fall of Mosul, when it took districts long disputed with the Arabs.

This left the KRG with a 600-mile-long frontier to defend against Isis, with the Peshmerga, whose high military reputation is based on battles against Saddam Hussein a quarter of a century ago.

"The Peshmerga didn't have the military equipment to face Isis," says Professor Gareth Stansfield, an expert on Kurdish and Iraqi affairs at the Institute of Arab and Islamic Studies at Exeter University. "They basically use Kalashnikovs and rocket-propelled grenade launchers."

Over the past two months Isis has captured an arsenal of weapons including tanks, artillery, heavy machine guns and hundreds of American Humvees. Professor Stansfield says the Arab population of the disputed territories has become more anti-Kurdish since the KRG took over. Powerful Sunni tribes sympathise with Isis in a bid to drive the Kurds out, even putting the oil city of Kirkuk at risk. The professor emphasises that if Kalak falls there will be little between Isis and Erbil airport.

President Obama will find that US military intervention in Iraq is likely to be more than a one-off mission. The long Kurdish front line is too thinly held to repel attacks. Likewise, the Iraqi army further south has failed to rally since its rout in Mosul and Tikrit two months ago.

Its one counter-attack to try to retake Tikrit on 15 July was ambushed and beaten back with heavy losses. Shia militia rushed to the front line when Isis first reached Baghdad, summoned by Grand Ayatollah Ali Sistani, the most influential Shia cleric. But many have since returned home, disillusioned by the government's failure to provide them with training, weapons and food.

Isis may not directly assault Baghdad, but it has been increasing its hold on Sunni villages and towns to the south of the capital, an area known during the American occupation as "the Triangle of Death". This would enable Isis to cut roads between the capital and the Shia provinces of the south. It could probably take over Sunni enclaves such as Abu Ghraib, Amariya, Khadra and Dora in the west of the city.

Shia are in the majority in Baghdad though many Sunni do not believe this and are likely to try to cap their recent victories by seizure of all or part of the capital. The hopes of Shia political leaders that the Isis-led coalition of Sunni military groups would fall apart because of the atrocities of the fundamentalists has been shown to be false. Despite the expulsion of the Christians and the blowing up of Sunni shrines in Mosul there has been no counter-reaction by more moderate Sunni factions.

The military crisis is matched by a political crisis in Baghdad. Despite military defeat and a well-established reputation for incompetence and corruption, Nouri al-Maliki is still clinging on as Iraq's Prime Minister. He has in the past blamed a Kurdish stab-in-the-back for the loss of Mosul, a charge that looks ever more fantastic as Isis invades the KRG.

Grand Ayatollah Sistani yesterday made his clearest call yet for Mr Maliki to go, his weekly sermon, read out by an aide, saying that politicians who cling to power "are making a grave mistake". Mr Maliki has been laying down conditions for his departure, such as: no prosecutions for corruption, officials he has appointed to stay in office, and personal protection. A former minister commented that it is "surreal" how Iraqi politicians have debated the future leadership of Iraq while half the country has been conquered by Isis.

Friday, 15 August 2014

THE WEST VACILLATES OVER IRAQ WHILE ISIS MAKES MAJOR GAINS IN SYRIA

As the West dithers about how to respond to the plight of Christians and Yazidis fleeing fundamentalist gunmen, the fighters of Isis, are making important gains hundreds of miles away in Syria.

In the past two days they have taken the towns of Turkmen Bareh and Akhtarin 30 miles from Aleppo, enabling them to take over the strategically valuable country on the way to the Turkish border. The Isis offensive started on Tuesday, reinforcing the position of the movement as the dominant force in the military opposition to President Bashar al-Assad. Isis already controls one-third of Syria, including most of its oil wells, while Sunni rebel groups hostile to Isis are fleeing, disintegrating or joining the victors.

These little-reported developments in Syria illustrate how far the US, UK and their allies are from developing a strategy to deal with Isis and the rapidly expanding caliphate, now encompassing much of northern Syria and Iraq. Western policy in the two countries remains contradictory and selfdefeating. In Iraq, the West supports the government in Baghdad and its counterparts in the quasi-independent KRG in their battle to stop Isis. But in Syria, Western policy is to weaken and displace Assad, though his government is the only force in Syria capable of battling Isis successfully. The West, Saudis, Turks and Qataris claim they are training and funding a "moderate" military opposition but this no longer exists in any strength on the ground.

The only other military force which can resist Isis in Syria is the militia of the 2.5 million-strong Kurdish minority. Divided into three enclaves, the Syrian Kurds have been holding off Isis attacks for weeks. Surely we should be helping these doughty fighters whom Isis cannot crush? Unfortunately, we do not do so because they are the military arm of the PYD, the main authority among the Syrian Kurds. The Syrian-Kurdish Democratic Union Party (PYD) is the Syrian affiliate of the Kurdistan Workers' Party (PKK), which the US, EU and Nato label as "terrorists". This is a pity because the PKK has plenty of recent military experience and rushed to combat Isis with some success when the armed forces of the KRG fled.

One of the revelations of the last week has been that the Peshmerga ("those who confront death" in Kurdish) did not deserve their high reputation as a military force. This should not have been the surprise it was. One veteran expert on Kurdish affairs has long referred to the Peshmerga as the "pêche melba". Brave self-sacrificing guerrillas they may have been in the 1980s, but they have not fought anybody for over a decade. Even in 2003, the last time they heard a shot fired in anger, the Peshmerga advanced slowly, supported by a massive US air umbrella battering Saddam Hussein's demoralised army that was not shooting back. It is even difficult to find out how many Peshmerga there really are, as Iraqi government officials discovered when the KRG asked the central government to pay for them.

Even if the Peshmerga were more effective, they would have difficulty in defending their 650-mile-long border with Isis-controlled territory. There were reports yesterday of Isis fighters massing at Qush Tappa for another push against the Kurds. But limited American air strikes have more effect than might be imagined because they help restore Kurdish morale. Nevertheless, Isis is gaining crucial ground around Baghdad in the Sunni towns to the south of the capital, enabling Isis potentially to surround the capital.

At Jafr al-Sakhar, a Sunni town 37 miles south-west of Baghdad, local men are joining Isis and are being paid between $400 and $500 a month, though payment may be irregular. Imad Farouq, a 22-year old local man, told the online magazine Al-Monitor that "the main reason why some young people are attracted to Isis is because they are looking for jobs and it is easy to join it. Isis has opened the door for Sunnis in the area that stretches from southern Baghdad to the outskirts of Fallujah, by providing a good salary." If Isis takes over this area, it will encircle Baghdad on three sides.

The Sunni Arabs in Iraq number five or six million and the evidence is that they still back the Isis-led revolt. They might split later - many Sunni are alienated by the bloodthirsty savagery and crude ideology of Isis - but there is no sign of this happening yet. Suspicion of a Shia-dominated Baghdad government runs high, particularly as the Sunni fear that, if it retakes their cities, its revenge for recent defeats will be merciless. Moreover, Isis is well prepared to prevent any stab in the back by its allies and has been swift to consolidate its power.

The replacement of Nouri al-Maliki by Haider al-Abadi as Prime Minister is not a magic wand that will suddenly make the Baghdad government acceptable to the Sunni. They are wondering how much has really changed. Ibrahim al-Shammary, the spokesman for the Islamic Army, a resistance group, asks in a tweet: "Whoever rejoiced about Abadi; how does he differ from Maliki?" After a decade of Shia rule, government apparatus is filled with adherents to Shia religious parties who have no intention of giving up power.

Baghdad and its Western allies have been over-optimistic about the chances of the departure of Mr Maliki opening the door to compromise with the Sunni. President Obama and the Europeans have spoken of great things that are to be expected from an "inclusive government", the phrase implying a real share in power for the Sunni. This might have worked in 2010 but not today when the Sunni have already seized power in Sunni-majority provinces. Sunni politicians in Baghdad hoping for top jobs dare not return to their home cities and towns where Isis is likely to cut their heads off.

Saturday, 16 August 2014

AL-MALIKI RESIGNS

After eight years as the Prime Minister of Iraq, Nouri al-Maliki, deserted by his allies, has finally stood down and will be replaced by Haider al-Abadi, who was not always a front-runner to succeed him.

Applause for the new Iraqi leader has come from individuals, parties and countries which normally detest each other, such as Iran, the US, the Kurds, Sunni politicians and Shia militia leaders. A commentator on Iraq caustically remarked: "Somebody is going to be disappointed."

Mr Maliki's stubbornness in clinging to power was finally overcome when Iran decided that there must be a new leader in Baghdad who was not detested by the Sunnis and the Kurds. Mr Maliki's Dawa party put forward Mr Abadi as a candidate who fitted this description and this was accepted by Tehran.

The ex-Prime Minister's speech ceding power late on Thursday may have been motivated by fear that, if he did not withdraw, he would be denounced at Friday prayers by Grand Ayatollah Ali Sistani, the vastly influential Shia clerical leader. The chorus of cheers inside and outside Iraq that has greeted Mr Maliki's departure is not unanimous.

The most significant of those who say the change will make no difference is Isis and Sunni armed groups who actually control the

Sunni provinces and whose fighters have recently been knocking on the gates of Baghdad and Irbil. They see Mr Abadi, a member of Mr Maliki's Dawa party, as one more representative of a Shia religious party who will seek to maintain Shia dominance over Iraq.

But cynicism can go too far and the departure of Mr Maliki removes a man who had become a hate figure for six million Sunni Muslims.

Sunday, 17 August 2014

FEAR BRINGS THE ENEMIES OF ISIS TOGETHER AT LAST

Fear of Isis is the new uniting factor for states in the Middle East and beyond who normally hate each other. The sudden emergence of Isis's still expanding caliphate, with its terrifying blend of brutality, bigotry and military effectiveness, provides a common enemy for the US, Iran, EU states, Saudi Arabia, Turkey and, in Iraq, Shia, Kurds and anti-Isis Sunni.

It was the capture of Mosul by Isis on 10 June which ended the eight-year rule of Nouri al-Maliki, who withdrew his candidacy for a third term as prime minister last Thursday. A diversity of Iraqi politicians and parties, intermittently supported by foreign powers, have been trying to get rid of him for years, but they failed because of their disunity and his control of the Iraqi state. It was Isis gunmen in their captured Humvees patrolling the roads an hour's drive from Baghdad that created the determination to finally get rid of Mr Maliki.

However deep the differences between Washington and Tehran, they were equally horrified by the prospect of Isis advancing on Baghdad and Erbil. Saudi Arabia has openly or covertly opposed Iran and Shia Islam since the overthrow of the Shah in 1979, but is seriously threatened by Isis, whose ideology is not much different from Saudi Wahhabism but challenges the legitimacy of the house of Saud. Last Friday in Mecca, the influential imam and preacher at the Grand Mosque, Sheikh Abdul-Rahman al-Sudais, called for a code of conduct to stop leaders, scholars and young people supporting violence and "terror". An implication of this is that Saudi Arabia will suppress pro-jihadi propaganda on the internet and satellite television which it has previously encouraged.

The Iranians are also facing a more menacing future as Isis fighters tighten their grip on Diyala province in Iraq, which is on the

Iranian border. A year ago a senior member of the IRGC explained how necessary it was for Iranian security to fight in Damascus although it is 870 miles from Tehran; but last week Isis, which considers Shia to be heretics worthy of death, captured the town of Jalawla, 25 miles from Iran. No wonder Iran was willing to say goodbye to Mr Maliki, whom it had so long defended, to end the political crisis in Baghdad.

The realisation of the danger posed by Isis did not come immediately with the fall of Mosul and Tikrit. In Baghdad, and abroad, there was wishful thinking that Isis was the fanatical shock-troop of an insurgent Sunni community in Iraq; and that once Mr Maliki was gone and reforms acceptable to the Sunni were implemented, then traditional tribal and non-Isis military leaders would reassert themselves and get rid of the dangerous zealots.

It was always a dubious argument, with much evidence to the contrary. Isis, after its experience in 2006 and 2007 when the Americans did succeed in splitting the Sunni insurgency, is wary of another stab in the back. It has taken precautions such as demanding a pledge of allegiance to the caliphate and, according to one account from Mosul, has seized 300 former Baathists and army officers as hostages. The lesson from Iraq and Syria is that in places it has conquered, Isis only shares power as long as it has to. So far, the chances of a counter-insurgency against it in Sunni provinces look bleak.

But this does not mean that Isis has not created a host of enemies for itself, and it is losing the advantage of its opponents' disunity. Within Iraq, relations between Erbil, the Kurdish capital, and Baghdad were "poisonous", the Iraqi foreign minister, Hoshyar Zebari, told me in early July. But the victorious Isis attack on Kurdish-held territory in August has made the Kurds less over-confident and more willing to cooperate with the Iraqi central government against the jihadis. Among the Kurds themselves there was a closing of the ranks as experienced fighters of the Kurdistan Workers Party (PKK) raced to help the Iraqi Kurdish forces with whom they had previously had hostile or very frosty relations.

With both the Shia and the Kurds feeling vulnerable, the US has restored much of its former influence in Iraq with a few air strikes. In contrast with American ignorance and arrogance in 2003, Washington is now much more knowledgeable and warier of the Iraqi quagmire. As states such as Saudi Arabia, Turkey and Iran find ferocious and battle-hardened Isis fighters on their borders, they are more likely to cooperate with each other and the US. In the words of Hillaire Belloc's poem, they're keeping "a-hold of Nurse, For fear of finding something worse."

This coming together of old rivals and enemies in opposition to Isis is happening in Iraq, but not yet in Syria where the US, Europeans, Turks, Saudis and Qataris continue with their old bankrupt policy. This is to get rid of or least weaken President Bashar al-Assad by backing a moderate military opposition that is supposedly going to fight both Mr Assad and Isis. Unfortunately, this group scarcely exists except as a propaganda slogan and a consumer of subsidies from the Gulf. Isis dominates the Syrian opposition and that domination grew greater last week as it captured the towns of Turkmen Bareh and Akhtarin, 30 miles from Aleppo.

The Sunni rebellion in Syria may soon be an Isis controlled project as it already is in Iraq. Given that Syria is 60 per cent Sunni Arab, compared to 20 per cent in Iraq, it is easier for Isis to increase its strength there. Any attempt to counter-attack Isis that focuses solely on Iraq is likely to fail because the caliphate straddles the two countries' border. The present US policy of leaving Mr Assad (backed by Hezbollah, Iran and Russia) to battle Isis alone poses high risks, says Anthony Cordesman, the national security analyst at the Center for Strategic and International Studies in Washington. He writes that US policy only works so long as the Assad forces do not lose territory and key cities to Isis and the caliphate "does not make major economic, military, political and religious gains". He adds that the present stance of the US and its Arab allies assumes the existence of a moderate Sunni resistance not dominated by Isis. If Isis is able to maintain its "sanctuary" in eastern Syria, the caliphate will be able to reinforce its "capabilities in Iraq and steadily increase the threat to Lebanon, Jordan, Saudi Arabia, Turkey and other neighbouring states".

In practice, none of the conditions for a successful US policy in Syria have been met. Since Isis expanded its caliphate to cover almost all of eastern Syria, its neighbours have every reason to be frightened. The nascent unity and cooperation of the opponents to Isis forged by the Iraq crisis may be too little and too late.

Sunday, 24 August 2014

FIRST STEP IS TO CLOSE THE JIHADIS' HIGHWAY

The murder of the US journalist James Foley by a British jihadi has reignited the barren debate in Britain about new government powers to tackle extremist Islamic groups. Dubious counter-terrorism specialists, the exact nature of their expertise frequently elusive, speak of the effectiveness of new controls in thwarting actual or potential jihadis. Much of what is said is irrelevant to the real circumstances in which Muslims leave Britain or other foreign countries to fight in Syria and Iraq. The discussion, driven by politicians responding to media hysteria, produces a sort of intellectual fog in which effective measures that can be taken swiftly disappear from view.

The point at which jihadis should be best identified, intercepted and stopped is not within Britain or even Europe but as they cross from Turkey into Syria. The Turks have a 560-mile-long border with Syria and it is across this that jihadis must travel if they are to reach their destination, primarily but not exclusively Isis, to offer their services. Those who head for Iraq must also take what Turkish journalists call "the Jihadist Highway", a network of roads across Turkey and Syria.

A glance at the map might appear to show that there are other ways of reaching the battlegrounds of Syria and Iraq, but in practice Turkey is the only feasible route for jihadis to the Sunni heartlands of both countries. They can no longer travel through Lebanon since the Syrian army and Hezbollah captured the land from Saudi territory to Iraq. Jordan, while trying as usual to keep in with all sides, has always been nervous of being in the front line of aiding the anti-Assad opposition in Syria.

It is down the "Jihadist Highway" through Turkey that the foreign fighters have flowed in their thousands over the past three years. Turkey's open border was crucial to sustaining the Sunni armed uprising which arose out of the mostly peaceful anti-government protests of 2011. It has played the same role as the open Pakistan-Afghan border does in sustaining the Taliban. So long as Taliban fighters could retreat back into Pakistan over the 1,500-mile-long frontier, they could have a safe haven or sanctuary to rest and resupply before returning to the war.

For the first two years of the Syrian civil war, the route of the foreign fighters was unimpeded. According to Iraqi intelligence officials, who interrogated captured fighters, they would arrive at Istanbul or Ankara airports, move to safe houses and then travel freely by car or bus through the border crossing points into Syria. Arms and ammunition for the rebels, mostly paid for by Qatar and private donors in the Gulf, took the same route, the whole supply operation monitored and to a degree orchestrated by the CIA.

It was only in the middle of 2013 that foreign governments began to get cold feet as it became evident that armed opposition movements in Syria had become dominated by home-grown and foreign jihadis. There was a surge of reports in the foreign media, which had previously been highly supportive of the Syrian uprising, that rebel wounded were being treated in Turkish hospitals. The online journal Al-Monitor quoted a Turkish MP from the border town of Reyhani as saying that "it's only after the Salafists [Sunni fundamentalists] took over the border crossings and the Obama administration took fright that the Western media decided to report on Turkey's support for extremist groups".

Over the past year, Turkey has done something but not nearly enough to close the border to jihadis. The problem is that the US, Britain, Turkey, Saudi Arabia and others have pretended that they are backing a powerful non-jihadi opposition movement capable of displacing Assad. This was the justification for keeping the border at least partly open. But the rebels are dominated by Isis, Jabhat al-Nusra, Ahrar al-Sham and other jihadis. The Turkish Prime Minister, Recep Tayyip Erdogan, has still not quite taken on board that his campaign to get rid of Assad by backing the jihadis is bankrupt and has failed. Countries such as the US and Britain are loath to admit that they went along with this policy for too long, contributing much to the rise of Isis, and the Turkish border may now be very difficult to close.

The Turkish government protests that it gets 34 million tourists a year and it cannot arrest everybody with a beard. But this excuse does not quite ring true since few of these tourists will be seeing the sites along the Syrian border.

Smuggling has become one of the few ways of eking out a living in these dangerous borderlands. There are 700,000 Syrian refugees in Turkey and a further 100,000 to 200,000 maintained by Turkey on the other side of the frontier. Fuel is heavily taxed in Turkey, so cheaper products from Isis-controlled oil wells, crudely distilled, is shipped back into Turkey. Smugglers, of course, are equally willing to use the same covert networks to move jihadis in and out of Syria.

Nevertheless, putting heavy pressure on Turkey to deploy its security forces to close this border is the most effective way to prevent Isis from establishing a network of adherents across the world. So far Turkey has built a few miles of wall in a token effort to secure the border, but this will not be enough. It is unlikely that the US and its allies will ever formally ally themselves with Assad, but to isolate Isis they will have to undermine those opposed to him. It has always been absurd to imagine that it is possible to draw a line distinguishing carefully vetted antijihadi rebels from Isis, Jabhat al-Nusra and the others.

The Foreign Secretary, Philip Hammond, has rebuffed the idea of an alliance or co-operation with Assad, but this was never likely or even necessary. In reality, the American and British policy of saying, as they did at the time of the Geneva 11 talks at the start of the year, that the only topic for negotiations should be about "transition" in Damascus never made much sense. Of the 14 provincial capitals in Syria, 13 are held by the government and the 14th, Raqqa, is ruled by Isis.

Assad was never going to step down voluntarily, and the rebels were never going to be strong enough to force him to do so. Demanding his departure as the only subject of negotiations has proved a recipe for the war continuing.

Isis, its caliphate, and the flood of foreign jihadis into Syria and Iraq are the children of this war. Towards the end of 2012 a senior British diplomat told me that he felt the belief that "the Syrian war will spread" was much exaggerated. This was the great miscalculation in Washington and London for which Iraqis, Syrians, Turks and many others are now paying a heavy price.

Wednesday, 10 September 2014

AMERICA'S WAR ON TWO FRONTS

The United States is reluctantly but decisively becoming engaged in the civil wars in Iraq and Syria as it seeks to combat Isis.

President Barack Obama will outline his plans in a speech today to create a grand coalition of Western and regional powers to contain and defeat Isis, which has established a quasi-state stretching from the frontiers of Iran to the outskirts of Aleppo.

The US is encouraged by the formation on Monday of what it sees as a more inclusive government in Iraq under Haider al-Abadi, the new Prime Minister. He replaces Nouri al-Maliki who, in his eight years in office, became a hate figure for the Sunni minority as the architect of Shia dominance and arbitrary power. Mr Maliki's government was notoriously corrupt and dysfunctional, its 350,000-strong army routed in June by a few thousand Isis fighters in northern and western Iraq. Fear of Isis has led former rivals and opponents such as the US and Iran, Kurdish parties and Shia and Sunni politicians in Baghdad, to sink some of their differences, though these have not gone away.

Mr Obama said after the Nato summit in Wales last week that "we are going to have to find effective partners on the ground to push back against Isil", using the US government's preferred name for Isis. But in seeking such partners in Iraq and Syria, the US will be taking sides in complex sectarian and ethnic struggles. Kamran Karadaghi, a Kurdish commentator and adviser to the former President Jalal Talabani, said: "It is still a sectarian government in Baghdad and Abadi had his ministers chosen for him by the different parties." He says the Kurds were pressured into agreeing to join it by the US and UN envoys sitting in on a decision-making meeting in Sulaymaniyah in the Kurdish region, though the main Kurdish demands have not been met. Among issues at stake are the sale of Kurdish oil, the future of Kirkuk and the central government's payment of the Kurdish share of Iraq's oil revenues. Mr Karadaghi says: "So far we have got nothing except some promises over payment of salaries."

The new government may be less divisive than the old one - it would be difficult to be more - but only to a limited degree. The most important security jobs of defence and interior minister have yet to be filled and there are many old faces in Mr Abadi's cabinet. Senior members of the Marjaiyyah, the Shia clerical establishment, are reported to be disappointed that there are not more people chosen by merit rather than party allegiance.

Commenting on the euphoric response by the US Secretary of State John Kerry to the new line-up in Baghdad, an Iraqi observer said he doubted if Mr Kerry's optimism would survive a meeting with Ibrahim al-Jaafari, notorious for his elusive style of conversation, who replaces Hoshyar Zebari, previously Iraq's highly effective Foreign Minister.

Most importantly, the new government may not convince Iraq's six million-strong Sunni community that they have any choice but to stick with Isis, which has seized the Sunni provinces. Aside from minorities in these areas, such as the Shia, Yazidi, Turkoman, Kurds and Christians, the Sunni are more terrified of the return of vengeful Iraqi government forces than they are of Isis.

They have reason to be frightened since revenge killing of Sunni are taking place in Amerli, the Shia Turkoman town whose two-month siege by Isis was broken last month by Shia and Kurdish fighters aided by US air strikes. Mass graves of Shia truck drivers murdered by Isis are being excavated and local Sunni are being killed in retaliation. The family of a 21-year-old Sunni man abducted by militiamen was soon afterwards offered his headless body back in return for $2,000 (£1,240).

In the 127 villages retaken by the Kurds from Isis under the cover of US air strikes, the Sunni Arab population has mostly fled and is unlikely to return. Often Sunni houses are burnt by Shia militiamen and in one village Kurdish fighters had reportedly sprayed over the word "apostate" placed there by Isis and instead written "Kurdish home".

This atmosphere of terror means that the favoured US policy of getting the Baghdad government to give enough concessions to the Sunni to lure them away from support for Isis may not work. The US succeeded in 2006 and 2007 in turning many Sunni tribes and neighbourhoods against al-Qa'ida in Iraq (AQI). But Isis is stronger and better organised than AQI and is wary of a stab in the back by fellow Sunni. To guard against this in Mosul it has taken 300 hostages, including senior Sunni retired generals. In Deir Ezzor province in Syria, one tribe called the al-Sheitaat staged an uprising against Isis last month only to be swiftly defeated with 700 tribal members rounded up and executed.

Isis will be difficult to defeat in Iraq because of Sunni sectarian solidarity. But the reach of Isis in Iraq is limited by the fact that Sunni Arabs are only 20 per cent of the 33 million population. In Syria, by way of contrast, Sunni Arabs make up at least 60 per cent of Syrians, so Isis's natural constituency is larger than in Iraq. Motorised Isis columns have been advancing fast here, taking some 35 per cent of the country and inflicting defeats both on other Syrian opposition fighters, notably Jabhat al-Nusra, the al-Qa'ida affiliate, and on the Syrian army. Isis is now within 30 miles of Aleppo, the largest city in Syria before the war.

The US and its allies face a huge dilemma which is largely of their own making. Since 2011 Washington's policy, closely followed by the UK, has been to replace President Bashar al-Assad, but among his opponents Isis is now dominant. Actions by the US and its regional Sunni allies led by Saudi Arabia, Qatar, Kuwait and Turkey, which were aimed at weakening Mr Assad, have in practice helped Isis. The 560-mile-long Turkish-Syrian border was left open by Ankara for jihadis to cross, enabling 12,000 foreign recruits to join the rebels, most becoming part of Isis. The US is now desperately trying to persuade Turkey to close the border effectively, but so far has only succeeded in raising the price charged by local guides taking people across the frontier from $10 to $25 a journey.

So far it looks as if Mr Obama will dodge the main problem facing his campaign against Isis. He will not want to carry out a U-turn in US policy by allying himself with President Assad, though the Damascus government is the main armed opposition to Isis in Syria. He will instead step up a pretence that there is a potent "moderate" armed opposition in Syria, capable of fighting both Isis and the Syrian government at once. Unfortunately, this force scarcely exists in any strength and the most important rebel movements opposed to Isis are themselves jihadis such as Jabhat al-Nusra, Ahrar al-Sham and the Islamic Front.

Their violent sectarianism is not very different to that of Isis.

Lacking a moderate military opposition to support as an alternative to Isis and the Assad government, the US has moved to raise such a force under its own control. The FSA, once lauded in Western capitals as the likely military victors over Mr Assad, largely collapsed at the end of 2013. The FSA military leader, General Abdul-Ilah al Bashir, who defected from the Syrian government side in 2012, said in an interview with the McClatchy news agency last week that the CIA had taken over direction of this new moderate force. He said that "the leadership of the FSA is American", adding that since last December US supplies of equipment have bypassed the FSA leadership in Turkey and been sent directly to up to 14 commanders in northern Syria and 60 smaller groups in the south of the country. General Bashir said that all these FSA groups reported directly to the CIA. Other FSA commanders confirmed that the US is equipping them with training and weapons including TOW anti-tank missiles.

It appears that, if the US does launch air strikes in Syria, they will be nominally in support of the FSA which is firmly under US control. The US is probably nervous of allowing weapons to be supplied to supposed moderates by Saudi Arabia and the Gulf monarchies which end up in the hands of Isis. The London-based small arms research organisation Conflict Armament Research said in a report this week that anti-tank rockets used by Isis in Syria were "identical to M79 rockets transferred by Saudi Arabia to forces operating under the FSA umbrella in 2013".

In Syria and in Iraq Mr Obama is finding that his policy of operating through local partners, whose real aims may differ markedly from his own, is full of perils.

Who's who: The groups fighting in Syria and Iraq

- **PKK Kurdish Workers Party**: Viewed as a terror group by the EU and US for its attacks in Turkey, its fighters are among the most effective in Syria and Iraq
- **Kurdistan Regional Government**: Had difficulty in withstanding the first attacks of Isis but new weapons from the West and training will revitalise them
- **PYD Democratic Union Party**: The Kurds in Syria have been successful in defending their territory in north east Syria from rebels and the Syrian army alike
- **Islamic State**: Supported by 12,000 foreigners but led by former Baathist Iraqi army officers, its emergence in Syria and Iraq has shocked and defeated traditional powers
- **The Army of Islam**: A consortium of small Syrian rebel groups which has largely been supported by Saudi Arabia
- **Jabhat al Nusra**: The original offshoot of al-Qaeda which remains an effective force despite defeats by its ideological allies but strategic rivals, Isis
- **Free Syrian Army**: The challengers to Bashar al-Assad which has been superseded by Islamic militias despite support from Europe and the US
- **Syrian Arab Army**: Assad's army remains the biggest military force in Syria but is stretched by attacks on all sides. Supported by Russia and Iran

- **Iraqi Army**: The Shia dominated army of the Iraqi state was reduced to a shambles by years of corruption and patronage
- **Badr Brigades**: An Iraqi Shia militia, which fought the US and its allies and terrorised the Sunni community, has re-emerged to take on Isis and its Sunni support

Sunday, 14 September 2014

THE 'DARK SIDE' OF SAUDI ARABIA

The rise of Isis has been aided by the continuing failure of the US Government to investigate the role of Saudi Arabia in the 9/11 attacks and its support of jihadi movements such as al-Qa'ida in the years since, says former Senator Bob Graham, the co-chairman of the official inquiry into 9/11.

Senator Graham, who chaired the Senate Intelligence Committee, said that successive administrations in Washington had turned a blind eye to Saudi support for Sunni extremists. He added: "I believe that the failure to shine a full light on Saudi actions and particularly its involvement in 9/11 has contributed to the Saudi ability to continue to engage in actions that are damaging to the US - and in particular their support for Isis."

Senator Graham, a distinguished elder statesmen who was twice Democratic governor of Florida before spending 18 years in the US Senate, believes that ignoring what Saudi Arabia was doing and treating it as a reliable American ally contributed to the US intelligence services' failure to identify Isis as a rising power until after it captured Mosul on 10 June. He says that "one reason I think that our intelligence has been less than stellar" is that not enough attention was given to Saudi Arabia's fostering of al-Qa'ida-type jihadi movements, of which Isis is the most notorious and successful. So far the CIA and other intelligence services have faced little criticism in the US for their apparent failure to foresee the explosive expansion of Isis, which now controls an area larger than Great Britain in northern Iraq and eastern Syria.

Senator Graham's criticism of the US policy towards Saudi Arabia is important because it comes amidst growing doubts in the US about the wisdom of President Barack Obama's plan announced on Wednesday to look to the Gulf monarchs as crucial allies in the US campaign to contain and, if possible, push back Isis after its victories in Iraq and Syria during the summer.

Under the plan, Saudi Arabia is to host a special training facility for "moderate" Syrian opposition which is to fight both Isis and the government of President Bashar al-Assad. A problem is that Saudi Arabia dislikes Isis today, whatever its role in its creation, but it gives priority to regime change in Damascus.

Senator Graham thinks it is wise to engage with Saudi Arabia because, despite Saudi denials, he says it has been "a central figure in financing Isis and extremist groups". But he is cautious about success from the US point of view because of the Saudi monarchy's long-term alliance with the Wahhabi clergy and its commitment to spread Wahhabism, the intolerant variant of Islam which denounces Shia as heretics and treats women as chattels under male control.

The Senator says that Saudi Arabia not only gives support to Sunni communities worldwide "but the most extreme elements among the Sunni".

The Saudi role in the 9/11 attacks on the World Trade Center in 2001 has long been public knowledge since 15 out of 19 of the hijackers were Saudis, and the leader of al-Qa'ida, Osama bin Laden, was a member of the Saudi ruling elite. The 9/11 inquiry found that, for financing, al-Qa'ida relied on a core group of private donors and charities in Saudi Arabia and the Gulf.

Despite the Saudi connections of the 9/11 conspirators, Saudi Arabia and its citizens were treated with extraordinary leniency in the wake of the attacks. Some 144 individuals, mostly from the Saudi aristocracy, were permitted to fly back to Saudi Arabia within days of the attacks without being questioned by the FBI. The influential Saudi

ambassador Prince Bandar bin Sultan was pictured in cheerful conversation with President Bush on the White House balcony a few days
after 9/11. Senator Graham recalls that "there were several incidents
[in which US officials] were inexplicably solicitous to Saudis". US officials who went to Saudi Arabia to investigate links to 9/11 found their
Saudi counterparts to be persistently obstructive.

Saudi obstructionism continued during the decade after 9/11: in
2007, Stuart Levey, the Under Secretary of the US Treasury in charge
of monitoring and impeding the financing of terrorism, told ABC News
that when it came to al-Qa'ida, "if I could somehow snap my fingers
and cut off the funding from one country, it would be Saudi Arabia".
He added that at that stage not one person identified by the US or the
UN as funding terrorism had been prosecuted by the Saudis. Eight
years after 9/11, the US Secretary of State, Hillary Clinton, wrote in a
cable leaked by WikiLeaks that "Saudi Arabia remains a critical financial support base for al-Qa'ida, the Taliban, LeT [Lashkar-e-Taiba in
Pakistan] and other terrorist groups."

As AQI began to reorganise and turn itself into Isis in the years
after 2010, politicians and security officials in Baghdad were convinced of the complicity of Saudi Arabia and the other Gulf monarchies
in funding jihadis in Iraq. They generally avoided public criticism of
these states as allies of the US, but in March 2014 Iraqi Prime Minister
Nouri al-Maliki identified Saudi Arabia and Qatar as the two countries
"primarily responsible for the sectarian, terrorist and security crisis
in Iraq". He said that Riyadh and Doha were "buying weapons for the
benefit of these terrorist organisations". Mr Maliki had his own share
of blame for persecuting the Sunni community in Iraq so it gave support to armed resistance by Isis, but Iraqi leaders all believed that the
monarchs of the Gulf were bankrolling Sunni opposition in Iraq and
would never accept a Shia-dominated government.

The most striking example of Washington's willingness to protect the Kingdom over complicity in 9/11 is the 28 pages of the official
inquiry that were censored and have yet to be published. Senator Graham is not allowed to reveal what is in the chapter that was redacted,
but other sources say that they are about connections between Saudi
government officials and the 9/11 attacks. Anthony Summers and
Robbyn Swan, in their book The Eleventh Day: The Full Story of 9/11,
quote a senior American official, who saw the 28 pages before they
were excised, apparently on the initiative of President Bush, as saying:

"If the 28 pages were to be made public, I have no question that the entire relationship with Saudi Arabia would change overnight."

Senator Graham has long campaigned to have the 28 pages of the 9/11 inquiry and other documents released. He says, knowing their content, that there is no national security justification for keeping them a secret 13 years after 9/11. He says that some government agencies, notably the FBI, have a motive in keeping information from the public about "their actions and their competence at the time of 9/11". In Sarasota, Florida, the FBI initially denied having any documents relating to hijackers who were based there but has now handed over 80,000 pages that might be relevant under the Freedom of Information Act, according to Tom Julin, the Miami-based attorney handling the FOI application.

Asked why the US government has been so eager since 2001 to cover up for the Saudis, Senator Graham says that one explanation is the longterm US strategic alliance with Saudi Arabia, going back to the Second World War. There is also the close personal relationship between the Bush family and the Kingdom. But what he finds more difficult to explain is why the "policy of covering up Saudi involvement [in 9/11] persisted under the Obama administration". Though Mr Obama had pledged to the families of the 9/11 victims during the 2008 presidential election campaign to release the 28 censored pages, it has failed to do so six years later.

Senator Graham does not suggest that the Saudis are directly running Isis, but that their support for Sunni extremists in Iraq and Syria opened the door to jihadis including Isis. Similar points were made by Sir Richard Dearlove, the former head of the British Secret Intelligence Service, and MI6, who said in a lecture at the Royal United Services Institute in London in July that the Saudi government is "deeply attracted towards any militancy which effectively challenges Shiadom". He said that rulers of the Kingdom tended to oppose jihadis at home as enemies of the House of Saud, but promote them abroad in the interests of Saudi foreign policy. Anti-Shi'ism has always been at the centre of the Saudi world view, and he quoted Prince Bandar, the ambassador in Washington at the time of 9/11 and later head of Saudi intelligence, as saying to him: "The time is not far off in the Middle East, Richard, when it will be literally 'God help the Shia'. More than a billion Sunni have simply had enough of them."

In allying itself with Saudi Arabia, the US automatically plugs itself into an anti-Shia agenda and limits its ability to monitor and take action against Sunni jihadis who are promoted by Riyadh. In Syria this has led to parts of a jihadi-dominated military opposition being relabelled as "moderate". President Obama intends to support this group, who scarcely exist on the map, to fight both Isis and the Assad government.

Senator Graham maintains that there is a "dark side" to Saudi Arabia exemplified by 9/11 and its aftermath that the American public need to know about and which has hitherto been concealed. The US and other Western governments have yet to explain why their "war on terror" has so demonstrably failed with the rise of Isis, but tolerance of Saudi complicity in 9/11 will surely be part of the answer.

Monday, 22 September 2014

TURKISH DELIGHT, WESTERN FRIGHT

Mystery surrounds the surprise release of 49 Turkish diplomats and their families held captive for three months by Isis. The Turkish government is denying any deal with the hostage-takers, making it unclear why Isis, notorious for its cruelty and ruthlessness, should hand over its Turkish prisoners on Saturday without a quid pro quo.

Hailed in Ankara as a triumph for Turkey, the freeing of the diplomats seized when Mosul fell to Isis on 10 June raises fresh questions about the relationship between the Turkish government and Isis. The Turkish President, Recep Tayyip Erdogan, says the release is the result of a covert operation by Turkish intelligence that must remain a secret.

He added yesterday that "there are things we cannot talk about. To run the state is not like running a grocery store. We have to protect our sensitive issues; if you don't there would be a price to pay." Turkey denies that a ransom was paid or promises made to Isis.

The freeing of the hostages comes at the same moment as 70,000 Syrian Kurds have fled across the border into Turkey to escape an Isis offensive against the enclave of Kobani, also known as Ayn al-Arab, which has seen the capture of many villages.

The assault on Kobani is energising Kurds throughout the region with 3,000 fighters from the PKK based in Iraq's Qandil mountains reported to be crossing from Iraq into Syria and heading for Kobani.

The Turkish security forces closed the border for a period yesterday after clashes between them and the refugees. They fired tear gas and water after stopping Kurds taking aid to Kobani according to one account, or because stones were thrown at them as they pushed back crowds of Kurdish onlookers, according to another. Most of those crossing are women, children and the elderly, with men of military age staying behind to fight.

Many Kurds are expressing bitterness towards the Turkish government, claiming that it is colluding with Isis to destroy the independent enclaves of the Syrian Kurds, who number 2.5 million, along the Turkish border. The pro-Kurdish Amed news agency asks "if Isis [is] the paramilitary wing of the of the neo-Ottomanism project of Turkey in the Middle East?" The Turkish government vehemently denies any collaboration with Isis.

Nevertheless, the strange circumstances of both the capture of the 49 Turks and their release shows that Ankara has a different and more intimate relationship with Isis than other countries. Pro-Isis Turkish websites say that the Turks were released on the direct orders of "the caliph" Abu Bakr al-Baghdadi. They had been moved to Raqqa, the Syrian headquarters of Isis from Mosul, and both men and women were well dressed and appeared to have suffered little harm from their imprisonment.

This is in sharp contrast to the treatment of Alan Henning, the British taxi driver seized when taking aid to Syria. A video has emerged of Mr Henning that shows him just hours before he was captured while travelling with an aid convoy in Syria.

In the footage, Mr Henning, whose wife Barbara has appealed for his captors to release her "peaceful, selfless" husband, says he has spoken to his family and "they are all OK". However he adds "it's hard". The aid worker who filmed the conversation told ITV News: "He's such a special man and you know everybody on the [aid] convoy holds him in high regard, everyone want him to come home."

As far as the Turkey situation is concerned, a number of factors do not quite add up: at the time the diplomats and their families were seized in June it was reported that they had asked Ankara if they could leave Mosul, but their request was refused.

Critics of Mr Erdogan say that since the first uprising against President Bashar al-Assad in 2011 he has made a series of misjudgements about developments in Syria. He made little effort to distinguish jihadi rebels crossing the 560-mile-long Syrian-Turkish border from the others. Some 12,000 foreign jihadis entered Syria and Iraq from Turkey.

Only at the end of 2013, under pressure from the US, did Turkey begin to increase border security making it more difficult for foreign or Turkish jihadis to pass through, though it is still possible. A Kurdish news agency reports that three Isis members, two from Belgium and one from France, were detained by the Syrian Kurdish militia at the weekend as they crossed into Syria from Turkey.

The hostages had no idea they were going to be freed until they got a phone call from the Prime Minister, Ahmet Davutoglu. While treated better than other hostages, they were still put under pressure, being forced to watch videos of other captives being beheaded "to break their morale," according to the Consul-General in Mosul, Ozturk Yilmaz.

He said that Isis did not torture people though it threatened to do so: "The only thing they do is to kill them."

The Turkish government may not be collaborating with Isis at this moment, but Isis has benefited from Turkey's tolerant attitude towards the jihadi movements. As with other anti-Assad governments, Ankara has claimed that there is a difference between the "moderate" rebels of the FSA and the al-Qa'ida-type movements that does not really exist on the ground inside Syria.

Thursday, 25 September 2014

BOMBS ALONE WILL NOT DEFEAT AN ENEMY THAT KNOWS HOW TO MELT AWAY

The US plan to weaken and ultimately destroy Isis has several political and military weaknesses undermining its long-term success. Air campaigns not supported by ground forces can damage the other side but they do not win wars on their own. Isis has already faced bombardment by US planes in Iraq since 8 August, but it is still fighting the Iraqi army around Baghdad.

Some of the weaknesses of the air war are already apparent since Isis had evacuated its leaders, fighters and heavy equipment from buildings that were targeted. Its fighters avoid large gatherings and mix with the civilian population. The shock effect of being bombed will be less because the Syrian air force has long been bombing rebel-held cities and towns.

Isis expertise is in guerrilla warfare and it is only recently that it has used columns of vehicles packed with gunmen and heavy infantry weapons. Air superiority over the fruit groves of Diyala province or the palm trees of northern Hilla is difficult to use effectively. Of course, in Syria and Iraq there are ground troops capable of taking advantage of the air strikes, but they mostly belong to armies and militias with whom the US is not meant to be cooperating.

In Syria, the most powerful armed group opposing Isis is the Syrian army, followed by Hezbollah and the Syrian Kurds. In Iraq, three months after the fall of Mosul, the Iraqi army still does not seem able to hold its own against Isis as recent fighting around Fallujah demonstrated. Advances that have taken place have generally been by Shia militiamen under the direction of Iranian Revolutionary Guards officers and Kurdish Peshmerga, though these did not distinguish themselves when Isis attacked Sinjar in August.

In Iraq, the US task is a little easier because at least it is allied to the elected government in Baghdad. But in Syria Isis is somehow to be attacked without aiding the Syrian government or groups that the US and Europeans have previously demonised, such as Hezbollah, from Lebanon, which has acted as shock troops for the Syrian government. Of course this detachment from military realities is not possible, but what is military common sense may be politically embarrassing.

The main Isis offensive at the moment is directed at the Syrian Kurdish enclave centred on the town of Kobani where half-a-million people had taken refuge. Some 200,000 Kurds have now fled across the border into Syria while their militia, the YPG, is fighting it out with Isis.

Air strikes hit eight villages captured by Isis early yesterday, but here the Americans face a political problem. The YPG is the Syrian branch of the Turkish Kurd PKK whom the US labels as "terrorists" and does not want to be associated with. But what does the US do if Isis responds to the air campaign against it by strengthening its forces trying to capture Kobani. It may want to send a message that it remains an enemy to be feared whatever the US does.

Air power can be made more effective at a tactical level by having forward air observers on the ground calling in air strikes. This worked in Afghanistan in 2001 and in northern Iraq in 2003. But use of these today in Iraq and Syria means the US getting further involved in some-body else's civil war.

There are other complications. Turkey now says that it is joining the anti-Isis coalition, but it does not want to strengthen the Syrian Kurds and the YPG or help to keep the Assad government in power. It would be interesting to know what the US has said to Turkish President Recep Tayyip Erdogan about their future plans for Syria.

Isis is strong because of its military expertise and religious fanaticism but there are more general reasons why it will be difficult to defeat. Many Sunnis in the areas controlled by Isis do not like it, but they are terrified of the return of the Syrian or Iraqi armies and accompanying sectarian militias.

Isis has been more successful than it ought to have been because of two vacuums which it has been able to fill. One is the vacuum left by the dysfunctional and corrupt Iraqi army and state. The other is the political vacuum created by the absence of leadership in the Sunni communities in Iraq and Syria which is capable of offering an alternative to Isis.

AUTUMN 2014: GLIMMER OF HOPE

US airstrike on Isis positions in Kobani, Syria, 24 October 2014

Sunday, 12 October 2014

US STRATEGY IN TATTERS AS ISIS MARCHES ON

America's plans to fight Isis are in ruins as the militant group's fighters come close to capturing Kobani and have inflicted a heavy defeat on the Iraqi army west of Baghdad.

The US-led air attacks launched against Isis on 8 August in Iraq and 23 September in Syria have not worked. President Obama's plan to "degrade and destroy" Islamic State has not even begun to achieve success. In both Syria and Iraq, Isis is expanding its control rather than contracting.

Isis reinforcements have been rushing towards Kobani in the past few days to ensure that they win a decisive victory over the Syrian Kurdish town's remaining defenders. The group is willing to take heavy casualties in street fighting and from air attacks in order to add to the string of victories it has won in the four months since its forces captured Mosul, the second-largest city in Iraq, on 10 June. Part of the strength of the fundamentalist movement is a sense that there is something inevitable and divinely inspired about its victories, whether it is against superior numbers in Mosul or US airpower at Kobani.

In the face of a likely Isis victory at Kobani, senior US officials have been trying to explain away the failure to save the Syrian Kurds in the town, probably Isis's toughest opponents in Syria. "Our focus in Syria is in degrading the capacity of [Islamic State] at its core to project power, to command itself, to sustain itself, to resource itself," said US Deputy National Security Adviser Tony Blinken, in a typical piece of waffle designed to mask defeat. "The tragic reality is that in the course of doing that there are going to be places like Kobani where we may or may not be able to fight effectively."

Unfortunately for the US, Kobani isn't the only place air strikes are failing to stop Isis. In an offensive in Iraq launched on 2 October but little reported in the outside world, Isis has captured almost all the cities and towns it did not already hold in Anbar province, a vast area in western Iraq that makes up a quarter of the country. It has captured Hit, Kubaisa and Ramadi, the provincial capital, which it had long fought for. Other cities, towns and bases on or close to the Euphrates River west of Baghdad fell in a few days, often after little resistance by the Iraqi Army which showed itself to be as dysfunctional as in the past, even when backed by US air strikes.

Today, only the city of Haditha and two bases, Al-Assad military base near Hit, and Camp Mazrah outside Fallujah, are still in Iraqi government hands. Joel Wing, in his study -"Iraq's Security Forces Collapse as The Islamic State Takes Control of Most of Anbar Province" - concludes: "This was a huge victory as it gives the insurgents virtual control over Anbar and poses a serious threat to western Baghdad".

The battle for Anbar, which was at the heart of the Sunni rebellion against the US occupation after 2003, is almost over and has ended with a decisive victory for Isis. It took large parts of Anbar in January and government counter-attacks failed dismally with some 5,000 casualties in the first six months of the year. About half the province's 1.5 million population has fled and become refugees. The next Isis target may be the Sunni enclaves in western Baghdad, starting with Abu Ghraib on the outskirts but leading right to the centre of the capital.

The Iraqi government and its foreign allies are drawing comfort, there having been some advances against Isis in the centre and north of the country. But north and northeast of Baghdad the successes have not been won by the Iraqi army but by highly sectarian Shia militias which do not distinguish between Isis and the rest of the Sunni population. They speak openly of getting rid of Sunni in mixed provinces such as Diyala where they have advanced. The result is that Sunni in Iraq have no alternative but to stick with Isis or flee, if they want to survive. The same is true northwest of Mosul on the border with Syria, where Iraqi Kurdish forces, aided by US air attacks, have retaken the important border crossing of Rabia, but only one Sunni Arab remained in the town. Ethnic and sectarian cleansing has become the norm in the war in both Iraq and Syria.

The US's failure to save Kobani, if it falls, will be a political as well as military disaster. Indeed, the circumstances surrounding the loss of the beleaguered town are even more significant than the inability so far of air strikes to stop Isis taking 40 per cent of it. At the start of the bombing in Syria, President Obama boasted of putting together a coalition of Sunni powers such as Turkey, Saudi Arabia, Qatar, Jordan, United Arab Emirates and Bahrain to oppose Isis, but these all have different agendas to the US in which destroying Isis is not the first priority. The Sunni Arab monarchies may not like Isis, which threatens the political status quo, but, as one Iraqi observer put it, "they like the fact that Isis creates more problems for the Shia than it does for them".

Of the countries supposedly uniting against Isis, by the far most important is Turkey because it shares a 510-mile border with Syria across which rebels of all sorts, including Isis and Jabhat al-Nusra, have previously passed with ease. This year the Turks have tightened border security, but since its successes in the summer Isis no longer needs sanctuary, supplies and volunteers from outside to the degree it once did.

In the course of the past week it has become clear that Turkey considers the Syrian Kurd political and military organisations, the PYD and YPG, as posing a greater threat to it than the Islamic fundamentalists. Moreover, the PYD has been fighting for Kurdish self-rule in Turkey since 1984.

Ever since Syrian government forces withdrew from the Syrian Kurdish enclaves or cantons on the border with Turkey in July 2012, Ankara has feared the impact of self-governing Syrian Kurds on its own 15 million strong Kurdish population. President Recep Tayyip Erdogan would prefer Isis to control Kobani, not the PYD.

Turkey is demanding a high price from the US for its co-operation in attacking Isis, such as a Turkish controlled buffer zone inside Syria where Syrian refugees are to live and anti-Assad rebels are to be trained. Mr Erdogan would like a no-fly zone which will also be directed against the government in Damascus since Isis has no air force. If implemented the plan would mean Turkey, backed by the US, would enter the Syrian civil war on the side of the rebels, though the anti-Assad forces are dominated by Isis and Jabhat al-Nusra.

It is worth keeping in mind that Turkey's actions in Syria since 2011 have been a self-defeating blend of hubris and miscalculation. At the start of the uprising, it could have held the balance between the government and its opponents. Instead, it supported the militarisation of the crisis, backed the jihadis and assumed Assad would soon be defeated. This did not happen and what had been a popular uprising became dominated by sectarian warlords who flourished in conditions created by Turkey. Mr Erdogan is assuming he can disregard the rage of the Turkish Kurds at what they see as his complicity with Isis against the Syrian Kurds. This fury is already deep, with 33 dead, and is likely to get a great deal worse if Kobani falls.

Why doesn't Ankara worry more about the collapse of the peace process with the PKK that has maintained a ceasefire since 2013? It may believe that the PKK is too heavily involved in fighting Isis in Syria that it cannot go back to war with the government in Turkey. On the other hand, if Turkey does join the civil war in Syria against Assad, a crucial ally of Iran, then Iranian leaders have said that "Turkey will pay a price". This probably means that Iran will covertly support an armed Kurdish insurgency in Turkey. Saddam Hussein made a somewhat similar mistake to Mr Erdogan when he invaded Iran in 1980, thus leading Iran to reignite the Kurdish rebellion that Baghdad had crushed through an agreement with the Shah in 1975. Turkish military intervention in Syria might not end the war there, but it may well spread the fighting to Turkey.

Wednesday, 15 October 2014
IRAQ'S SECTARIAN SLAUGHTER WORSENS

Iraq is descending into savage sectarian warfare as government-backed Shia militias kill, torture and hold for ransom any Sunni whom they detain. Isis is notorious for its mass killings of Shia, but retaliation by Shia militiamen means that Iraq is returning to the levels of sectarian slaughter last seen in the Sunni-Shia civil war of 2006-07 when tens of thousands were murdered.

The Shia militias have become the main fighting force of the Baghdad government since the Iraqi army was defeated by Isis when it took northern Iraq in June. According to a detailed Amnesty International report published yesterday, the militias enjoy total immunity in committing war crimes against the Sunni community, often demanding large ransoms but killing their victims even when the money is paid.

The re-emergence of the Shia militias and the failure to rebuild the Iraqi army is torpedoing the US and British policy of supporting a more inclusive and less sectarian government in Baghdad. The aim was to create a government that could reach out to Iraq's five or six million-strong Sunni community and seek to turn it against Isis. But, since the militias treat all Sunni men as Isis fighters or supporters, the Sunni are left with no choice but to stick with the jihadi militants.

The report cites a member of the Asa'ib Ahl al-Haq, one of the largest militias, on duty at a checkpoint north of Baghdad, saying: "If we catch 'those dogs' [Sunni] coming down from the Tikrit we execute them; in those areas they are all working with Daesh [Isis]. They come to Baghdad to commit terrorist crimes. So we have to stop them."

In addition to sectarian motives, militias such as Asa'ib Ahl al-Haq, the Badr Brigades, Kata'ib Hezbollah and Saraya al-Salam are thoroughly criminalised. One mother said: "I begged friends and acquaintances to lend me the ransom money to save my son, but after I paid they killed him and now I have no way to pay back the money I borrowed, as my son was the only one working in the family."

Moving on the roads has become lethally dangerous for Sunni even before Isis launched its summer offensive. On the afternoon of 30 May two cousins, Majed, a 31-year-old ministry of education employee and father of three, and Nayef, an engineer, were abducted at a checkpoint when they went to Tikrit from Baghdad to pick up furniture.

A $90,000 (£56,000) ransom was demanded and paid but they were later found handcuffed and shot in the head. A Sunni businessman called Salem, 43, was kidnapped from his factory at al-Taji and, though a ransom was paid, his body was later found with his head smashed in either by a large calibre bullet or some form of club.

American and British ministers have lauded the new government in Baghdad under Prime Minister Haider al-Abadi as being less sectarian than that of his predecessor, Nouri al-Maliki, whom he replaced in August.

But in practice, Mr Abadi's administration is much like the old. "For now nothing is different," says Donatella Rovera, Amnesty International's senior crisis response adviser. "Shia militias are way more important than the army and are running the show." Even if it wanted to the government would have difficulty in bringing them under control. Ms Rovera says: "In terms of sectarian violence we are back to the levels of 2006-07."

The militia gunmen frequently act in co-ordination with the police and army. Their victims are Christian as well as Sunni. One Christian family, threatened with death by three militiamen unless they paid a large sum, fled the country but without telling the police.

The report comments that the fact that the family thought it would be unsafe and unwise to tell the police "speaks volumes about the atmosphere of lawlessness in the capital, where [Shia] militias know they can act with impunity."

One reason the Sunni community first protested and supported armed resistance against the government has been the knowledge that they could be detained and tortured by government forces at any time.

Uda Taha Kurdi, 33, a lawyer, was arrested at the Baghdad Central Court on 10 June. Two weeks later his family was told he had suffered from "a health problem" and had died, a judge alleging that he was "from a terrorist family" and was "from the IS leader-ship". A forensic examination of Mr Kurdi's body concluded that he had probably been killed by electrical torture with electrodes attached to his calf and little toe.

The overall plan of Mr Obama and his allies to find a reliable ally on the ground in Baghdad who could woo the Sunni has failed to make progress, despite the departure of Mr Maliki. Mr Abadi has still to get his choice for the defence and interior ministries accepted by parliament.

Meanwhile, Isis has seized all of Anbar province west of Baghdad, defeating the Iraqi army despite the support of US airpower. One of the last two army bases in Anbar fell on Monday as Isis began moving towards west Baghdad.

The inability of the Baghdad government to field a national army and its reliance on militias means that Iraq is in the last stages of disintegration. The few mixed Sunni-Shia areas are disappearing.

In places where the army and militias have retaken towns such as Amerli, north of Baghdad, the inhabitants of nearby Sunni villages have fled. The final break-up of Iraq has become a fact.

Wednesday, 12 November 2014

'WE WILL SAVE KOBANI'

Kobani cannot now be captured by the fighters of Isis but a million people in another Kurdish enclave in Syria are facing a mounting threat of being massacred or forced to flee by advancing jihadis, according to the Kurdish guerrilla leader overseeing the defence of Syrian Kurds.

In an exclusive interview with *The Independent* in his headquarters in the Kandil mountains in Iraqi Kurdistan, Cemil Bayik, the top field commander of the PKK, the Kurdish guerrilla organisation in Turkey, and also of its Syrian affiliate, says: "Kobani will not fall. We are advancing on the eastern and southern fronts."

He said that the Syrian Kurdish fighters had succeeded in "taking back the municipal building and Isis was forced to blow up a mosque it held".

He added that US jets were regularly bombing the top of the strategic hill overlooking Kobani through which Isis fighters first entered the city. But the fighters "disappear into houses on the hillside when the bombing is going on and reoccupy their positions later." Other reports suggest that Isis holds half the city after a siege of 63 days.

Bayik says there is a growing danger to the Kurdish enclave or canton of Afrin, 120 miles to the west of Kobani which has a population of one million people, including 200,000 refugees. The Syrian al-Qa'ida branch, Jabhat al-Nusra, after defeating more moderate Syrian rebels in recent weeks, is moving towards Afrin.

"They are approaching its borders," says Bayik. "They are calling villagers by telephone, saying, 'Runaway or we will kill you'. Like Isis they use psychological war, first creating panic among the people and then attacking."

Bayik accuses Turkey of having covert links with Jabhat al-Nusra and encouraging the jihadis to threaten Afrin. It is one of three Syrian Kurdish enclaves, all strung along Syria's border with Turkey, and all of which have come under attack from jihadis.

He says that if Kobani falls or Jabhat al-Nusra attacks then "it will no longer be possible for the peace process to go on with Turkey", and the 18-month-old ceasefire which started in March 2013 may end. He believes that Turkey has sufficient influence over Jabhat al-Nusra to prevent it attacking Afrin. "Kurds will not accept Kobani and Afrin being under threat of genocide and massacre."

Even if the ceasefire does not end, the siege of Kobani has provoked anger among the 15 million Turkish Kurds against their government whom they accuse of aiding Isis. Protests and rioting provoked by fear that Kobani was about to fall in early October left some 44 people dead. A similar threat to Afrin would probably lead to outbursts of rage from the 30 million Kurds in the region who live mostly in Turkey, Iraq, Iran and Syria.

The Turkish President, Recep Tayyip Erdogan, has said that Isis is no worse than the PKK or PYD, though on 20 October Turkey agreed under American pressure to allow Iraqi-Kurdish Peshmerga forces to reinforce Kobani.

While international attention has been focused on the fate of Kobani, the Yazidis trapped on Mount Sinjar by Isis, whose fate helped fuel public support for US air strikes in August, are under renewed pressure. The jihadis have once more cut all roads leading to their mountain.

Bayik, who has guerrilla fighters on the mountain, agreed that there was a greater danger of Sinjar falling to Isis than Kobani.

"There are 10,000 people on the mountain and they are in need of everything from food to medical care," said Bayik. "Winter is coming and Isis is attacking once more."

He added that Sinjar is strategically important because it is close to important road links: "If you hold this area, you can control the roads between Iraq and Syria and cut Isis's communications between the two countries." He said the Yazidis trapped on the mountain, which they regard as holy, needed to be resupplied by plane or helicopter or a corridor should be driven through Isis positions so the Yazidis could be reinforced or evacuated.

Bayik is careful to stress that the PYD and the YPG, the People's Defence Units, are not directly controlled by him, though he heads the PKK umbrella organisation, the KCK, which unites PKK affiliates in different countries. All follow the same leader, Abdullah Ocalan, who has been in prison in Turkey for 15 years, and they are organised along similar lines.

A further reason for Bayik to put distance between himself and the PYD is that the US has labelled the PKK, but not its Syrian affiliate, a "terrorist" organisation. Bayik says: "The PKK is not in touch with the Americans directly but the YPG and PYD are."

The battle for Kobani and the PKK's role in helping the Yazidis trapped on Mount Sinjar resist Isis has increased the movement's popularity and prestige among Kurds in Turkey and elsewhere. The determination of their fighters to resist Isis successfully is in contrast to the failure of the Iraqi army, Syrian army, Syrian rebels and Iraqi Kurdish Peshmerga, all of whom had been routed over the last five months by the jihadis. Although the number of male and female fighters in Kandil has been put at only between 3,000 and 5,000, they are having a significant impact on the politics of the region.

The Kurds complain that they are the nation which was the prime victim of the Sykes-Picot agreement that left them without a state. But they have been playing an increasing role in the region. The defeat of Saddam Hussein by a US-led coalition in 1991 and again in 2003 allowed the Iraqi Kurds to create a quasi-independent state more powerful than many members of the United Nations.

The PKK has fought an on-off guerrilla war with the Turkish army since 1984 and, while it has failed to create liberated zones, the Turkish state has failed to eliminate it. The 2.2 million Syrian Kurds were a persecuted and largely invisible minority, 10 per cent of the Syrian population, until the Syrian civil war. In July 2012 the Syrian army pulled out of Kurdish areas in northern Syria, allowing the creation of three autonomous enclaves centred on the towns of Qamishli, Kobani and Afrin. Somewhat to their own surprise the Syrian Kurds became important players in the Syrian civil war. When Isis attacked the Iraqi Kurds this August, they too began to play a central role in the US-led campaign against Isis.

There are some signs that the US campaign is beginning to have some impact, with the Iraqi army fighting its way into the refinery town of Baiji yesterday. This is still some way from the refinery itself, which is the largest in Iraq and has been fought over since the first Isis onslaught in June. Isis may be feeling the strain of fighting on too many fronts in Syria and Iraq and having diverted many of its fighters to Kobani where they are vulnerable to US air strikes.

Bayik confirmed that Kurds in Kobani are in direct contact with the US air force in order to call in air strikes: "If there were no contacts or people on the ground to give coordinates then the US would not be able to send arms and ammunition or carry out bombing missions."

He says that the US air drop of arms and ammunition on 19 October was of immense value to the defenders because of its effect on their morale. Other sources say the Kurds were close to running out of ammunition.

Bayik sees much of what happens in the region through the prism of Turkish-Kurd relations and is convinced Turkey has a strong influence over Isis and Jabhat al-Nusra and has been able to manipulate them against the Kurds. This may be overstated, though Turkey's tolerance of jihadis crossing from Turkey into Syria between 2011 and 2013 was a factor in strengthening Isis and Jabhat al-Nusra. Mystery also reigns over why 46 Turkish diplomats stayed in the Turkish consulate in Mosul when Isis captured it on 10 June and were later released by Isis in exchange for Isis prisoners held in Turkey.

But regardless of the real level of complicity between the jihadis and Turkey, the long struggle for Kobani has created a wave of feeling against the Turkish government among Kurds everywhere. Small though the siege is it compares to other sieges in history from Derry to Stalingrad which have acquired significance as symbols of courage and determination. The Kurdish belief that they won despite the best efforts of Ankara will not create a conciliatory mood in which Turkish Kurds might negotiate a measure of self-rule. A study just published by ICG called Turkey and the PKK: Saving the Peace Process says that the process is at a turning point: "It will either collapse as the sides squander years of work, or it will accelerate as they commit to real convergences."

The furious rhetoric on both Turkish and Kurdish sides because of Kobani makes real negotiations more necessary but less likely. The PKK accuses the Turkish state of being hand-in-glove with Isis, something President Erdogan roundly denies. When a Turkish flag was taken down by demonstrators during the funeral of two young Kurdish protesters in Diyarbakir, President Erdogan said: "The fact that [the demonstrator] was a child does not concern us. He will pay the same price as those who sent him there."

Saturday, 15 November 2014

THE KURDS STRIKE BACK

Iraqi forces have recaptured the refinery town of Baiji and broken the siege of the giant oil refinery nearby, say officials in Baghdad - in the most important success for the Iraqi government since Isis seized a third of Iraq in June.

Isis fighters, after their spectacular victories in Iraq and Syria over the summer, are overstretched as they seek to extend or defend the vast territories they have seized. A Kurdish general, Najat Ali, commanding Peshmerga soldiers in the town of Makhmour, 50 miles north of Baiji, said yesterday that "Isis has big administrative problems in supplying food and ammunition to its forces in the front line".

Makhmour, a Kurdish town of 12,000 people, lies just to the east of the Tigris River and was briefly captured by Isis in its offensive in August that led to the start of US air strikes. It too is back in Kurdish hands.

A shattered 120mm artillery piece, captured by Isis from the Iraqi army but later destroyed by US bombers, lies abandoned near the town's main grain silo. Kurds were shocked and frightened at the time by the speed with which Isis columns defeated the Peshmerga in blitzkrieg attacks and came close to capturing the Kurdish capital Irbil, which is only 45 minutes' drive from Mahkmour.

From the top of a mound defended by a machine-gun post on the outskirts of the town, the Peshmerga watch the Isis front line, which is in a treeline and an abandoned village in the middle distance.

They speak respectfully of the deadly accuracy of Isis snipers, but the Peshmerga morale has rebounded since they fled before the advance of small Isis units five months ago. Dasko, one of the Peshmerga fighters at the post, said that "American air strikes will prevent Daesh [the Arabic acronym for Isis] from advancing again".

The return of Kurdish self-confidence may be premature. Isis may be feeling the strain, but is by no means on the run. In the past six weeks it has captured most of Anbar province, covering a great swathe of western Iraq, defeating the Iraqi army in a series of engagements.

It has inflicted savage punishment on the Sunni Arab Albu Nimr tribe which fought against it in central Anbar. The tribe says that 497 of its members, including 20 women and 16 children, were executed by Isis in massacres aimed at deterring other tribes from resisting Isis. The Albu Nimrs' desperate appeals to Baghdad for help in the shape of weapons, ammunition and air strikes met with no response.

In the wake of these defeats, the new Iraqi Prime Minister, Haider al-Abadi, has this week purged the top command of the Iraqi army, sacking 26 senior officers, retiring another 10 and making 18 new appointments.

Among those removed is General Rashid Flaih, head of the Anbar Operations Command, who presided over a series of debacles that has left 80 per cent of Anbar under Isis control. He had been criticised for failing to get supplies to a besieged Iraqi army base at Saqlawiyah, north of Fallujah, whose 700-strong garrison he described as "whingers". It was ultimately overrun in a surprise assault on 21 September by Isis fighters in disguise, wearing Iraqi army uniforms and driving captured American Humvees. The garrison thought this was an Iraqi army relief force until it was too late.

Since then the Iraqi army's position in Anbar has continued to deteriorate. An aid worker says that "some 100,000 people are besieged and entirely cut off by Isis in the Sunni city of Haditha on the Euphrates. The US air force dropped some 7,000 meals but they have received no other supplies." General Martin Dempsey, Chairman of the US Joint Chiefs of Staff, told Congress this week that 80,000 efficient troops would be needed to defeat Isis.

If Isis is overstretched, so too are its opponents, particularly the Kurds who have to defend a 650-mile-long frontier with the new "caliphate" declared by its leader Abu Bakr al-Baghdadi on 29 June. A leader of the Patriotic Union of Kurdistan, one of the two main Kurdish parties, Saadi Pira, says that "on 10 June we woke up and found we had a new neighbour in the shape of Isis, whose territory stretches from Iran to Syria".

He believes that Isis is weaker than it was at the height of its success, when it had won an unbroken series of military victories and was generally supported by Iraq's Sunni community, which had been persecuted by the former Prime Minister Nouri al-Maliki during his eight years in power.

Mr Pira says: "The Sunni community was willing to co-operate with the devil to punish Maliki." Many Sunni may have come to regret their previous support for Isis, but they are equally terrified of the return of the Iraqi army, the Shia militias or the Kurds.

The Isis force that captured Makhmour on 8 August was only about 150 strong, according to Porat, an official of the PKK at a Turkish Kurd refugee camp at Makhmour, whose inhabitants fled from Turkey in 1998.

A peculiarity of this part of Iraq is that the political and military situation in every district is determined by the varying local political, ethnic and sectarian balance. In Makhmour, the 12,000 Kurds in the camp are an important factor in the local balance of power. The PKK evacuated them in the face of the Isis offensive, but summoned some 200 PKK guerrillas from their base in the Kandil Mountains in northeast Kurdistan who had plenty of recent military experience in fighting the Turkish army. Fighting together with the Iraqi Kurdish Peshmerga, the PKK drove Isis out of the town.

For long ignored or demonised by the rest of the world, the PKK militants unexpectedly find themselves lauded for their heroic defence of Kobani, Mount Sinjar and towns like Makhmour. At the entrance to their camp workers were labouring yesterday to build a large plinth for a statue or picture of their leader, Abdullah Ocalan, imprisoned by Turkey since 1999.

The Iraqi Kurdish authorities are somewhat irritated by the praise being lavished on the PKK's military prowess but for the moment fear and hatred of Isis is a strong bond for all the Kurds. One PKK official in Makhmour said, "I should really thank Daesh because they have united the Kurds and publicised our cause before the world."

Najat Ali, the Kurdistan Democratic Party commander in Makhmour, says that Isis is weakened by being no longer able to use its captured heavy artillery and Humvees because of US air strikes. Knowledge that US air power is protecting them had done a lot to raise Kurdish morale. He says: "Isis's psychological tactics, spreading terror through their atrocities, no longer works as [they] once did."

The recapture of Baiji refinery after months of fighting would boost the morale of the Iraqi government, though its most effective units are often Iranian-backed Shia militiamen.

Each side, if it concentrates its forces, can punch through the thinly held battle lines anywhere in Iraq and win a local success.

But such is the degree of sectarian and ethnic hatred that these little victories lead to mass flights of people who support the losing side.

Thursday, 4 December 2014

IRAN JOINS 'GREAT SATAN'S' WAR ON ISIS

The United States says Iranian F-4 Phantoms have carried out bombing raids against Isis north-east of Baghdad, a claim that appears to be confirmed by film of the aircraft taken from the ground.

Iran, however, denies that any of its planes are carrying out combat missions in Iraq. The raids are said to have taken place in Diyala province on the border with Iran, where there has been heavy fighting for months between Isis fighters, Shia militias and Kurdish Peshmerga. Isis has recently been driven out of the towns of Jalawla and Saadiyah.

An Iraqi security expert, Hisham al-Hashimi, told a news agency that 10 days ago: "Iranian planes hit some targets in Diyala. Of course, the government denies it because they have no radars." Film appears to show an F-4 in action, a type of aircraft only used by Iran and Turkey.

It is not clear why Iran should have used its air force for the first time in Iraq, though it has been giving heavy publicity to the role of Qasem Soleimani, the head of the Quds Force of the Islamic Revolutionary Guards, in inspiring and organising Shia militias.

Having long remained in the shadows, Mr Soleimani began to allow himself to be photographed and filmed in company with militia commanders. The militias are the main fighting force of the Baghdad government whose 350,000-strong army disintegrated when attacked by Isis in northern and western Iraq over the last six months.

The US and Iran were quick to deny that they are coordinating military action against Isis, though they are pursuing parallel policies in seeking to defend the governments in Baghdad and Irbil. The Pentagon spokesman Rear Admiral John Kirby told a news briefing on

Tuesday that the United States was not coordinating its military activities with Iran, and added that it was up to the Iraqis to manage Iraqi air space.

"It's the Iraqi air space and [Iraq's] to deconflict. We are not coordinating with nor are we deconflicting with Iranian military," Admiral Kirby said. However, it is likely that, if Iranian aircraft were in action, Iran would have told Baghdad what they were doing and the Iraqi military would have passed this on to the Americans.

John Kerry would not confirm that Iran had launched the strikes, saying it was "up to them or up to the Iraqis to do that, if indeed it took place". He said that if Iran did decide to launch strikes against Isis then the "net effect is positive".

US-Iranian policy in Iraq has been a mixture of open confrontation and covert cooperation since the overthrow of Saddam Hussein, whom both governments opposed in 2003. Today, they both want to stop and, if possible, eliminate Isis and at the same time expand their own influence.

The recently displaced Prime Minister Nouri al-Maliki remained in power for eight years because he was able to win the support of Washington and Tehran despite the extreme incompetence and corruption of his government. The US and Iran both eased the process of forcing him to leave office though he remains a force. He recently made a trip to Iran, where was received at the highest level.

The Iranian denial that its planes had conducted air raids was categorical as it was its rebuttal of any suggestion that it is co-operating with the US in Iraq. "Iran has never been involved in any air strikes against Daesh [Isis] targets in Iraq. Any co-operation in such strikes with America is also out of the question for Iran," a senior official said.

The Iraqi Prime Minister, Haider al-Abadi, in Brussels for a meeting of the US-led coalition against Isis, said he was not aware of any Iranian air strikes. The US Secretary of State, John Kerry, said the US-led coalition had inflicted serious damage on Isis, carrying out around 1,000 air strikes so far in Iraq and Syria, but the fight against the militants could last years.

Both Washington and Tehran were horrified when the Iraqi government suffered a complete defeat at Mosul on 10 June when attacked by much smaller Isis forces.

The US had spent years training the Iraqi army only to see it dissolve without fighting. Mr Maliki was increasingly seen as being under

Iran's influence, but it was a severe blow to Iran to watch the Shia-dominated government in Iraq collapse as the Sunni Arabs revolted. This brought America back as an important player in Iraq whose aid was once more badly needed by Baghdad and Irbil.

The Baghdad government now rules a Shia rump state that does little without conferring with Iran. When Isis attacked the Iraqi Kurds on 1 August and defeated the Peshmerga, so threatening Irbil, the US stepped in with air strikes and Iran sent advisers and artillery, say Kurdish sources.

The knowledge that at the end of the day the US and Iran will step in to prevent an Isis victory has done much to restore Iraqi army and Kurdish morale that had been undermined by Isis's terror tactics and surprise assaults.

WINTER 2015: SPREADING TERROR

Charlie Hebdo demonstrators, Paris, France, 10 January 2016

Thursday, 8 January 2015

VIOLENCE WAS BOUND TO SPREAD TO WESTERN EUROPE

There is a feeling of inevitability about the attack in Paris.

The likelihood must be that the killers were Islamic fanatics, the murder of the journalists and police underlining the degree to which the ferocious religious war being waged in Iraq and Syria now affects all of the world. Regardless of whether or not those who attacked the Charlie Hebdo office have any direct connection with this conflict, it has provided an ideal seedbed for Islamic extremism.

It was culpably naive to imagine that sparks from the Iraq-Syrian civil war, now in its fourth year, would not spread explosive violence to Western Europe. With thousands of young Sunni Muslims making the increasingly difficult journey to Syria and Iraq to fight for Isis, it has always been probable that some of them would choose to give a demonstration of their religious faith by attacking targets they deem anti-Islamic closer to home.

One way of measuring the spread of al-Qa'ida-type groups is to look at suicide bombings over the last week. Several of them have inflicted heavier casualties than at Charlie Hebdo, though little reported. For instance, in the heart of the Yemeni capital, Sanaa, yesterday, a suicide bomber driving a minibus packed with explosives killed 33 police cadets. On Tuesday, another suicide bomber killed 23 Iraqi soldiers and pro-government Sunni tribesmen in a town in Anbar province north-west of Baghdad.

The day before, gunfire and a suicide bombing killed the general heading the Saudi border control force and two others on the Saudi-Iraq frontier. On 30 December, a suicide bomb blew up outside the internationally recognised antijihadi Libyan government building in Tobruk.

Regardless of who carried out the Paris massacre, it would be surprising if West European states remained unaffected. One of the characteristics of the modern jihadi movement has been to commit highly public atrocities as intimidation and as a demonstration of their religious commitment.

This was a feature of 9/11, suicide bombings in Iraq, Syria and Afghanistan and the ritualised murder of journalists and aid workers on camera.

An added benefit from the jihadis' point of view comes if they can tempt the government of the country under attack into an overreaction that helps spread their cause.

Thus George Bush and Tony Blair played straight into the hands of al-Qa'ida by responding to 9/11 by sending armies to Iraq and Afghanistan. The American prison wardens of Abu Ghraib, by mistreating prisoners, and the CIA by torturing them, acted as recruiting sergeants for movements similar to al-Qa'ida. The countereffectiveness of that strategy is demonstrated by the surging growth of al-Qa'ida type jihadi movements 14 years after 9/11.

Can anything be done to reverse the trend towards the spread of Islamic fanaticism? Catching and punishing those responsible for the Charlie Hebdo massacre is not going to deter people who have martyrdom as a central feature of their faith. But bringing to an end, or even just de-escalating the war in Syria, would begin to drain the waters in which violent jihadism flourishes. Such a de-escalation means the US, Britain, France and their regional allies accepting that they are not going to overthrow President Bashar al-Assad and Assad accepting that he is not going to win back all of Syria. There should be local ceasefires between government and non-jihadi rebels. Power would not be shared at the top but divided geographically within Syria and, for the first time, governments in Damascus, Baghdad and Paris, could unite against violent Sunni jihadism.

Tuesday, 13 January 2015

TRAINING TERRORISTS IN YEMEN

After making rapid gains across Syria and Iraq last year, Isis has grabbed a great deal of attention from those who fear that parts of the Middle East are slipping into chaos, but the focus has moved away from Yemen where an already bad situation has continued to deteriorate.

Al-Qa'ida in Yemen is becoming more powerful because it provides the shock troops for a Sunni community that feels under increasing threat from a Shia insurgency that has seized much of the country. Its increased strength has nothing to do with foreign jihadis like Chérif and Saïd Kouachi, who killed 12 people in Paris last week and received training from AQAP based in Yemen in 2011 Aqap is finding support among Sunni tribes that previously fought against it but are now under pressure from the Houthis, who belong to a branch of Shia Islam known as the Zaidis. About a third of Yemenis are reckoned to belong to the sect which dominated the country for 1,000 years before the revolution of 1962. In September, the Houthis captured the capital, Sanaa, and have been pushing south against Sunni tribes ever since. These are increasingly looking to Aqap to provide experienced fighters and suicide bombers to battle the Houthi militiamen.

The Houthi advance "is only increasing al-Qa'ida membership," said an Aqap member interviewed by the Associated Press news agency. He added that the group's strategy was to fight the Houthis in central Yemen far from their strongholds in the north, and "drag them into a long war, and force them to retreat". He claimed that al-Qa'ida has spread to 16 out of 21 Yemeni provinces. There have been frequent bomb attacks against the Houthis around the city of Radaa, once held by al-Qa'ida militants in 2012, and now the centre of heavy fighting. A tribal leader in Radaa, Sheikh Ahmed al-Jabri, told the news agency that "it's a matter of vendetta against the Houthis. Tribes can even ally with the devil". The development is a serious blow to the long campaign by the US using drones against Aqap camps and militants.

Yemen has traditionally been more divided by tribal and regional allegiances than by sectarian differences between Shia and Sunni. But this is now changing, with Iran giving support to the Houthis and the Sunni states of the Gulf helping their opponents.

Different though Yemen is from Syria and Iraq, it is benefiting from many Sunnis looking to it as a source of experienced and fanatical fighters to defend their community when it comes under attack. The Yemeni government, always weak, has virtually collapsed, with President Abed Rabbo Mansour Hadi exercising little authority since the Houthis captured Sanaa on 21 September.

The Kouachi brothers covertly visited Yemen in 2011 and stayed two weeks. A Yemeni official said they met the US-born Aqap preacher Anwar al-Awlaki, who was killed in an American drone strike in September of that year. Saïd Kouachi is reported to have shared a room in Sanaa with Farouk Abdulmutallah, who later tried to blow up a plane with explosives hidden in his underwear.

Nevertheless, it is likely that Aqap is much more interested in exploiting the opportunities offered to it by the civil chaos and intermittent warfare in Yemen than it is in taking operational control of attacks in Paris. Despite claims that the Kouachi brothers received military training, little would have been needed to murder unarmed journalists and policemen caught by surprise.

The Yemeni President Ali Abdullah Saleh, who was forced to step down in 2011 after 33 years in power, once said that "ruling Yemen was like dancing on the head of snakes". The state has never been strong and its authority has depended on seeking the backing of tribes and foreign allies. But Yemenis now being sucked into the Sunni-Shia confrontation in the region with Saudi Arabia and the Sunni monarchies of the Gulf nervous of the influence of Iran and the Shia in Baghdad, Damascus, Beirut and now Sanaa. An Iranian leader has said the Houthis play the same role in Yemen as Hezbollah in Lebanon but the movement has always been much more than a pawn of Iranian foreign policy.

The growing strength of Aqap in Yemen means that there are now at least six countries in the wider Middle East and North Africa where jihadis from Europe can expect to receive support. These are areas held by the Taliban in Afghanistan, by Isis and other al-Qa'ida type groups in Iraq and Syria, and parts of eastern Libya, as well as in Yemen and Somalia. Given the numbers of foreign jihadis visiting these widely dispersed countries, it is an impossible task for Western security agencies to monitor and intercept them all.

Monday, 19 January 2015

RAPE AND SUICIDE

Many girls from the Yazidi community in Iraq are committing suicide after being raped and sold into sexual slavery by Isis fighters who captured them last August. Two hundred Yazidis were freed over the weekend because they were sick or old, and report continuing mistreatment of those still captive.

"They are very bad people," said Gawre Semo, 69, who reached the Kurdish-held town of Altun Kupri. "They took our children and they took our women."

A surprise Isis offensive in August led 50,000 Yazidis to flee into territory held by the KRG. But an unknown number, amounting to many thousands, were massacred or detained; many women were raped or sold as slaves. Isis says that such treatment of the Yazidis, whose ancient religion is drawn from Islam, Christianity and Zoroastrianism, is permissible under sharia.

Some 300 women who have escaped have given accounts to Amnesty International about how they were raped and sold as slaves. One girl, 20-year-old Luna, described how Jilan, 19, had committed suicide: "We were 21 girls in one room, two of them were very young, 10 to 12 years. One day we were given clothes that looked like dancing costumes and were told to bathe and wear these clothes. Jilan cut her wrists and hanged herself. I think she knew she was going to be taken away by a man and that is why she killed herself."

Arwa, who is 16, was abducted from her village south of Mount Sinjar in August along with relatives and neighbours. She described how she was moved around between Syria and Iraq until finally she was held in a house in Rambussi, south of Sinjar, with five other girls. She said: "They did to me what they did to many other girls. I was raped ... The men were all Iraqis. They said that if we killed ourselves they would kill our relatives."

Despite these threats, many girls kill themselves. The Amnesty International report "Escape from Hell: Torture and Sexual Slavery in Islamic State Captivity in Iraq" describes how Wafa, 27, and her sister tried to kill themselves after being told they were to be sold as slaves. She said: "We tied scarves around our necks and pulled away from each other, until we fainted." Wafa and her sister only survived because two other girls sleeping in there attempted suicide.

"Hundreds of Yazidi women and girls have had their lives shattered by the horrors of sexual violence and sexual slavery in captivity," said Donatella Rovera of AI, who spoke to 40 former captives.

"Many of those held as sexual slaves are children - girls aged 14, 15 or even younger." Captives are often forced to convert to Islam.

Isis launched a surprise attack on 3 August against KRG forces in Nineveh province around Mosul and Sinjar, where the Yazidi were heavily concentrated. The area contains some of their holiest sites.

The KRG Peshmerga fled immediately, often without telling Yazidi villagers that they were leaving. The first that many Yazidis knew of the offensive was when Isis arrived in their villages and it was too late to flee. A KRG counteroffensive in December has retaken part of Sinjar, but few Yazidis have returned to their homes.

Yesterday, General Shirko Fatih, commander of Kurdish forces in Kirkuk, said almost all of the freed prisoners were in poor health and bore signs of abuse and neglect.

The militants transported the captives from Tal Afar, where they were held for five months, and dropped them off at the Khazer Bridge, near the Kurdish regional capital of Irbil. "It probably became too expensive to feed them and care for them," said General Fatih.

Thursday, 22 January 2015

UNSTOPPABLE FLOOD OF JIHADI VOLUNTEERS

The tide of foreign volunteers crossing from Turkey into Syria to fight for Isis cannot be stopped, the Turkish Prime Minister has warned, with authorities unable to close the porous 510-mile border between the two countries.

Ahmet Davutoglu, whose government has been accused of not doing enough to stop jihadi fighters from Britain and other countries crossing into Syria, told *The Independent* that Turkey could not put "soldiers everywhere on the border". He added: "In any case, there isn't any state on the other side [of the frontier]."

Turkey plays a crucial role in the Syrian crisis because of its long border with the country, part of which is now controlled by Isis. Mr Davutoglu described how Turkey's close relations with Bashar al-Assad - "I visited there 62 times in 10 years" - soured in 2011 when "Assad started to kill his own people".

Mr Davutoglu said Isis was the creation of the war in Iraq and the US occupation after 2003. And Turkey - which is home to 1.5 million refugees who fled President Assad, and a further 500,000 who fled from Isis in Syria and Iraq - had nothing to do with the rise of Isis.

Barack Obama says the US will go on the offensive in Iraq, providing air support to the Iraqi army when it attacks Isis forces. But Iraqi sources say the army, badly beaten by Isis last summer, is failing to reconstitute itself despite US efforts to retrain it. Even when supported by air strikes, it has made little headway and many of its combat units remain grossly under-strength. This suggests that Isis is likely to continue to rule most of the territory it has seized in Iraq and Syria because its enemies are failing to unite and act decisively against it.

Thursday, 29 January 2015

ISIS ENEMIES DISUNITED

Isis is surviving attempts to defeat it and holds about the same amount of territory in Iraq and Syria - an area larger than Great Britain - as it did at the end of its blitzkrieg offensives last year. Its enemies are numerous, but disunited and without a common plan. Neither the Iraqi nor the Syrian armies, its chief military opponents, are strong enough to overrun the jihadist state. So long as Isis continues to exist, it retains the capacity to dominate the political and media agenda for days at a time by threatening the public execution of hostages. These grizzly events, as we have seen with the Japanese and Jordanian hostages, are stage managed in order to gain maximum publicity and inspire general terror.

Isis has suffered setbacks, but has also had successes. This week, its forces were finally driven out of the Syrian Kurdish town of Kobani after a siege lasting 134 days, in which it suffered heavy losses from 606 US air strikes. But elsewhere in Syria, Isis has been advancing towards the city of Homs as well as gaining strength south of Damascus and at al-Qalamoun, close to eastern Lebanon. By one account, Isis has won control of territory since last September where one million Syrians live, in addition to the area it already held.

In Iraq, government forces have made advances in the provinces around Baghdad, but earlier this week bullets hit a plane and wounded passengers over Baghdad International Airport, forcing major airlines to stop flying there. This isolates the Iraqi capital and, though the airport is not completely closed, Isis could probably achieve this at any moment. The Iraqi government's victories against Isis have largely been the work of sectarian Shia militias. Iraqi sources say that regular army brigades, with a nominal strength of 3,000, may have only a few hundred in the front line. Iraqi Kurdish Peshmerga have been winning back territory around Mosul from Isis as they advance behind a curtain of US air strikes. But Kurdish officials say their forces would never assault a Sunni Arab city like Mosul, because this would infuriate Sunni Arabs in general.

The failure of the Iraqi army to reconstitute itself after shattering defeats at the hands of Isis last summer has important political and military consequences. If the Baghdad government's main fighting force consists of Shia militiamen then it will be difficult to get Sunni support for the government. The militias tend to treat all Sunni as actual or potential Isis members. In recent fighting in Diyala province north-east of Baghdad and in Hilla - south-west of the capital - Sunni villages and towns taken from Isis have been emptied of their inhabitants. Where the Iraqi army has had successes and captured ground, it does not have enough men to hold it unless local commanders hand over to the militiamen. An Iraqi army with some Sunni soldiers is essential if Mosul is to be recaptured, say Iraqi observers.

Isis victories last summer frightened many countries and parties, hostile to each other in normal times, into coming together. In the battle for Kobani, the US at first kept its distance from the YPG - because they are ultimately commanded by the PKK which the US has called "terrorists". It was only when Kobani was on the verge of being captured by Isis in mid-October that the US began close air support for the YPG.

Retired US General James Mattis told the Senate Armed Services Committee this week that in the war against Isis, the US has a "strategy-free" stance. He said that in Syria, America's political objectives were uncertain and the time for supporting "moderate" Syrian rebels had passed. The Syrian armed opposition is increasingly under the control of Isis and its rival, the al-Qa'ida affiliate, Jabhat al-Nusra. President Bashar al-Assad is losing the important military advantage of fighting a fragmented rebel movement which, at one time, the US said consisted of 1,200 different groups.

Western political, military and security policies point in different directions and often contradict each other. The aim of the US and its allies is to defeat Isis, but also to get rid of Assad, though his fall would probably lead to the break-up of the Syrian army and benefit Isis and Jabhat al-Nusra. Turkey is an important ally against Isis, but its Prime Minister Ahmed Davutoglu told *The Independent* last week that it is impossible to close the 510-mile-long Turkish Syrian border to jihadists because the terrain is too difficult. According to the International Centre for the Study of Radicalisation and Political Violence, the number of foreign fighters joining Isis in Iraq and Syria has risen from 15,000 last October to 20,000 today. A fifth of these come from Western Europe. Isis has also conscripted fighters in the territories it controls.

Isis is being squeezed militarily and economically, but there is no sign of it imploding. Even its loss of Kobani is not necessarily a sign of weakness, since it held on for months despite fighting the highly motivated and well-organised Syrian Kurds, backed by an intensive US air bombardment in a confined place.

Western analysts are encouraged by the number of experienced Isis commanders killed last year, but its ideology is built around martyrdom, and the high casualty rate among leaders shows that they fight in the front line. President Obama says America's main effort is in Iraq but unless it can rebuild the Iraqi army then it will be near impossible to defeat Isis there. And so long as Isis continues, so too will high profile hostage-taking and executions.

FRACTURES THAT FAVOR ISIS

Isis is still receiving significant financial support from Arab sympathisers outside Iraq and Syria, enabling it to expand its war effort, says a senior Kurdish official. The US has been trying to stop such private donors in the Gulf oil states sending to Isis funds that help pay the salaries of fighters who may number well over 100,000.

Fuad Hussein, the chief of staff of the Kurdish President, Massoud Barzani, told *The Independent* on Sunday: "There is sympathy for Da'esh in many Arab countries and this has translated into money - and that is a disaster." He pointed out that until recently financial aid was being given more or less openly by Gulf states to the opposition in Syria - but by now most of these rebel groups have been absorbed into Isis and Jabhat al-Nusra, the al-Qa'ida affiliate, so it is they "who now have the money and the weapons".

Mr Hussein would not identify the states from which the funding for Isis comes today, but implied that they were the same Gulf oil states that financed Sunni Arab rebels in Iraq and Syria in the past.

Dr Mahmoud Othman, a veteran member of the Iraqi Kurdish leadership who recently retired from the Iraqi parliament, said there was a misunderstanding as to why Gulf countries paid off Isis. It is not only that donors are supporters of Isis, but that the movement "gets money from the Arab countries because they are afraid of it", he says. "Gulf countries give money to Da'esh so that it promises not to carry out operations on their territory."

Iraqi leaders in Baghdad privately express similar suspicions that Isis could not be financially selfsufficient, given the calls on its limited resources.

Islamic State is doing everything it can to expand its military capacity, as the Iraqi Prime Minister, Haider al-Abadi, and the US Central Command (CentCom) threaten an offensive later this year to recapture Mosul. Regardless of the feasibility of this operation, Isis forces are fighting in widely different locations across northern and central Iraq.

On Tuesday night they made a surprise attack with between 300 and 400 fighters, many of them North Africans from Tunisia, Algeria and Libya, on Kurdish forces 40 miles west of the Kurdish capital, Irbil. The Kurds say that 34 Isis fighters were killed in fighting and by US air strikes. At the same time, Isis was battling for control of the town of al-Baghdadi, several hundred miles away in Anbar province. Despite forecasts by a CentCom spokesman last week that the tide has turned and that Isis is on the retreat there is little sign of this on the ground.

On the contrary, Isis appears to have the human and financial resources to fight a long war, though both are under strain. According to interviews by *The Independent* with people living in Mosul reached by phone, or with recent refugees from the city, Isis officials are conscripting at least one young man from every family in Mosul, which has a population of 1.5 million. It has drafted a list of draconian punishments for those not willing to fight, starting with 80 lashes and ending with execution.

All these new recruits receive pay, as well as their keep, which until recently was $500 (£324) a month but has now been cut to about $350. Officers and commanders receive much more. A local source, who did not want to be named, says that foreign fighters, of whom there are an estimated 20,000 in Isis, get a much higher salary - starting at $800 a month.

"I know three foreign fighters," said Ahmad, a 45-year-old shopkeeper still working in Mosul. "I usually see them at checkpoints in our neighbourhood: one is Turkish and the others are Europeans. Some of them speak a little Arabic. I know them well because they buy soft drinks from the shops in our neighbourhood. The Turkish one is my customer. He says he talks to his family using the satellite internet service that is available for the foreigners, who have excellent privileges in terms of salaries, spoils and even captives."

Ahmad added: "IS fighters have arrested four high-school teachers for telling their students not to join IS." Islamic State fighters have entered the schools and demanded that students in their final year join them. Isis has also lowered the conscription age below 18 years of age, leading some families to leave the city. Military bases for the training and arming of children have also been established.

Given this degree of mobilisation by Islamic State, statements from Mr Abadi and CentCom about recapturing Mosul this spring, using between 20,000 and 25,000 Baghdad government and Kurdish forces, sound like an effort to boost morale on the anti-Isis side.

The CentCom spokesman claimed there were only between 1,000 and 2,000 Isis fighters in Mosul, which is out of keeping with what local observers report. Ominously, Iraqi and foreign governments have an impressive record of underestimating Isis as a military and political force over the past two years.

Mr Hussein said at the end of last year that Isis had "hundreds of thousands of fighters", at a time when the CIA was claiming they numbered between 20,000 and 31,500. He does not wholly rule out an offensive to take Mosul but, as he outlines the conditions for a successful attack, it becomes clear that he does not expect the city to be recaptured any time soon. For the Kurdish Peshmerga forces to storm Mosul they would need far better equipment "in order to wage a decisive war against Isis and defeat them", he says. "So far we are only defeating them in various places in Kurdistan by giving our blood. We have had 1,011 Peshmerga killed and about 5,000 wounded."

The Kurds want heavy weapons including Humvees, tanks to surround but not to enter Mosul, snipers' rifles, because Isis has many highly accurate snipers, as well as equipment to deal with improvised explosive devices (IEDs) and booby traps, both of which Isis uses profusely.

Above all, Kurdish participation in an offensive would require a military partner in the shape of an effective Iraqi army and local Sunni allies. Without the latter, a battle for Mosul conducted by Shia and Kurds alone would provoke Sunni Arab resistance. Mr Hussein is dubious about the effectiveness of the Iraqi army, which disintegrated last June when, though nominally it had 350,000 soldiers, it was defeated by a few thousand Isis fighters. "The Iraqi army has two divisions to protect Baghdad, but is it possible for the Iraqi government to release them?" asks Mr Hussein. "And how will they get to Mosul? If they have to come through Tikrit and Baiji, they will have to fight hard along the way even before they get to Mosul."

Of course, an anti- Isis offensive has advantages not available last year, such as US air strikes, but these might be difficult to use in a city. The US air force carried out at least 600 air strikes on the Isis-held part of the small Syrian Kurdish city of Kobani before Isis finally retreated after a siege of 134 days. In the most optimistic scenarios Isis splits or there is a popular uprising against it, but so far there is no sign of this and Isis has proved that it exacts merciless vengeance against any individual or community opposed to it.

Mr Hussein makes another important point: difficult and dangerous though it may be for the Kurds and the Baghdad government to recapture Mosul, they cannot afford to leave it alone. It was here that Isis won its first great victory and Abu Baqr al-Baghdadi declared the caliphate on 29 June last year.

"Mosul is important politically and militarily," he says. "Without defeating Isis in Mosul, it will be very difficult to talk about the defeat of Isis in the rest of Iraq."

At the moment, Peshmerga forces are only eight miles from Mosul. But Isis fighters are likewise not much further from the Kurdish-held oil city of Kirkuk, which Isis assaulted last month.

Given the size of Iraq and the small size of the armies deployed, each side can inflict tactical surprises on the other by punching through scantily held frontlines.

There are two further developments to the advantage of Islamic State. Even in the face of the common threat, the leaders in Baghdad and Irbil remain deeply divided. When Mosul fell last year, the government of Prime Minister Nouri al-Maliki claimed that the Iraqi army had been stabbed in the back by a conspiracy between Kurds and Isis. The two sides remain deeply suspicious of each other and, at the start of last week, a delegation led by the Kurdish Prime Minister Nechirvan Barzani failed to reach an agreement in Baghdad on how much of Iraq's oil revenues should go to the Kurds in exchange for a previously agreed quantity of oil from Kurdish-held northern oilfields.

"Unbelievably, the divisions now are as great as under Maliki," says Dr Othman. Islamic State has made many enemies, but it may be saved by their inability to unite.

Saturday, 28 February 2015

DESTROYING OUR PAST

Isis militants may next target for destruction the remains of the ancient Assyrian city of Nimrud after smashing statues and artefacts in Mosul museum. The men, who used sledgehammers and electric drills to destroy archaeological treasures, are quoted as telling bystanders that they would continue their work in Nimrud. One of the great cities of the Assyrian empire some 2,500 years ago, Nimrud lies in Isis-held territory east of the Tigris river, 30 miles south of Mosul.

Archaeologists are worried that the Isis-made video, showing the destruction of the antiquities and denouncing them as idols and against Islam, will encourage mass looting of the remains of ancient cities and palaces across northern Iraq and eastern Syria. The final scene in the video is shot outside at the so-called Nirgal Gate of the Assyrian city of Nineveh, which is intertwined with modern Mosul. A black-clad man is drilling into a massive stone winged bull, which the Assyrians commonly placed at the entrance to their cities, palaces and throne rooms. The man says: "Muslims, these artefacts that are behind me were idols and gods worshipped by people who lived centuries ago instead of Allah."

"I am fearful that there will be mass looting as in Syria," says Katharyn Hanson, a postdoctoral fellow at the University of Pennsylvania's Cultural Heritage Centre and a specialist in Mesopotamian archaeology, who is visiting Irbil. She says that Nineveh, Nimrud and other cities of the Assyrian empire, which once stretched from the Gulf to the Mediterranean, will "become like Dura-Europos on the Euphrates, a moonscape of craters [from looters' pits]." Dura-Europos is a Hellenistic city whose site used to be known as "the Pompeii of the Syrian desert".

The five cities most under threat from Isis are Nineveh, Nimrud, Ashur, Khorsabad and Hatra, all of which stand in the territory of the self-declared "Islamic State". A government official is quoted by Al Jazeera as saying that those breaking up the statues "told the people they will go next to Nimrud" to continue the destruction. Ms Hanson says she recalls Isis officials making similar threats against the Greco-Roman city of Hatra last year, although there is no evidence of destruction from there.

Fortunately, the most famous surviving monument of Nimrud is the great winged bull that is now in the British Museum, brought there by Austen Henry Layard in the mid-19th century. The golden treasure of Nimrud, 613 pieces of gold and precious stone excavated in the 1990s, is in Baghdad. But other artefacts at Nimrud could be vandalised and destroyed. It is already in some danger from its proximity to the battle lines between Isis and the Kurds, where there has been much fighting and heavy US air strikes in recent weeks.

Unlike most other public buildings there, on the day the Mosul museum was taken by the Kurds in 2003 it was not looted because its staff had persuaded looters not to. At that time, it contained only a limited number of important antiquities because they had been taken to Baghdad for safekeeping after the Kurdish and Shia uprisings of 1991 when provincial museums across the country had been ransacked.

Ms Hanson says that at first she "felt that the damage could have been a lot worse" until she saw the winged bull of the Nirgal Gate being destroyed with a drill and realised that all such sites are at risk. Iraq has 12,000 registered archaeological sites, of which 1,800 are in Isis-held territory.

Ms Hanson says that the video does not show what has happened to the prehistoric or Islamic galleries in the museum and fears that items there might be sold to dealers. Also in danger from looters are cuneiform tablets that can be easily sold on the international black market.

Isis in Syria started destroying ancient monuments long before the movement started doing the same thing in Iraq. In early 2014 it blew up Byzantine mosaics near Raqqa, Isis's Syrian capital, because they portrayed the human form. The systematic destruction of antiquities in Syria and Iraq by Isis is the worst disaster for ancient monuments since the Taliban in Afghanistan dynamited the giant statues of Buddha at Bamiyan in 2001 for similar ideological reasons.

In Syria many ancient remains along the Euphrates and in the north of the country are vulnerable because they were left in situ.

Professor Maamoun Abdulkarim, general director of antiquities and museums at the ministry of culture in Damascus, said then that extreme Islamic iconoclasm was a calamity. An expert on the Roman and early Christian periods in Syria, he added: "I am sure that if the crisis continues in Syria we shall have the destruction of all the crosses from the early Christian world, mosaics with mythological figures and thousands of Greek and Roman statues." His predictions have turned out to be all too true.

Monday, 16 March 2015

INSIDE THE ISLAMIC STATE

The so-called Islamic State wants to force all humanity to believe in its vision of a religious and social utopia existing in the first days of Islam. Women are to be treated as chattels, forbidden to leave the house unless they are accompanied by a male relative. People deemed to be pagans, like the Yazidis, can be bought and sold as slaves. Punishments such as beheadings, amputations and flogging become the norm. All those not pledging allegiance to the caliphate declared by its leader, Abu Bakr al-Baghdadi, on 29 June last year are considered enemies.

The rest of the world has watched with fascinated horror over the past eight months as the Islamic State, also known as Isis, imposed its rule over a vast area in northern Iraq and eastern Syria inhabited by six million people. Highly publicised atrocities or acts of destruction, such as burning to death a Jordanian pilot, decapitating prisoners and destroying the remains of ancient cities, are deliberately staged as demonstrations of strength and acts of defiance. For a movement whose tenets are supposedly drawn from the religious norms of the 7th century CE, Isis has a very modern and manipulative approach to dominating the news agenda by means of attention-grabbing PR stunts in which merciless violence plays a central role.

These are not the acts of a weird but beleaguered cult, but of a powerful state and war machine. In swift succession last year, its fighters inflicted defeats on the Iraqi army, the Iraqi Kurdish Peshmerga, the Syrian army and Syrian rebels. They staged a 134-day siege of the Syrian-Kurdish city of Kobani and withstood 700 US air strikes targeting the small urban area where they were concentrated before finally being forced to pull back. The caliphate's opponents deny it is a real state, but it is surprisingly well organised, capable of raising taxes, imposing conscription and even controlling rents.

Isis may be regarded with appalled fascination by most people, but conditions inside its territory remain a frightening mystery to the outside world. This is scarcely surprising, because it imprisons and frequently murders local and foreign journalists who report on its activities. Despite these difficulties, *The Independent* has tried to build up a complete picture of what life is like inside the Islamic State by interviewing people who have recently lived in Sunni Arab cities like Mosul and Fallujah that are held — or, in the case of Ramadi, the capital of Anbar province, 80 per cent held - by Isis.

Christians, Yazidis, Shabak and Shia, persecuted by Isis as heretics or idolaters, fled or were killed last year, so almost all of those interviewed are Sunni Arabs living in Iraq, with the exception of some Kurds still living in Mosul.

The aim of the investigation is to find out what it is like to live in the Islamic State. A range of questions need to be answered. Do people support, oppose or have mixed feelings about Isis rule and, if so, why? What is it like to live in a place where a wife appearing on the street without the niqab, a cloth covering the head and face, will be told to fetch her husband, who will then be given 40 lashes? How do foreign fighters behave? What is the reaction of local people to demands by Isis that unmarried women should wed its fighters? More prosaically, what do people eat, drink and cook, and how do they obtain electricity? The answers to these and many other questions show instances of savage brutality, but also a picture of the Islamic State battling to provide some basic services and food.

A point to emphasise is that none of those interviewed, even those who detest it, expect Isis to go out of business any time soon, although it is coming under increasingly effective pressure from its many enemies. These include the US, Iran, the Iraqi army, Shia militias, Iraqi Kurdish Peshmerga, Syrian Kurds and the Syrian army, to name only the main protagonists. Anti-Isis forces are beginning to win significant victories on the battlefield and the odds are heavily stacked against the Islamic State. Over the past week 20,000 Shia militiamen, 3,000 Iraqi security forces, 200 defence ministry commandos and 1,000 Sunni tribesmen have been fighting their way into Tikrit, Saddam Hussein's home town.

"The numbers are overwhelming," said General Martin Dempsey, chairman of the US Joint Chiefs of Staff, claiming that there are only "hundreds" of Isis fighters pitted against this massive pro-government force, although other reports suggest it may be closer to 1,000.

The fall of Tikrit would be a serious reversal for the Islamic State, though it is easy to exaggerate its impact. Isis claims that its victories are divinely inspired, but it has never felt duty-bound to fight to the last man and bullet for its every stronghold. It describes its strategy of fluid manoeuvre as "moving like a serpent between the rocks". Long a purely guerrilla force, it is at its most effective when it launches unexpected attacks using a deadly cocktail of well-tried tactics such as suicide bombers, IEDs and snipers. These are accompanied by well-made films of atrocities broadcast over the internet and social media, directed at frightening and demoralising its enemies. Isis may be retreating, but it can afford to do so, since last year it seized an area larger than Great Britain. Its strength is not just military or geographical but political - and this is a point raised by many of those interviewed. The dislike and fear that many Sunni Arabs feel for Isis is balanced and often outweighed by similar feelings towards Iraqi government forces. At the heart of the problem is the fact that last year Isis seized the leadership of the Sunni Arab communities in Iraq and Syria through its military victories.

So far no credible Sunni alternative to Isis has emerged. An assault by Iraqi government, Shia militia or Kurdish Peshmerga on Mosul would probably be resisted by the Sunni Arabs as an attack on their community as a whole.

"The Kurds cannot fight for Mosul alone because they are not Arabs," says Fuad Hussein, chief of staff of Kurdish President Massoud Barzani. "And I don't think the Shia militias would be willing to fight there; and in any case, local people would not accept them."

If no alternative to Isis emerges for the Sunni to rally to, then all the six million or so Sunni Arabs in Iraq may be targeted as Isis supporters, regardless of their real sympathies. In the long term, Isis could turn out to be the gravedigger of the Sunni Arabs in Iraq, where they are 20 per cent of the population, by stoking the hostility of the other 80 per cent of Iraqis, who are Shia or Kurds.

The Islamic State was declared in the weeks after the capture of Mosul, Iraq's second city, by Isis on 10 June 2014. It was only then that countries around the world began to wake up to the fact that Isis posed a serious threat to them all. Reorganised under Abu Bakr al-Baghdadi in 2010 after the death of the previous leader, Isis took advantage of the Syrian uprising of 2011 to expand its forces and resume widespread guerrilla warfare. Sunni protests against mounting repression by the Baghdad government transmuted into armed resistance. In the first half of 2014 Isis defeated five Iraqi divisions, a third of the Iraqi Army, to take over most of the giant Anbar province. A crucial success came when Isis-led forces seized the city of Fallujah, 40 miles west of Baghdad, on 3 January 2014 and the Iraqi army failed to win it back. This was the first time that Isis had ruled a large population centre and it is important to understand how it behaved and how and why this behaviour became more extreme as Isis consolidated its authority. The stories of two men, Abbas (generally known as Abu Mohammed) and Omar Abu Ali, who come from the militant

Sunni strongholds of Fallujah and the nearby town of al-Karmah, explain graphically what happened during those first crucial months
when Isis was in power.

Abbas is a 53-year-old Sunni farmer from Fallujah. He recalls the
joyous day when Isis first entered the city: "At the beginning... we
were so happy and called it 'the Islamic Conquest'. Most of the people
were offering them feasts and warmly welcoming their chief fighters."

Isis told people in Fallujah that it had come to set up an Islamic
state, and at first this was not too onerous. A Sharia Board of Authority
was established to resolve local problems. Abbas says that "everything was going well until Isis also took Mosul. Then restrictions on
our people increased. At the mosques, local imams started to be replaced by people from other Arab states or Afghanistan. During the
first six months of Isis rule, the movement had encouraged people to
go to the mosque, but after the capture of Mosul it became obligatory
and anybody who violated the rule received 40 lashes."

A committee of community leaders protested to Isis and received
an interesting reply: "The answer was that, even at the time of the
Prophet Mohamed, laws were not strict at the beginning and alcoholic
drinks were allowed in the first three years of Islamic rule." Only after
Islamic rule had become strongly entrenched were stricter rules enforced. So it had been in the 7th century and so it would be 1,400 years
later in Fallujah.

Abbas, a conservative-minded community leader with two sons
and three daughters in Fallujah, said he had no desire to leave the city
because all his extended family were there, though daily life was tough
and getting tougher. As of this February, "people suffer from lack of
water and electricity which they get from generators because the public supply only operates three to five hours every two days". The price
of cooking gas has soared to the equivalent of £50 a cylinder, so people
have started to use wood for cooking. Communications are difficult
because Isis blew up the mast for mobile phones six months ago, but
"some civilians have managed to get satellite internet lines".

However, it was not harsh living conditions but two issues affecting his children that led Abbas to leave Fallujah hurriedly on 2 January
this year. The first reason was a new conscription law under which
every family had to send one of their sons to be an Isis fighter. Abbas
did not want his son Mohammed to be called up. (Previously, families
could avoid conscription by paying a heavy fine but at the start of this

year military service in Isis-held areas became obligatory.) The second concerned one of Abbas's daughters. He says that one day "a foreign fighter on the bazaar checkpoint followed my daughter, who was shopping with her mother, until they reached home. He knocked on the door and asked to meet the head of the house. I welcomed him and asked: 'How can I help you?' He said he wanted to ask for my daughter's hand. I refused his request because it is the custom of our tribe that we cannot give our daughters in marriage to strangers.

"He was shocked by my answer and later attempted to harass my girls many times. I saw it was better to leave."

Abbas is now in the KRG area with his family. He regrets that Isis did not stick with its original moderate and popular policy before the capture of Mosul, after which it started to impose rules not mentioned in Sharia law. Abbas says that "we need Isis to save us from the government but that doesn't mean that we completely support them". He recalls how Isis prohibited cigarettes and hubblebubble pipes because they might distract people from prayer, in addition to banning Western-style haircuts, T-shirts with English writing on them or images of women. Women are not allowed to leave home unaccompanied by a male relative. Abbas says that "all this shocked us and made us leave the city".

A more cynical view is held by Omar Abu Ali, a 45-year-old Sunni Arab farmer from al-Karmah (also called Garma) 10 miles north-east of Fallujah. He has two sons and three daughters and he says that, when Isis took over their town last year, "my sons welcomed the rebels, but I wasn't that optimistic". The arrival of Isis did not improve the dire living conditions in al-Kharmah and he didn't take too seriously the propaganda about how "the soldiers of Allah would defeat [Iraqi Prime Minister Nouri al-] Maliki's devils". Still, he agrees that many people in his town were convinced by this, though his experience was that Saddam Hussein, Maliki or Isis were equally bad for the people of al-Kharmah: "They turn our town into a battlefield and we are the only losers."

Al-Kharmah is close to the front line with Baghdad and endures conditions of semi-siege in which few supplies can get through. A litre of petrol costs £2.70 and a bag of flour more than £65. Omar tried to buy as much bread as he could store to last his family a week or more "because even the bakeries were suffering from lack of flour". There was constant bombardment and in February the last water purification plant in town was hit, though he is not clear if this was done by artillery or US air strikes: "The town is now in a horrible situation because of lack of water."

Omar spent five months working for Isis, though it is not clear in what capacity, his main purpose being to prevent the conscription of his two sons aged 14 and 16. Rockets and artillery shells rained down on al-Karmah, though Omar says they seldom hit Isis fighters because they hid in civilian houses or in schools. "The day I left a school was hit and many children were killed," he recalls.

He says US air strikes and Iraqi army artillery "kill us along with Isis fighters. There is no difference between what they do and the mass killings by Isis". Omar had been trying to flee for two months but did not have the money until he managed to sell his furniture. He is now staying outside Irbil, the Kurdish capital, where his sons and daughters work on local farms which "is at least better than staying in al-Kharmah". He says the Americans, Iraqi government and Isis have all brought disaster and lists the wars that have engulfed his home town in the last 10 years. "All of them are killing us," he says. "We have no friends."

Tuesday, 17 March 2015

A GIFT FROM ALLAH

Hamza is a 33-year-old from Fallujah, a city ruled by Isis 40 miles west of Baghdad, who became an Isis fighter last year after being attracted by its appeal to his religious feelings. Two months ago, however, he defected, after being asked to help execute people he knew - and being appalled by invitations to join in what amounted to rape of captured Yazidi women.

In an interview with him, given in the safety of another country, Hamza gives a vivid account of why he joined Isis, what it was like to be a member of the jihadist group - and why he left.

He reveals extraordinary details about how the army of Isis operates, the elaborate training that its fighters receive in Iraq and Syria and the way in which taking part in executions is an initiation rite, proof of the commitment and loyalty of fighters.

An intelligent, idealistic, well-educated and religious man, Hamza defected from Isis after six months as a trainee and a fighter because he was deeply upset by the executions in Fallujah. He became conscious that if he stayed in Isis he would soon have to carry out an execution himself. "I don't like Shia, but when it comes to killing them, I was shocked," he says.

He refused to execute some Sunnis accused of working with Iraq's mostly Shia government "or what they [Isis] call 'the pagan government'," he said. Surprisingly, he was not punished for this, but was told by his commander that he would be asked to carry out an execution later and, in the meantime, foreign jihadis would do the job.

Hamza gives a fascinating insight into the lives led by Isis fighters. "I was paid 400,000 Iraqi dinars (£231) a month in addition to many privileges, including food, fuel and, more recently, access to the internet," he says. His disillusionment stemmed not only from his future role as an executioner, but the offer of sex with captured Yazidi women, something which he considered to be the equivalent of rape.

"It was in the first week of December 2014 when they brought about 13 Yazidi girls," he said. "The commander tried to tempt us by saying that this is Halal [lawful] for you; a gift from Allah that we are allowed to satisfy ourselves without even marrying them because they are pagans. "On the other hand, there were some Tunisian Muslim girls who came from Syria. Those Muslim girls were sleeping with some commanders under a marriage contract for a week only and then they were divorced and married to another one. I asked one of them how she had come to be in Syria and she answered that she had travelled first to Turkey and then across the Turkish-Syrian border." The three British schoolgirls who likewise crossed into Syria may well find that they are similarly treated by Isis.

Hamza does not want his real name or location disclosed, though he believes that for the moment he is safe. He asked for certain details about his escape in January be concealed, but otherwise is open about how he came to join Isis forces and what he did.

In many cases what he says can be confirmed by other witnesses from Fallujah interviewed by *The Independent*, though none of these were fighters.

"It's a complicated story," he says, when asked how he came to join Isis. Last year, the group captured Fallujah, where Hamza and his family were living.

"They were kind to people in general and did not force them to join their military service," he recalls. "They had many ways of gaining people's goodwill and support.

"For example, they would go house to house, asking those living there if they needed anything and offering services such as education, saying, 'We will enlighten your children, so don't send them to the government's schools.' In addition, they were giving small lectures and sermons after prayers.

"Most of the lecture topics were about how to reform and improve society, using the Koran and Hadith [traditional Islamic teachings] to support their arguments.

"This was like some kind of brainwashing, but it happened slowly over six months. I was attending many of those lectures and, after a time, I was preparing in advance the Koranic verses and Hadith texts relevant to the topics.

"There were weekly competitions between groups of youths. I won two competitions on these religious topics and each time I received 300,000 Iraqi Dinars."

Last July, his family left Fallujah for Baghdad, but he remained behind.

"After winning two prizes, I felt I liked their system," he says. "When my family left, my father asked me not to stay and told me not to be too influenced by the prizes I had won. He said the situation would get worse. He was not very opposed to Isis, but he is so old and cannot cope with the hard life in Fallujah after conditions deteriorated - in terms of work, electricity, water, food and the militarisation of life."

Hamza told his family that he would follow them to Baghdad within a few days, but had decided at this moment, July 2014, to join Isis. His motive was primarily religious and idealistic. He says that he "decided to join them willingly because I was convinced that [Isis] is the ideal state to serve, and to work for, Allah and the after-life, which is the surest part of life".

He was accepted immediately by Isis, his preacher recommending him to a military commander, though he was not at first sent to a military unit.

The details Hamza gives of his induction and training by Isis are significant because they help explain how it has created such a formidable military machine.

First, he was told to do exercises to get him into good physical shape.

"The exercises I did in July and August 2014 were physical activity exercises, fitness training and abdominal exercises," he says. "After that, I was transferred to a military unit outside Fallujah for a month and then I was sent for a month and a half to Raqqa [in Syria] where I was taught military skills through intensive training courses.

"In Fallujah, I had learned to shoot using Kalashnikov rifles and how to throw grenades. It was a more advanced level of training in Raqqa where I, together with a group of volunteers, learned to use RPG [rocket propelled grenade] launchers and different kinds of machine guns."

Asked why Isis had taken him and other volunteers to Raqqa for military training, Hamza has an interesting response. "The reason wasn't because training is not available in Iraq. All kinds of training, equipment and facilities are available in Fallujah, but we were taken to Raqqa to increase our sense of what is called 'patriotism towards the caliphate lands' and to introduce us to a new experience and a new revolution.

"When they took us to Raqqa, all the fighters became convinced that the boundary between Syria and Iraq is fake and we are all united under the rule of the Caliphate. Psychologically speaking, I was so relaxed and happy to go there because it was a nice feeling to destroy the borders between two governments and pass through them. This was really a great achievement."

Executions play an important role in the life of Isis, not only as a means of intimidating enemies but as an initiation rite and proof of faith by new fighters. Hamza says that in Raqqa trainees like him were sent to watch public executions: "I attended three executions in Raqqa and others in Fallujah. One was of a man believed to be working with the Syrian regime. He was just shot."

In Fallujah, captured Shia soldiers of the Iraqi Army were executed.

"This was the first time that I witnessed a beheading," he said. "I had been shown some videos made with impressive visual and audio skill. After watching many of these, we were being taken to attend public executions."

Asked if he had carried out any executions himself, Hamza said that he had not and explained why. "I was not ordered to do so because according to Isis rules, the trainee needs more than six months to be ready to carry out an execution. But this is not the only criterion. The trainee should also show additional skills in his religious education and military tactics as well as many other tests.

"However, the problem was that I was a little bit shaken after attending those executions. I don't like Shia but when it came to killing them, I was shocked. Although they were showing us videos of Shia militias killing Sunni people, we were troubled when we attended real executions.

"In November, a large number of Sunni men were taken prisoner on the grounds that they were working with the government.

"In the fourth week of November there were some executions to be carried out. One of our commanders asked me and my fellow fighters to bring our guns to be used in an execution the following day.

"But the victims were Sunnis, some of whom I knew.

"I couldn't endure what we were going to do. I tried to explain that, if they were Shia I would do it immediately. The commander said: 'I will give you another chance later. For now we have Mujahideen [jihadis] to carry out the killing.'" It may also have been that Hamza had not served the full six months normally required in Isis before becoming a fully-fledged executioner. It was shortly after he had refused to execute Sunni prisoners that Hamza and other Isis volunteers were offered the 13 Yazidi girls for sex. He says that the two events together shattered his idealistic enthusiasm for Isis and created doubts in his mind. He gives a compelling description of his mental turmoil at this time, thinking of "the executions, or more horribly the beheadings, as well as the raping of the non-Muslim girls. These scenes terrified me.

"I imagined myself being caught up in these shootings, executions, beheadings and raping, if I stayed where I was."

Now he started to plan his escape, but he knew that this would be difficult and dangerous. He says one Isis fighter had tried to run away but was caught and executed for treason. "The problem is that no one was trustworthy, not even close friends," he says. Nevertheless, he managed to make arrangements with a friend outside the caliphate to help him using the instant messaging service Viber, taking advantage of the satellite internet connection that was available to fighters in Fallujah for three hours at a time, three days a week.

Mobile phones evidently worked in at least part of Fallujah (though Isis has blown up mobile masts elsewhere as a security measure), but only some particularly trusted fighters were allowed to have them. "I told my commander that I needed a mobile to talk to my family and he agreed, saying that I will be given more privileges as I prove my loyalty and courage," Hamza says.

This enabled him to arrange his escape, through friends and smugglers whom he paid to help him. He made his move one early January night when he was put on guard duty on the outskirts of Fallujah, enabling him to slip away easily. It took him five days to reach a place of safety. He has given *The Independent* details of his itinerary, but publication of these might compromise his security. He is not sure if Isis will pursue him actively and says that he has held back some information about the group because he fears their reaction.

He admits that there are also limits to what he does know: "For example we, the fighters, were not able to enter what they call the operation rooms, which have many computers and foreign experts, though sometimes my comrades would use the internet nearby and get the wi-fi passwords through giving money to the technicians," he said.

As a recently recruited fighter, he did not meet any senior members of Isis or lieutenants of its leader, Abu Baqr al-Baghdadi. "No, they were always moving from one place to another," he says. "And they keep talking about al-Baghdadi, saying that he is still living. I am sure and have been told that they [the Isis leadership] are Iraqis only."

Asked if he thinks Isis will be defeated, he says that this will not be easy, even though coalition air strikes mean "they cannot advance now".

Hamza says he is now entirely disillusioned with Isis. "At the beginning I thought they were fighting for Allah, but later I discovered they are far from the principles of Islam. I know that some fighters were taking hallucinatory drugs. Others were obsessed with sex. As for the raping, and the way different men marry by turn the same woman over a period of time - this is not humane.

"I left them because I was afraid and deeply troubled by this horrible situation. The justice they were calling for when they first arrived in Fallujah turned out to be only words."

'THEY POKE THEIR NOSES INTO EVERYTHING'

It was on 4 October last year that Isis captured the small city of Hit, seizing complete control in the space of just a few hours. For the city's 100,000 mostly Sunni residents the takeover by the self-proclaimed Islamic State has brought changes that some support, but others deeply resent.

Among those living in Hit when Isis rolled in was Faisal, a 35-year-old government employee who is married with two children, and a keen observer of all that has befallen the agricultural centre and former transport hub over the past five months.

He recently fled to the Kurdish capital, Irbil, where he described to *The Independent* the rule of Isis and its impact on Hit, starting with the day the city was captured.

"First let me tell you how Isis entered the city," he says. "At 4am we heard an explosion; Isis had exploded a bomb at the main checkpoint. Then they started fighting inside and outside the city. This was because some of their fighters were attacking from outside but others were locals, who belonged to sleeper cells and attacked the Iraqi security forces from behind. They captured all the police stations, aside from two that resisted until 5pm, after which Isis had total control."

Faisal, not his real name, says he had no problems with Isis checkpoints even during the first days after the jihadist group captured Hit, because they were often manned by his neighbours who knew who he was. They had lists of wanted people and they sometimes checked ID cards.

One of the first things that happened was that the electricity went off. This was because 90 per cent of power in Anbar province comes from a hydroelectric power station, the largest in Iraq, at Haditha, 50 miles up the Euphrates river from Hit. Isis had seized most of the province but not Haditha.

Faisal explains: "When Isis took Hit, they stopped food being sold to people in Haditha because it was still held by the government. In response, Haditha cut off the supply of electricity to Hit and many other cities which had come under Isis control."

This stopped all projects in Hit dependent on electricity, including the water-treatment stations, so there was a water shortage. People had to obtain their water from the heavily polluted Euphrates.

Because Hit is at the centre of an agricultural area there continues to be plentiful food available at cheap prices. The problem is that, although food is inexpensive, many cannot afford to buy it because all paid work has stopped and nobody is earning any money. Paradoxically, the only people still paid are Iraqi government employees, because even though it has lost control of the city, Baghdad wants to retain their loyalty - Isis does not want to prevent earnings that it can tax.

Isis provides some services itself by taking domestic gas cylinders, almost invariably used in Iraq for cooking, to be refilled in the group's Syrian capital Raqqa.

Faisal particularly resents Isis's vigorous intervention in every aspect of daily life in Hit. "They poke their noses into education, mosques, women's clothes, taxes on shops (Zakat), and many other aspects of life," he said. "My parents and brothers told me yesterday via satellite internet call that there are about 2,000 men appointed to check the shops in the city and collect the taxes under the name of Zakat, not just from the shops, but from employees' salaries.

"In education they changed the courses taught before and brought in new ones, that are being taught now in Raqqa and Fallujah. Some courses are modified or cancelled, like philosophy and chemistry. They cancelled classes in art, music, geography, philosophy, sociology, psychology and Christian religion, and asked mathematics teachers to remove any questions that refer to democracy and elections.

"Biology teachers can't refer to evolution. Arabic classes are not allowed to teach any 'pagan' poems." (Isis refers to anything outside the boundaries of its self-declared Caliphate, established on 29 June last year, as the Pagan World.) Faisal says petrol and oil products are available in Hit, but they are expensive and of poor quality. "This is because the crude oil available in Raqqa [Isis captured most of the Syrian oilfields] is refined in a rough-and-ready way and then exported to Iraqi regions under Isis control. These poor-quality oil products ruin car engines, machinery and generators."

Isis is paranoid about mobile phones and the internet being used to communicate information about it, giving away the location of its leaders and military units which could then be destroyed by US air strikes. Until February, mobile phones were working in Hit, but then there was heavy fighting in the nearby town of al-Baghdadi and Isis, fearing spies, blew up the mobile telephone masts.

The internet has not worked in Anbar Province for the past eight months, compelling people to use satellite internet connections that are monitored by Isis. More recently the group offered a limited internet service, though this is only available in internet offices and other locations monitored by the jihadist group. There is no internet access from private homes, while in the public locations, Faisal says, "Isis can spy on computers so they can see what you are surfing and to whom you are talking".

Predictably, Isis focuses on religion and spreading its variant of Islam. Faisal says: "Many preachers (imams) were replaced by foreign preachers from the Arab world, mostly Saudis, Tunisians and Libyans, as well as Afghans. Some new imams are appointed temporarily just for Friday speech and prayer, while others are permanent appointments. Isis removed some of the old preachers who have left for Baghdad or KRG (the Kurdish-controlled region). These are often Sufis, whose beliefs are rejected by Isis."

There are many other signs of Isis imposing its cultural agenda in Hit. Faisal says that "at the entrance to every main street and bazaar, there are Isis groups holding black dresses that cover the whole body including the face and head. If a woman does not have one, she must buy one [for about £8] and the money goes to the Isis treasury."

Are people joining Isis in Hit? Faisal says they do, often for economic reasons. "I know many people in my neighbourhood in Hit who joined Isis," he says. "They are paid little money, about 175,000 dinars (£80), but they say that the salary is enough because they also enjoy many privileges, including free fuel, cooking gas, sugar, tea, bread, and many other foodstuffs and services.

"Isis still has a strong financial basis. It confiscates the houses of the people who were previously employed in the police, courts, and security forces. These houses, and any furniture in them, are confiscated by the Sharia (legal or religious) court, where the judges are Libyan and Tunisian, though the other staff are locals. The ruling authority in Hit is headed by the military governor, the religious [legal] governor, the security governor and finally the administrative governor."

Faisal's account of life in Hit is confirmed by eyewitnesses from other parts of the Islamic State. Isis at first benefited from widespread popular relief that the Iraqi Army was gone, but there is deepening resentment against the enforcement of outlandish rules on personal behaviour that is contrary to local religious and social traditions. These include women being forced to wear the niqab (covering their faces), obligatory attendance at prayers and the destruction of mosques, such as the Younis mosque in Mosul, deemed by Isis to be un-Islamic shrines.

There is also the fear of conscription of young men to fight for the Islamic State, an obligation that is increasingly difficult to avoid and is leading many families to try to leave Isis-controlled territory, which is not easy to do.

But despite resentment by many at its takeover of mosques and schools, Isis is able to use these to propagate its views and to make converts - something that may strengthen the forces of the Islamic State. Conscription does not seem to have diluted the fanaticism of Isis fighters, or their willingness to take heavy casualties, according to Kurdish commanders who have come under attack by Isis units in recent months.

Local eyewitnesses confirm that the unpopularity of Isis is not universal. Sameer, a Kurdish shopkeeper in Mosul, told *The Independent* last November that "in spite of the coalition air strikes every night and every morning, Isis increases in terms of the number of its men and the territory they occupy".

Since then, Isis has retreated from much of the Sinjar area west of Mosul, but Ali Hussein Mustafa, a 21-year-old university student who left Mosul last month, says that "many Isis men were much better than the fighters of the Iraqi Army in dealing with people and helping them".

He says this better behaviour was not invariable and criticised Isis fighters at some checkpoints who harassed or swore at women whose faces were not hidden. He added, however, that many people had now concluded that "Isis rule is no better, and maybe worse, than what they endured before [when the US or Iraqi government was in charge of Mosul from 2003 to 2014]".

When discussing the origins and motivations of Isis as a movement, Faisal, hitherto factual and down-to-earth, falls back on conspiracy theories. Because he believes that the actions of Isis will be very damaging to the Sunni in the long term, he is convinced that it must be under the control of the Sunni's traditional enemies. "To me,

Isis is an Iranian-American project and, when its mission ends, Isis may leave the region," he says. "Most of the Sunni people who experience the rule of Isis do not believe it is establishing a state, but intends to destroy Sunni areas."

More realistically, Faisal detects a lack of seriousness in Baghdad's efforts to drive out Isis, saying that "so long as corruption prevails, any solution to the problems of the country, including the recapture of cities taken by Isis, will not work". As for the impact of US air strikes, "they are limiting the movement of Isis a little bit and weakening it, but not more".

How does Isis compare with its predecessor, al-Qa'ida in Iraq? Faisal has strong opinions on this: "I remember when we were dealing with al-Qa'ida in 2005 and 2006. Al-Qa'ida men are angels compared to the demons of Isis. In Hit 10 years ago, there were many military operations by al-Qa'ida, but nobody thought of leaving the city as many do today. The old al-Qa'ida was much better than Isis. We hate the government, but Isis is not the appropriate substitute. We hate Isis, but imagine if the Shia militia were the substitute for it! The situation would be more horrible. Every substitute is worse than the previous one."

Thursday, 19 March 2015

A BLEAK FUTURE IN IRAQ FOR SUNNIS

Mahmoud Omar, a young Sunni photographer, is angered though not entirely surprised by the way in which the Baghdad government continues to mistreat his fellow Sunnis. Political leaders inside and outside Iraq all agree that the best, and possibly the only, way to defeat Isis is to turn at least part of the Sunni Arab community against it.

The idea is to repeat the US success in 2006-07 in supporting the Sunni "Awakening Movement" which weakened, though it never destroyed, al-Qa'ida in Iraq, the predecessor of Isis. Now as then, many Sunnis hate the extremists for their merciless violence and enforcement of outlandish and arbitrary rules on personal behaviour that have no connection to even the strictest interpretation of sharia. The fact that so many Sunnis are alienated from or terrified by Isis should present an opportunity for Baghdad, since Prime Minister Haider al-Abadi's government is meant to be more inclusive than that of his predecessor, Nouri al-Maliki. Increasingly aggressive sectarian policies pursued by Mr Maliki during his eight years in power are now blamed for turning peaceful protests by Sunnis into armed resistance and pushing the Sunni community into the arms of Isis. This is an over-simplified version of recent history, but with the new government lauded internationally for its non-sectarian stance, the Sunni hoped they would face less day-to-day repression. "Isis has shocked many Sunni by its actions," says Mahmoud. "But instead of the government treating us better to win us over, they are treating us even worse."

As an example of this he cites the behaviour of police in Ramadi, the capital of the vast and overwhelmingly Sunni province of Anbar. His family comes from the city, which used to have a population of 600,000. Now 80 per cent have fled the fighting as Isis and government forces battle for control. Isis launched seven almost simultaneous suicide bomb attacks last week and was already holding 80 per cent of Ramadi.

The situation inside the government-held enclave is desperate, with shortages of food, fuel and electricity. Trucks bringing in supplies have to run the gauntlet of Isis checkpoints and ambushes. Food prices have risen sharply and in outlying cities, like al-Qaim and al-Baghdadi, Mahmoud says that "the people are reduced to eating fodder."

Schools are closed to pupils because they are full of refugees. But in the midst of this crisis, Mahmoud - who asked for his real name not to be published - says the local police are as predatory and corrupt as ever when it comes to dealing with the Sunni.

He says that in one police station in the government held part of Ramadi "the police go on arresting Sunni, torturing them and refusing to release them until their families come up with a bribe. I know one man who was in there for a week before his family paid the police $5,000 to get him released."

All the old methods of surveillance remain in place with shop-keepers forced to spy on their customers and hand in daily reports to the police. Predictably, Mahmoud dismisses as "promises and words" the pledges of the new Abadi government to be more even-handed - intentions the Americans and Europeans apparently take at face value.

As a photographer and educated member of a politically moderate, well-off family, Mahmoud would be seen by Isis as a natural enemy.

His family have lost much because of the jihadist group's takeover of Anbar. His father only stayed in Ramadi until recently because he wanted to safeguard two houses he owned. A third house in Fallujah has been taken over by Isis and the family doesn't know what has happened to it; Isis sends officials door to door and, if the owner of a house has fled, they give him 10 days to return or they confiscate the property. But for all his dislike of Isis, Mahmoud would have great difficulty trusting the Baghdad government. This is because a relative, Muad Mohammed Abed, who was a teacher and has a wife and daughter, has been in prison since 2012, under sentence of death for murder.

It is a crime he and his family vehemently deny he committed, saying that the only evidence against him is a confession obtained after torture. They have photographs of Muad taken after his interrogation, showing him covered in bruises and burns. His sentence was ultimately quashed, but he remains in jail. A promised retrial may be a long time coming because there are 1,500 similar cases to be heard by a court before his turn comes. His wife, who visits him in prison, says that he is kept in a cell four metres square with seven other prisoners. They are forbidden to have a radio or television.

Muad's experience is fairly common. Many of the young Sunni men from villages near Fallujah are in prison awaiting execution because they have been tortured into confessing to capital crimes. The only way for them to be freed is through a large bribe to the right official.

Mahmoud recalls that in 2012 he investigated 12 cases in which people were tortured to death, "including a pharmacist who was arrested when he refused to supply drugs to soldiers and police at checkpoint near his pharmacy".

Most of Mahmoud's family have now fled to Kurdistan. He sees their misfortunes as mirroring the suffering of the Sunni community as a whole. He fears that the Iraqi Sunnis will be ground to pieces in the struggle between Isis and the government and that, as Isis is pushed back, the Sunni community will share in its defeat so "we will end up like the Christians who are being forced out of the country".

Yet for all Mahmoud's passionate sense of injustice, his belief that the government is irredeemably anti-Sunni is only part of the story. Sunni and Shia have both used mass violence against one another's communities in the past 50 years, but the Sunni have most often been the perpetrators. The explosive growth of sectarian killings in 2012 to 2014, when 31,414 civilians were killed according to Iraqi Body Count, very much reflects the growth of Isis.

The group carried out massacres of Shias and Yazidis as a matter of policy, and then broadcast videos of the murders. Isis bombers targeted bus queues, funerals, religious processions and anywhere else where Shia gathered and could be killed. The obvious motive was anti-Shia and a desire to destabilise the government, but there was also a carefully calculated policy at work of provoking Shia into retaliation against Sunni.

Isis knew that this would leave the Sunni with no alternative but to fight and die alongside them.

As Isis's columns advanced last year, its fighters carried out massacres to spread fear just as Saddam Hussein had done against the Kurds and Shia a quarter of a century earlier. When the government's Badush prison, near Mosul, was captured by Isis, its fighters slaughtered 670 Shia prisoners. At Camp Speicher, outside Tikrit, 800 Shia cadets were lined up in front of trenches and machine gunned. Pictures of the scene resemble those of atrocities carried out by the German army in Russia in 1941. In August, when Isis fighters stormed into Kurdish-held regions, they targeted the Yazidis as "pagans" to be murdered, raped and enslaved. The Isis advance in Iraq had largely ended by last October. Since then it has retreated, though not very far. Where Shia militias or Kurdish Peshmerga have successfully counter-attacked, the Sunni have generally fled before their towns and villages were recaptured - or they have been subsequently expelled. It is not surprising that the Shia and Kurdish commanders fighting back are not in a forgiving mood. There is an almost universal belief among last year's victims - be they Shia, Yazidis, Christians or Kurds - that their Sunni Arab neighbours collaborated with Isis.

Where Isis is beaten back, the Sunni may hold on to their strongholds where they are the great majority, but where populations are mixed they are likely to be losers. A final ethnic and sectarian shake-out in Iraq seems to be under way.

Is the defeat of Isis, and with it the Sunni, inevitable? In the long term it is difficult to see any alternative outcome in Iraq because they make up only a fifth of the population and their more numerous ene-mies are backed by the US and Iran. The land mass held by Isis may be large, but it was always poor and is becoming more impoverished.

There is little electricity. In Mosul, Ahmad, a shopkeeper in the Bab al-Saray area, says: "We are getting only two hours of electricity every four days." There are private generators, he says, "but since there are no jobs, people have no money to pay their electricity bills or for generator supply services".

This has had the effect of reducing some prices because there is no power for fridges and freezers, meaning food cannot be stored for long.

Deteriorating living conditions mean that many want to leave Mosul, but they are prevented by Isis, which does not want to find that its greatest conquest has become a ghost town. In any case, it is not clear where the one million people still in Mosul would go.

As the fighting intensifies across Iraq this spring, the Sunni cities and towns are likely to be devastated. Mahmoud may well be right in thinking that the Sunni will be forced to take flight or become a vul-nerable minority like the Christians.

Even if the government in Baghdad wanted to share power with the Sunni, Isis has ensured through its atrocities that this will be near impossible. For its part, Isis has been raising tens of thousands more fighters - they may now number well over 100,000 in Iraq and Syria. The so-called Islamic State will not go down without fierce resistance and, if it does fall, the Sunni community will be caught up in its de-struction.

Friday, 20 March 2015

THE DIVIDE THAT LETS TERROR RULE

The Islamic State still rules most of the territories it captured last year in Iraq and Syria. It may no longer be expanding, but it is little diminished, despite 2,500 US air strikes hitting its military forces and economic infrastructure.

The much-heralded offensive by some 25,000 Iraqi government forces aimed at recapturing the small city of Tikrit has come to a halt over the past week, though American officials say the city is held by only a few hundred Isis fighters. The faltering assault, though it may

ultimately succeed, bodes ill for plans to recapture the much larger
city of Mosul later in the year.

The battle for Tikrit illustrates one of the great strengths of Isis:
the divisions of its many enemies.

In this case, the attack force is made up of 20,000 Shia militia
armed and directed by Iran. There are only 3,000 Iraqi army soldiers.
The US says it is not supporting the advance with air strikes because
it has not been asked to do so.

It is also concerned about its aircraft becoming the flying artillery
for anti-Sunni sectarian cleansing by Shia militias. Iran and the US may
both be combating the so-called Islamic State, but they are conducting
very different wars. Consequently, Tikrit has been a long time falling
despite Isis being so wholly outnumbered.

Preservation of Isis depends on its powers of resistance and the
strength of the forces battering at its outer defences. The inability so
far of the US-led coalition, including the UK, France, Saudi Arabia and
other regional powers, to win victories against Isis, is explained by
failures that are political rather than military.

Crucially, the US and its allies are not giving air support to the
Shia militias and the Syrian army which are the two largest ground
forces opposing Isis.

The importance of ground-air cooperation was made plain by the
siege of the Syrian-Kurdish town of Kobani which Isis failed to take
thanks to cooperation between Syrian Kurdish fighters and American
aircraft which carried out 700 air strikes. Likewise, in Iraq the only
place where the US and its allies were able to help drive back Isis was
in Sinjar, where their aircraft were cooperating with Iraqi Kurdish
Peshmerga.

The Islamic State can probably hold out against attacks from a
US-backed coalition or an Iranian backed one if each fights separately,
but not against a combination of the two. American and western European leaders may feel that they have done enough to pen Isis into
the admittedly vast area it conquered last year. Certainly, it has made
no significant advances since last October and has lost some territory,
but the belief that it can safely be left to its own barbaric devices is
short-sighted. The Islamic State is not going to implode because of
mounting popular discontent within its borders. Its enemies may de-
ride its pretensions to be a real state, but in terms of the ability to

conscript troops, raise taxes and impose its brutal variant of Islam, it is stronger than many neighbouring countries.

In recent weeks *The Independent* has sought to discover the real state of feeling among people living within that portion of the Islamic State inside Iraq. In a series of interviews published this week we have spoken to Iraqis who have just left the self-declared caliphate and can tell from recent experience what it is really like. We asked people from Sunni Arab towns and cities along the Tigris and Euphrates rivers such as Mosul, Fallujah, Ramadi, Karnah and Hit what their lives are like and how they rate the chances of the Islamic State surviving.

Many express detestation or disillusionment with their present rulers, but none predicted their imminent defeat. Almost all those questioned are Sunni Arabs and many said that, bad though Isis might be, the alternative in the shape of a corrupt and sectarian government might be even worse. "We hate Isis, but imagine if the Shia militia were the substitute for it," said Faisal, a former government employee from Hit, on the Euphrates, west of Baghdad. "The situation would be more horrible. Every substitute is worse than the previous one."

Isis feels itself under growing military and economic pressure, but it has also shown itself capable of rising to the challenge. It has long borders to defend, requiring many more soldiers than the 5,000 or so it fielded before the capture of Mosul on 10 June last year. Its front line with the Iraqi Kurds alone is 600 miles long (compare this with the Western Front in 1914 which was 440 miles long). The response by Isis is to conscript one man of military age from every family living in territory under its control and, since the population it rules numbers about six million, this means that it is becoming a far larger military organisation than it was last year.

Of course, seeing their sons disappear into an army from which they may never return is not popular with their families. Many interviews conducted by *The Independent* were with people who had recently fled Islamic State territory because military service has become obligatory (previously men who paid a large fine were excused service).

Ali Hussein Mustafa, a student in Mosul, explains that his family finally left because Isis recently amended the conscription law to include men under 18, which meant that his younger brother became liable for military service. Society within the self-declared caliphate is being militarised.

The standard of living within the Islamic State is deteriorating, but this will not necessarily weaken its authority because what resources there are go to its fighting forces. Hamza, the fighter who defected and was cited in Tuesday's article, says that while he was not particularly well paid (the equivalent of £231 a month), this did not matter because the money was "in addition to many privileges, including food, fuel and, more recently, access to the internet". The same view is repeated by Ahmad, a shopkeeper in Mosul, who adds that foreign fighters do even better with excellent privileges in terms of salaries, spoils and even captives. The new recruits are well trained. The Islamic State continues to blend religious fanaticism with military expertise. Kurdish commanders who have come under attack in recent weeks say that Isis units fight as well as ever and are able to sustain heavy casualties without flinching.

At the same time, Islamic rule is becoming more unpopular because of its bizarre religious ideology, conscription, falling standards of living and its extreme violence. This might seem to provide fertile soil for a movement to resist Isis as happened in 2006-7 when the US succeeded in turning many of the tribes against AQI which, like Isis today, had become hated and feared by many Sunni.

But today there is unlikely to be a repeat of the anti-al-Qa'ida Awakening Movement because Isis is stronger than its predecessor and there is no American army in Iraq to fund, arm and protect an anti-Isis Sunni armed opposition.

The terrible fate of tribes and all others who oppose Isis was explained in an *Independent* interview earlier this year with Sheikh Na'eem al-Gu'ood, the leader of the previously powerful Albu Nimr tribe of western and central Iraq. Last year, the Albu Nimr did rise up against Isis, much as they had done against AQI eight years earlier. They fought for almost 11 months before they ran out of ammunition and were overwhelmed.

Sheikh Na'eem says that since the first killings of Albu Nimr, which began on 25 October last year "the total number of victims in our tribe has reached 864 dead. In addition to which there are many missing whose numbers we don't know."

He describes it as genocide directed against a single tribe. Nobody was spared Isis's vengeance, with women and children being killed and thrown into wells. Survivors have fled into the desert or other parts of Iraq.

Asked why Isis has been able to take over the giant Anbar province in so short a time, Sheikh Na'eem says: "The main reason is that 90 per cent of the tribes in Anbar collaborated with Isis or joined them except for ourselves." He complains bitterly that the Albu Nimr got no support from the Iraqi government or the Americans, which led to the mass killings. He says the situation is very different from 2006 when his tribe fought alongside the US army. "Later, when Isis came, they considered us the friends and allies of the Americans," he says. "That is why Isis fights us and considers the killing of our men, women and children lawful."

Isis doesn't only target hostile tribes but anybody who has worked for the Iraqi government as soldiers or policemen. At Harshem refugee camp on the outskirts of Irbil, Sunni Arabs explain why they fled there. Ghanim, a 60-year-old former Iraqi soldier who supports himself on a crutch because he lost a leg fighting in the Iran-Iraq war, says: "I fled because my son is fighting in the Iraqi army today and Isis would punish us for this."

Isis likes to demonstrate that its vengeance is unrelenting. Abu Ahmed, a community leader who fled to Irbil when Isis took over in Mosul last June, says he left his 100-year-old mother behind in his house in Mosul. One day last September: "Isis men came and took my mother out of the house. Then they blew it up and placed a video on Facebook to show me the destruction of my home."

SPRING 2015: BARBARIANS

Wednesday, 8 April 2015

MASS GRAVES ARE EXHUMED

Mass graves containing the bodies of some 1,700 Iraqi military cadets slaughtered by Isis fighters last June are being opened up by forensic teams which have gained access to them since the capture of the nearby city of Tikrit.

The unarmed cadets from the base at Camp Speicher were taken prisoner by Isis forces as they swept through northern and western Iraq during their blitzkrieg advance last year. Videos showed them forced to lie face down by a shallow trench where they were sprayed with machine gun bullets. Others were taken to the bank of the Tigris River and shot in the back of the head before being thrown in.

The massacre took place on 12 June last year and was known about immediately because Isis filmed their atrocities. But the mass graves were previously inaccessible because Tikrit and the area around it was controlled by Isis until about a week ago, when 25,000 Shia militiamen and soldiers recaptured it after a month-long siege.

Weeping Iraqi soldiers were digging at eight locations yesterday as the first bodies were exhumed. The graves are mostly inside a complex of palaces built by Saddam Hussein, who came from the Tikrit area. It has never been explained why so many cadets who were in the old American air base at Camp Speicher were ordered to change into civilian clothes and go to their homes in Baghdad and further south. In other mass killings by Isis, the militants have first separated Shia from the others before massacring them. By one account the cadets were at first told that they were going to be part of a prisoner exchange. It was only later that they were divided up into batches to be more easily murdered.

Kamil Amin from Iraq's Human Rights Ministry told reporters that 12 bodies had been exhumed on Monday and laboratory tests will be carried out to determine their DNA. Families of the victims have already given DNA samples so the bodies of their relatives can be identified. Digging up all the bodies is expected to take months. Mr Amin said that "the work is continuing and we expect to discover more mass graves. We expect huge numbers of bodies to be unearthed."

The Tikrit area is still insecure with some Isis fighters holding out in the north of the city. A purpose of the massacres carried out by Isis against Iraq's Shia majority, aside from sectarian bloodlust, is to provoke a reaction against the Sunni community as a whole. This means that even those Sunni who do not like Isis and the self-declared "Caliphate" will be treated as Isis supporters by Shia militia and police. While retaliation against Isis by the Shia is nothing like on the scale of the Camp Speicher massacre, the Sunni complain that they are being driven from their villages and individual Sunnis have been murdered or kidnapped at pro-government checkpoints.

Camp Speicher was not the only massacre carried out by Isis last year. The first mass killing during their June offensive took place outside Mosul city when it captured Badush prison and immediately split up Sunni and Shia prisoners. Some 600 of the latter were then murdered. Other mass killings include the Albu Nimr tribe which fought against Isis for almost a year before being overwhelmed. Tribal leaders say that since last October 864 tribal members have been killed.

ISIS BRIDES BRAINWASHED INTO BECOMING SUICIDE BOMBERS

It was when Isis issued a fatwa saying a wife should obey her husband in all matters, including becoming a suicide bomber, that Aysha, a 32-year-old mother of two children, decided to flee her home in Mosul. She recalls that her husband did not ask her directly to be a suicide bomber, but gradually started talking about it. "He was coming home once a week," she told *The Independent*, "but recently he came home every day, and finally asked me to attend a new course showing how a Muslim woman could support Muslim society with her soul and body".

Aysha, which is not her real name, attended the course for two days along with many other women. She was appalled by what she heard. She says "the course was a sort of brainwashing, teaching women to sacrifice cheap worldly things - blood, flesh, soul - for the victory of more precious things - religion, Allah, the Prophet, and, most importantly, the eternal afterlife".

But instead of being persuaded by these teachings, Aysha was thinking about her children and how to rescue them from the situation she found herself in. On the third day of the course she pretended to be ill and claimed that her son had flu so she had to stay at home. She says that on 3 April "at the time of the Friday prayers I took my children and told them that we were going to visit their aunt in the same district, al-Rifa'ey, that we lived in, but in fact I had already arranged what to do through my cousin. He lives in Zakho [in north-west of the KRG zone] and he has helped many people to escape Mosul". She added that the cousin knew many smugglers in Mosul and KRG. "It cost me about $1,200 (£760) to flee with my son and daughter," she says.

Aysha was forced to pledge total obedience to her husband, even when it came to suicide bombing. What happened to her illustrates the complete subjection of women under the rule of the self-proclaimed "Islamic State". Their status has been reduced to that of chattels without rights or independence. A woman is not allowed to leave her house without being accompanied by a male relative. If she does so and is stopped by Isis fighters or officials, they take her back to her home and her husband is given between 40 and 80 lashes for allowing her out alone. All women going outside must wear the niqab, a cloth covering the head and face. In no other society on earth are women treated like this, not even in Saudi Arabia, where they are forbidden to drive, or in Afghanistan, where girls' schools have been attacked and burnt.

Aysha's story gives an insight into marriage and daily life within Isis. She gives a fascinating account of the last months of her marriage and her relations with her husband, whom she does not want to name because this might compromise the safety of her children. Prior to Isis forces unexpectedly capturing Mosul, a mainly Sunni Arab city with a population of two million, on 10 June last year, her husband had been an officer in the Iraqi army. Isis kills many of its opponents who are Shia or Yazidi and has driven Christians out of Mosul and surrounding towns, but it offers forgiveness to Sunni Muslims who publicly repent working for the Iraqi army or government.

Aysha says that her husband announced his repentance and offered his services to Isis as a soldier, though it was five months before they trusted him enough to accept him into their ranks where he became a unit commander. Aysha was never sure exactly what he did. "He never told me anything," she says, "and I didn't dare ask him because when I once did so his answer was: "Don't poke your nose into things." She found drops of blood on his uniform and suspected he took part in killings. He was earning a lot of money and had his share of spoils, property and valuables confiscated by Isis from those it deems to be its enemies. Aysha stole part of her husband's savings, recalling that "when I left home, I had about $6,000 in addition to my jewellery, but I paid a lot to get out of the city [Mosul] and I paid in advance to get to Turkey".

After her husband was accepted into Isis as a military officer, Aysha found that his behaviour began to change and he became more aggressive. She says that recently he had started to ask her for obedience "even when it comes to the sacrifice of the soul and body, otherwise I will not win paradise in the afterlife and hell will be my place. In this life I may be punished or be taken to jail." She responded to these threats by pretending to be wholly obedient to him and to sharia. Aside from pressure on her to become a suicide bomber, she feared that if her husband were killed she would be compelled to marry another Isis commander. It was when her husband was absent on some military operation that Aysha fled to Irbil, the capital of the KRG. She has had no contact with him since her escape.

Becoming a martyr in the cause of defeating the enemies of religion is at the heart of the Isis ideology as Aysha was taught during the course her husband insisted she attend. Suicide bombing is an effective military tactic, turning fanatical but untrained volunteers into lethal weapons. Families across the "Islamic State", which has a population of six million, are fearful that their children will be brainwashed into this self-sacrifice.

This was why Noura, a 36-year-old married woman, fled Mosul with her husband and six children. Isis had established camps where young teenagers were trained for suicide bombing. Noura, who wants her real name kept secret, reached Irbil on 22 March. She told *The Independent* in an interview that the main reason she and her family left is that "my children were under threat because Isis decided to establish camps for adolescents between 12 and 16 to educate and train them for suicide bombing". She says the preachers did not speak of "suicide bombing" but of "martyrdom honour". When these camps were first established it was possible for families to pay a fine instead of sending their children to them, but later attendance became compulsory.

Unlike Aysha, Noura had little money and her husband was jobless. This was a further reason for them and their family to leave Mosul. She explains that "people don't find jobs, so they offer their services to Isis for food. The problem is that many jobless people start to be attracted to the idea of working with Isis, not because they are happy with it, but because it is the only option available even if it is undesirable."

Aside from the threat of her children being trained as suicide bombers, Noura found day-to-day living difficult in Mosul. She says there was no public supply of electricity "and we didn't have the money to pay for the [electric] generators so it was terrible". Cooking-gas cylinders were expensive, costing 80,000 Iraqi dinars (£44), and tomatoes and potatoes each cost 15,000 dinars (£8) a kilo. There was a lack of clean water. More recently, she has heard by phone from her parents, who are still in Mosul, that things have improved a little and there are two hours' electricity per day and the price of gas has halved.

Isis must have received more money, says Noura.

Her father told her that wheat farmers around Mosul will sell their harvest this year to Isis because it is the only buyer and has promised to pay a high price. Aysha tells much the same story about the lack of electricity - only three hours every two days in her district and none at all in others. There is no shortage of food because Isis imports it from Syria "so we have many products from Aleppo and Raqqa in addition to Iraqi products". Isis has blown up the mobile phone masts, but mobiles still get a signal in high buildings.

Aysha and Noura's accounts of life under Isis corroborate each other, but on one point they disagree. Aysha does not think that Isis will be defeated "because, although they are in financial crisis, they have solutions to their crises". They impose fines on people and on those leaving Mosul: some leave with permission after paying a lot of money, though others are not allowed out for security reasons. Aysha had to pay smugglers to get her out.

Noura, on the contrary, believes that Isis will be defeated because it is running out of money and becoming more corrupt. She says bribery has become rampant but she does not think that US air strikes will defeat Isis. "The devastating factor internally is corruption - bribery, nepotism, favouritism - that will be the final blow." Significantly, neither woman speaks of any armed resistance to Isis despite its moves to recruit women and children as suicide bombers.

Tuesday, 19 May 2015

BATTLE NOW IS TO DEFEND THE ROAD TO BAGHDAD

The fall of Ramadi is the worst military disaster suffered by the Iraqi government since it lost the north of Iraq to an Isis offensive almost a year ago. One local councillor in Ramadi described the situation as "total collapse". Shia militiamen will not attempt to block the road to Baghdad after Isis fighters defeated elite units of the Iraqi armed forces as they captured the city of Ramadi, 70 miles west of the capital.

Burned bodies litter the streets and there are reports of massacres of policemen and tribesmen opposed to the selfproclaimed "Islamic State". Armoured vehicles belonging to the Iraqi army's so-called "Golden Division", considered its best unit, could be seen streaming out of Ramadi in a retreat that looked, at times, as if it had turned into a rout. Heavy equipment, including armoured Humvees and artillery, was abandoned.

Some 500 soldiers and civilians have been killed in fighting in Ramadi over the past few days as Isis closed in on the remaining government outposts, suicide bombers destroying fortifications by ramming them with vehicles packed with explosives. Up to 25,000 people have fled Ramadi, though they have had difficulty getting past army and militia checkpoints in Baghdad where displaced Sunni are suspected of being Isis sympathisers. Omar, a journalist from Ramadi, told The Independent that Isis fighters regard the majority of people in Ramadi as hostile to them and were telling them: "Get out! We don't need you!" He blamed the fall of his city, which had a population of 600,000, on the failure of Baghdad to send military aid. "For a year-and-a-half we have been calling for help from Baghdad," he said.

The fall of Ramadi may turn out to be a decisive event, changing the political and military landscape of Iraq and Syria. In some respects, it is a worst defeat for the Iraqi government than the capture of the northern Iraqi city of Mosul in a surprise Isis attack last year. The Isis pressure on Ramadi has been ongoing since April and a further assault was fully expected. Moreover, the garrison of the city consisted of some of the best troops in the Iraqi army and they were supported by US air strikes. US generals have been downplaying the extent of the calamity, but the US policy of rebuilding the Iraqi army and aiding it with US air power is in ruins.

The Baghdad government now has little choice but to deploy the Hashd al-Shaabi, the Shia paramilitaries which the US sees as being under Iranian influence and has not wanted to see in the frontline fighting in Sunni areas like Ramadi, the capital of the giant Anbar province. The latest victory of Isis, which had been portrayed inside and outside Iraq as having lost momentum since a run of victories between June and October last year, will strengthen its appeal to Sunni people as a winner. It is already causing dismay among the opponents of the Sunni jihadists who had hoped that the military situation had stabilised and Isis was on the retreat.

Isis lost Tikrit, the home town of Saddam Hussein, earlier this year and failed to take the Syrian Kurdish town of Kobani in a 134-day siege despite suffering heavy losses.

Fuad Hussein, chief of staff to President Massoud Barzani, the Kurdish leader, said he was concerned at what the fall of Ramadi meant for the Kurdish region and the rest of Iraq. He was particularly worried that Isis would follow up its latest victory by attacks on the vast Iraqi army base at al-Assad, which is full of weapons, as well as the Haditha Dam that controls the water level of the Euphrates.

Isis has been fighting for Ramadi since early 2014 when it took over much of Anbar province, including the city of Fallujah. Five Iraqi army divisions were unable regain the province, but government forces still held on to the central administrative complex in Ramadi. After a carefully planned assault that began on Thursday, the last pockets of government resistance were eliminated on Sunday with an attack on the Malaab district of south Ramadi.

Four suicide bombers killed at least 10 police and wounded 15, including Colonel Muthana al-Jabri, the chief of the Malaab police station. Later in the day, three suicide bombers drove cars packed with explosives into the gate of the Anbar Operation Command, the military headquarters for Anbar province, killing a further five soldiers and wounding 12. A police officer who was stationed at the headquarters said retreating troops left behind about 30 army vehicles and weapons that included artillery and assault rifles. The best Iraqi military units such as the Golden Division and Swat forces number perhaps 5,000 men and have been rushed from crisis point to crisis point over the past year and are reported to be suffering from desertions.

Iran has offered to aid the Baghdad government in its hour of need. A senior Iranian official said his country would provide any help necessary. The US has conducted 19 air strikes in the vicinity of Ramadi in the last 72 hours. But the most crucial development could be comments from Ali al-Sarai, a spokesman for the Shia militia, Hashid Shaabi. He told Reuters in Baghdad that "the Hashid has received the order to march forward, they will definitely take part. They were waiting for this order and now they have it". However, it is doubtful if the Hashid have the strength to recapture Ramadi.

Among senior leaders in Baghdad there is a growing feeling that they have no choice but to look to Shia militias for their salvation, even if this angers the US and alienates the Sunnis. One former minister said: "I think there is growing pressure to throw away the straitjacket that the US has imposed on the government's relationship with the Hashid. It is pretty clear that they are the only fighting force that can confront Isis."

AREAS OF CONTROL

● ISIS ◉ KURDISTAN GOVERNMENT ● CONTESTED AREA

SOURCES: ISW, US DEPARTMENT OF DEFENCE

Saturday, 23 May 2015

ISIS DEFEATED IN BATTLE OF MOUNT ABDULAZIZ

In a house on the lower slopes of the pine-clad Mount Abdulaziz, five Isis fighters are under siege by Syrian Kurdish fighters. "They can't get out," says a voice cutting through the crackle on the field radio. "But one of those bastards just shot and wounded one of our men."

This was a mopping-up operation, a day after a major battle for
Mount Abdulaziz had ended with the defeat of some 1,000 Isis fighters
who had been besieged. The mountain was one of the jihadists'
strongholds in this corner of north-east Syria, from which they could
fire artillery into the nearby Kurdish city of Al-Hasakah and menace a
fertile Kurdish enclave with a population of one million.

Isis fighters did not leave much behind in their retreat - a few
freshly painted slogans in praise of Isis, and some burned-out hulks of
cars that had been used as bombs. Crisp new cards lie discarded on
the floor of one building, saying "Office of Zakat (obligatory tax for
benefit of the poor) and Insurance", which appear to be ration cards
requiring the listing of names, numbers and other details. The cards
underline the extent to which Isis is well organised - and confirm that
its leaders have renamed the Syrian provinces, changing Al-Hasakah
to Barakat.

The defeat of Isis in the battle which started on 6 May is in sharp
contrast to the jihadist group's victories over the Iraqi army at Ramadi
and the Syrian army at Palmyra over the past week. The difference in
the outcome of the three battles may be because the Syrian Kurdish
forces are highly motivated, disciplined and come from the area in
which they are fighting. The Kurdish commander General Garzan
Gerer, interviewed by *The Independent* beside a pine forest just below
the mountain, said: "We fight better than the Syrian army at Palmyra
because we have strong beliefs and we are defending our own land."

There is another, more material, reason why the Kurds won and
Isis lost. Young Kurdish fighters resting in a captured Isis command
post, painted in green, cream and brown camouflage colours, are open
about how much they benefit from US air strikes. Botan Damhat, a
smoothfaced squad commander aged only 18, said: "Without the
American planes it would have been much harder to take the mountain. We would have won in the end, but we would have lost a lot more
men."

Kurdish commanders were unclear yesterday about casualties,
saying they had buried 300 bodies of Isis fighters but many more had
been carried away. They put their own fatalities at 25 to 30, the disparity perhaps being explained by the effectiveness of US air strikes.
Asked why some Isis headquarters had not been bombed, Botan Damhat said that, on the whole, Isis had hidden in the pine forests on the
slopes of the mountain "and the Americans knew that so they did not

destroy the buildings". In some cases, Isis set fire to its buildings before retreating.

General Gerer said the two main problems in capturing the mountain were the terrain and the fact that "many of the local villages are Arab and they often supported Daesh [Isis]". He said, also, that there were 25 Assyrian Christian villages where the jihadists had stopped people leaving so they could be used as hostages if the Kurds attacked. He did not think that more than a few of the Arabs who had supported Isis would be returning. As we left we saw a party of Arabs with their belongings returning to their house in a village. They waved frantically as we drove past in a military vehicle, as if uncertain about how they would be treated by the victorious Kurds.

Who were the Isis fighters holding Mount Abdulaziz? The Kurds insisted that their opponents were Muslims from all over the world, one of three of those captured turning out to be Chinese. In a headquarters building they had found neat little notebooks with translations of different words into a variety of languages, and drawings of a desk and chair with their names in minute handwriting.

Yalmaz Shahid, 25, another squad leader, said Isis had fought well. "We were particularly afraid of their suicide bombers and booby traps." Another fighter, who gave his name as Ernesto, said "they are very professional snipers".

The victory at Mount Abdulaziz is the biggest Kurdish success since the four-and-a-half-month siege of the town of Kobani on the Turkish border which ended earlier this year. In the town of Amuda, a few miles from Al-Hasakah, there was the rattle of festive gunfire well into the night and parties of children patrolled the streets singing patriotic songs in celebration.

But not all the news this week is good for the Kurds. With the fall of Palmyra, Isis holds half of Syria and part of the rest is held by Jabhat al-Nusra, the Syrian affiliate of al-Qa'ida that has fought the Kurds in the past. Overall, Isis is much stronger than it was pre-Ramadi and Palmyra in terms of morale and prestige among the Sunni Arabs, not to mention captured equipment.

In an interview with *The Independent*, Amina Osse, deputy foreign affairs manager for the region Kurds call Rojava, said she feared Isis was expanding fast "and may soon threaten to take all of Aleppo", Syria's largest city. She added that, as with the fall of Mosul last year,

Isis had captured a lot of arms and ammunition. This would allow them to renew their assault on the Syrian Kurds when they want to.

She did not have much confidence in President Bashar al-Assad's Syrian army, saying it was exhausted and suffered from the old Baath party tradition of having few links with, and thus little support from, the people where they were fighting. She recalled that in one battle last year the Syrian army had abandoned 35 tanks after rejecting offers of Kurdish help against Isis.

The problem for the Syrian Kurds is that, although their discipline and commitment backed by American air power has been effective, they number only about 2.2 million, or 10 per cent of the Syrian population. They will have difficulty holding off an emboldened Isis able to draw on resources in Syria and Iraq and having recently defeated the regular armies of both countries. The Kurdish cantons strung along the Turkish border are isolated and economically besieged from all sides.

The region is fertile, with wheat fields now being harvested, and the roads are full of vehicles carrying harvesting equipment. There are also more than 1,000 "nodding donkeys", the pumps which once produced oil but which are now almost all unused and rusting.

The outcome of the battle for Mount Abdulaziz shows the Syrian Kurds can hold their own against Isis in a way that Syrian and Iraqi soldiers cannot. But, in the long term, their de facto independent enclaves, ruling themselves for the first time in history, are very vulnerable to whoever turns out to be the winner in the Syrian civil war.

Tuesday, 26 May 2015

DRIVING OUT ISIS IS A JOB FOR A WOMAN

The Kurdish soldiers relax half a mile behind the front line, where they have been battling Isis forces west of the Syrian town of Ras al-Ayn. The women have no doubt about why they are fighting.

Nujaan, who is 27 and has been a soldier for four years, says that Isis's "target is women". She says: "Look at Shingal [in Iraq] where they raped the women and massacred the men. It is a matter of honour to defend ourselves first and then our families and lands." Sitting beside her is Zenya, 22, who adds that she also "is fighting for myself and my family."

Overhead there is the drone of US aircraft and Nujaan says there have been several air strikes that morning as well as ground fighting.

She says that several Kurdish soldiers have been killed and wounded, though she did not know the details. She adds that the YPJ Kurdish women's militia, to which she belongs, is gradually driving Isis towards the west. She and the other women appear remote and detached from what they are saying, possibly because they are exhausted from days in the front line.

In fact, the push westwards mentioned by Nujaan is of great military and possibly political significance because the Syrian Kurdish armed forces are closing in on a crucial Isis-controlled border crossing point from Syria into Turkey at Tal Abyad. The Syrian Kurds note bitterly that Turkey has closed the crossing points into Kurdish-held territory, but has kept open those used by Isis.

But now Tal Abyad, the northern end of the road that leads straight to Raqqa, the Isis Syrian capital, is threatened by a pincer movement by Kurds advancing from both the east and west. Some are advancing from the battered town of Ras Al-Ayn in the main Kurdish canton of al-Jazeera and, from the west, some are coming from Kobani, the town that withstood a four-and-a-half month Isis siege.

Sehanok Dibo, adviser to the leaders - Saleh Muslim and Asya Abdullah - of the PYD, the ruling party in the three Kurdish cantons on the Turkish border that make up the statelet of Rojava, told *The Independent* in an interview that Tal Abyad is the next Kurdish military target. "We are 18km from Tal Abyad in the east and 20km in the west," he said. "We hope to liberate it soon." If this does happen, it will be a serious blow to Isis and also to Turkey, which will see even more of the Syrian side of its southern frontier controlled by Kurds. Mr Dibo takes it as a matter of proven fact that "Turkey supports Daesh."

He stresses that he is not part of the Syrian Kurdish military command structure, but his opinion about Isis's future strategy is significant because the Syrian Kurds are the only military force in Iraq and Syria to consistently defeat the jihadis. He says: "I think their next target will be Dayr Az Zawr [the provincial capital on the Euphrates partly held by Syrian government forces] because the people in the city are Sunni Arabs and tribal. Isis will get support there."

In the longer term Mr Dibo expects Isis and other jihadist groups, such as Jabhat al-Nusra, to try to capture the half of Aleppo that is still

held by President Bashar al-Assad and the Syrian army. He sees Assad's military strength ebbing by the day.

Despite savage rivalries between Isis and Jabhat al-Nusra, he believes that in most respects they are just the same. "They are the
children of al-Qa'ida," he says. The leaders of the Syrian Kurds are jubilant this week because of their victory over Isis at Mount Abdulaziz
last week. Trucks full of cheering soldiers are returning from the front.
The Kurds in this north-east corner of Syria know, somewhat to their
own surprise, that, encompassed by enemies though they may be,
they are living in the safest part of Syria. The territory behind the front
line where Nujaan and Zenya are fighting is full of farmers bringing in
the wheat harvest, without the undercurrent of terror you find in the
rest of Syria.

Of course, the greater safety in this triangular-shaped Kurdish
enclave only stands out because of the contrast with everywhere else
on the borders of the "Islamic State". But, for the moment, there are
no car bombs, kidnappings, bandit gangs at check points or fear of
massacre. The PYD and its militia, the YPG, has an effective monopoly
of power here as it does in the two other Kurdish cantons on the Turkish frontier that gained de facto autonomy when the Syrian army
withdrew on 19 July 2012. Though its militarised rule is not popular
with all Kurds, its militiamen and women do provide genuine protection - unlike the Syrian or Iraqi armies. It may not last and it has not
come easily. Ras al-Ayn, a town of about 30,000 people, still looks
shattered by heavy fighting in 2012 and 2013 when it was at the centre of fighting between the Kurds and extreme jihadists led by Jabhat
al-Nusra, then the Syrian branch of Isis and now the official affiliate of
al-Qa'ida in Syria. Everywhere in this shabby little town there are
bombed out ruins and surviving walls are peppered with the pock
marks made by machine gun bullets.

Ibrahim and Jamil, two middleaged PYD representatives, give a
guided tour of their town, pointing to the border crossing with Turkey
across which Jabhat al-Nusraled forces poured across on 11 November 2012. They say that "at first we welcomed them because they were
against the Assad regime and then we were shocked to find they were
all jihadis".

They enforced compulsory attendance at the mosque, stole
Christian houses and attacked and killed all who opposed them. Captured officers from the ruling Allawi sect were massacred and the

regime in Damascus responded with random bombing that killed many civilians and levelled rows of houses. The battle for Ras al-Ayn went on from November 2012 to July 2013 and has similarities with the struggle within the opposition to the regime between the jihadis and secular forces. The difference is that here in Ras al-Ayn the anti-jihadis were well-armed and militarily experienced since the PYD is effectively the Syrian branch of the PKK, which has been fighting the Turkish army since 1984.

Ibrahim says that the final stage of this complex battle, which had many ceasefires interrupted by new bouts of street fighting, came on 16 July 2013. Rojna, the leader of the women fighters known as the YPJ, was buying material for uniforms in the bazaar, when she and her guards were attacked by al-Nusra militants infuriated by the sight of a female military leader. "It was then we decided to finally drive them out," says Ibrahim.

The Kurdish canton of al-Jazeera is a well defended island in a sea full of sharks. Turkey has demanded a "buffer zone" in Syria, allowing it to occupy the Kurdish enclaves along the border. Mr Dibo says it is difficult to predict what will happen next. "The balance of power in the war in Syria can be changed abruptly by the actions of one of the outside powers".

SUMMER 2015: ONE YEAR OF ISIS

Friday, 26 June 2015

ISIS ONE YEAR ON

The "Islamic State" is stronger than it was when it was first pro-claimed on 29 June last year, shortly after Isis fighters captured much of northern and western Iraq. Its ability to go on winning victories was confirmed on 17 May this year in Iraq, when it seized Ramadi, the cap-ital of Anbar province, and again four days later in Syria, when it took Palmyra, one of the most famous cities of antiquity and at the centre of modern transport routes.

The twin victories show how Isis has grown in strength: it can now simultaneously attack on multiple fronts, hundreds of miles apart, a capacity it did not have a year ago. In swift succession, its forces defeated the Iraqi and Syrian armies and, equally telling, nei-ther army was able to respond with an effective counter-attack.

Supposedly these successes, achieved by Isis during its summer offensive in 2014, should no longer be feasible in the face of air strikes by the US-led coalition. These began last August in Iraq and were ex-tended to Syria in October, with US officials recently claiming that

4,000 air strikes had killed 10,000 Isis fighters. Certainly, the air campaign has inflicted heavy losses, but it has made up for these casualties
by conscripting recruits within the caliphate.

What makes the loss of Ramadi and Palmyra so significant is that
they did not fall to surprise attacks, the means by which a few thousand Isis fighters unexpectedly captured Mosul, Iraq's second largest
city, in 2014.

That city had a garrison estimated to number about 20,000 men,
though nobody knows the exact figure because the Iraqi armed forces
were full of "virtual" soldiers, who did not physically exist but whose
pay was pocketed by officials. Baghdad later admitted to 50,000 of
these. There were, in addition, many soldiers who did exist, but kicked
back at least half their salary on the condition that they perform no
military duties.

Yet the outcome of the fighting at Ramadi, a Sunni Arab city which
once had a population of 600,000, should have been different than at
Mosul. The Isis assault in mid-May was the wholly predictable culmination of attacks that had been continuous in the eight months since
October 2014. What was unexpected was a retreat that was close to
flight by government forces and, in the longer term, the same old fatal
disparity between the nominal size of the Iraqi armed forces and their
real combat strength.

A crucial feature of the political and military landscape in Iraq is
that the Iraqi army never recovered from its defeats of 2014. To meet
Isis attacks on many fronts it had fewer than five brigades, or between
10,000 and 12,000 soldiers, capable of fighting while "the rest of the
army are only good for manning checkpoints" - in the words of a senior Iraqi security official. Even so, many of these elite units were in
Ramadi, though their men complained of exhaustion and of suffering
serious casualties without receiving replacements.

In the event, even the presence of experienced troops was not
enough. Just why the forces were defeated is partly explained in an
interview with *The Independent* by Colonel Hamid Shandoukh, who
was the police commander in the southern sector of Ramadi during
the final battle. The colonel says: "In three days of fighting, 76 of our
men were killed and 180 wounded." Isis commanders used a lethal
cocktail of well-tried tactics, sending fanatical volunteers driving vehicles packed with explosives to blow themselves up. Suicide bombing

on a mass scale was followed by assaults by welltrained infantry. Colonel Shandoukh, himself a Sunni Arab, says the root of the problem is that neither the Iraqi security forces nor pro-government tribal forces received reinforcements or adequate equipment. He says that the central failure is sectarian and happened "because of fear that, as the people of Anbar are Sunni, mobilising them will threaten the government later". He complains that sophisticated weapons are reserved for Shia militias and counter-terrorism units, while the predominantly Sunni Arab police in Anbar received only seven Humvees, far fewer than the number captured by Isis in Mosul.

I am a little wary of Colonel Shandoukh's explanation that Isis's victory was thanks to superior weapons denied to his own troops by the Shia dominated Baghdad government. Lack of arms is an excuse invariably used by Iraqi and Kurdish leaders to explain reverses inflicted on them. But this claim is frequently contradicted by videos shot by Isis after it has captured positions, showing heaps of abandoned weaponry.

At Mosul last year and again at Ramadi almost a year later, there was the same breakdown in morale among government commanders leading to a panicky and unnecessary withdrawal. In the sour words of General Martin Dempsey, the chairman of the US Joint Chiefs of Staff "the Iraqi security forces weren't "driven from" Ramadi, they "drove out of Ramadi".

Colonel Shandoukh regards distrust between Sunni and Shia as the main cause of the rout. Others blame the corruption and overall dysfunctional nature of the Iraqi state in a country in which people's loyalty is to their sectarian or ethnic community. Iraqi nationalism is at a discount.

A more precise reason for the military disintegration may be that the Iraqi army, and this also applies to the Kurdish Peshmerga, have become over-dependent on US air strikes. In Iraqi Kurdistan, Peshmerga respond to Isis attacks by giving their location to the US-Kurdish Joint Operations headquarters in Erbil which calls in air strikes. Significantly, it was an impending sandstorm that would blind US aircraft and drones and prevent their use that was apparently the reason why the order was given for Iraqi forces to abandon Ramadi.

General Dempsey's ill-concealed anger at the debacle at Ramadi may stem from his understanding that the disaster involves more than just the loss of a single city, but discredits the whole American strategy towards Islamic State. The aim was to use US air power in combination with local ground forces to weaken and eliminate Isis. It was a policy that Washington had persuaded itself was working effectively right up to the moment it fell apart on 17 May.

Proof of this is a spectacularly illtimed briefing given on 15 May by Brigadier General Thomas D Weidley, the chief of staff for Combined Joint Task Force Operation Inherent Resolve, as the US-led air campaign to defeat Islamic State is known. "We firmly believe [Isis] is on the defensive, attempting to hold previous gains, while conducting small-scale, localised harassing attacks [and] occasionally complex or high-profile attacks to feed their information and propaganda apparatus," he said.

Keep in mind that on the very day the General was making his upbeat remarks, Isis was over-running the last government strongholds in Ramadi. The US generals were not alone in their over-optimism. The capture of Tikrit, the home city of Saddam Hussein, by the Iraqi army and Shia militias led to exaggerated assumptions that Islamic State was on the retreat. On 1 April the Iraqi Prime Minister, Haider al-Abadi, walked down the main street of Tikrit, basking in the plaudits of his triumphant troops.

The loss of Ramadi has exposed Western policy for defeating Isis in Iraq as a failure and no new policy has been devised to take its place. If the same thing has not happened in Syria, it is simply because the West never had a policy there to begin with or, put more charitably, in so far as there was a policy, it was so crippled by contradictions as to rob it of any coherence or chance of success. The West would like to weaken President Bashar al-Assad, but is frightened that, if he goes, his regime will collapse with him and thereby create a vacuum.

Western-backed moderates play only a marginal role among opposition fighters. Robert Ford, the former US ambassador to Syria, and a long-time supporter of the rebel moderates, changed his stance earlier this year announcing that the reality in Syria is that "the people we have backed have not been strong enough to hold their ground against the Nusra Front".

After capturing Palmyra, Islamic State is now threatening Deir Ezzor, a Sunni Arab tribal city, one of the few strongholds still held by the government in eastern Syria. Isis is getting closer to Aleppo, once Syria's largest city, and probably hopes to take it at some point in the future. According to the Syrian Observatory for Human Rights, Islamic

State "has seized more than 50 per cent of Syria and is now present in 10 of its 14 provinces". It adds that Isis now holds the majority of Syria's oil and gas fields.

This calculation gives a slightly exaggerated idea of Islamic state control in Syria since its dominance is mostly in the scantily-populated regions of the east. It is under pressure from the well-organised Syrian Kurds, fighting against whom it suffered its biggest defeat when it failed to take the city of Kobani despite a four-and-a-half-month siege. On 16 June, Isis lost the important border crossing into Turkey at Tal Abyad after an attack by the Kurds backed by US air power. Earlier this week they were reportedly driven out of the town of Ayn Isa, just 30 miles north of Raqqa.

Once again, this led to over-optimistic talk of Isis weakening, though it did not try very hard to hold either town as they were encircled by Kurdish troops. As in Iraq, Kurdish willingness and ability to advance into Sunni Arab majority areas is limited, so the Kurds will not inflict a decisive defeat on Islamic State. Yesterday there were reports of Isis advancing in other areas. Isis has more long-term opportunities in Syria than Iraq because some 60 per cent of Syrians are Sunni Arabs, compared to only 20 per cent in Iraq. It has yet to dominate the Sunni opposition in Syria to the extent it does in Iraq, but this may come. As sectarian warfare escalates, Isis's combination of fanatical Sunni ideology and military expertise will be difficult to overcome.

Saturday, 27 June 2015

HAIRCUTS CAN BE A MATTER OF LIFE AND DEATH

Even in a city as dangerous as Fallujah, 40 miles west of Baghdad, Salem had a peculiarly dangerous occupation which meant that he was at risk of corporal punishment and financial ruin every day he lived there.

A 35-year-old man, who, like everybody else in this article, does not want his real name published, he is the sole breadwinner of his family and also cares for his sick and elderly father. At the time Isis took over Fallujah in January last year, he was earning his living as a barber.

During the first six months of Isis occupation, the militants were generally moderate in their enforcement of Islamic fundamentalist regulations. Isis did not have a complete monopoly of power in the city and did not want to alienate its people. But on important issues of principle, such as the correct Islamic haircut, the militants were adamant from the beginning. Beards were obligatory: no man could be clean shaven and Western haircuts were forbidden.

"Shaving was prohibited and the punishment for shaving someone was severe," says Salem. Isis closed most of the barber salons in Fallujah, but not Salem's "because mine was a simple poor salon without posters so they didn't close it". Even though his salon remained open, there were strict limits on what Salem could do for his customers so he did not make enough money to feed his family. He tried supplementing his income by selling vegetables in the market and only worked as a barber when he got a call from old customers, friends and relatives.

He had no trouble until the day of his cousin's wedding when disaster struck. He says: "My cousin came to my salon and asked me not only to dress his hair, but to shave his beard." Salem was horrified by such a dangerous proposal because he was conscious of the punishment Isis was likely to inflict on any barber ignoring the shaving ban. He turned his cousin down flat, but the man then asked for his hair to be cut short in a modern way rather than left to grow long as Isis demanded. The cousin argued that "nobody would notice because it was the afternoon and the street was empty". Unwillingly, Salem complied with his cousin's request and "dressed his hair, adding gel to make it look good".

Salem and his cousin soon found out that they had badly underestimated how closely Isis monitored illicit haircuts. Four days after the wedding, Salem learned that his action had been reported by an Isis informant to the local religious authority. He was arrested and then sentenced to 80 lashes to be administered in public and, in addition, his salon was to be closed. In the event, he had received only 50 lashes, when "I fainted and was taken to hospital".

Deprived of his ability to make a living in Fallujah, Salem went first to Ramadi, the capital of Anbar province, which was mostly under Isis control and where he had a brother. But the city was being bombarded by the Iraqi air force and Shia militias, so he left for Baghdad and finally Irbil, the capital of Iraqi Kurdistan, where he hopes to find a job. He is one of many arrivals from Isis-controlled territory to be interviewed by *The Independent* in order to build up a picture of day-to-day life in the self-declared caliphate.

Over the past six months, we have spoken to everybody from fighters to farmers and tribal leaders to mothers of families about their experiences. We tried to reach beyond the routine denunciations of their former rulers by displaced Sunni Arabs seeking to allay the suspicions of their Kurdish hosts.

Eyewitness testimony includes an Isis fighter who called himself Hamza and fled Fallujah because he believed he would be asked to execute people he knew and he had been offered Yazidi girls for sex, something he felt was no different from rape.

The wife of an Iraqi army officer turned Isis commander left because she thought her husband wanted her to become a suicide bomber.

Many of those who sought refuge in the KRG were trying to escape poor living conditions and violence. Others cited two specific reasons for flight: they were frightened that their sons would be conscripted as Isis fighters or that their unmarried daughters would be forcibly married to Isis fighters. The so-called Islamic State is a militarised state whose military forces always get priority.

The five or six million people living in Isis-controlled territory exist in a world full of prohibitions and regulations. Breach of these divinely inspired rules is savagely punished. The aim is to model human behaviour on the way it was in the days of the Prophet in the seventh century. Rules closely define who is a Muslim and who is not, with Shia and Yazidis demonised as "apostates" and "pagans" who can be massacred or enslaved.

Relations between men and women are minutely regulated, with the latter reduced to the level of chattels. Salem says that nobody in Fallujah is ignorant of Isis rules because they were previously read out in public every day, though this has now been reduced to three times a week. Speaking from memory, he gave a number of examples:

❖ Girls are not allowed to wear jeans and must wear Islamic dress (abaya and veil).

❖ Makeup is prohibited.

❖ No smoking of cigarettes or hubble-bubble. The punishment is 80 lashes, but may include execution if there are repeated violations.

- ❖ Using the word "Daesh", the Arabic acronym for Isis, is forbidden and the punishment is 70 lashes.
- ❖ Women's sewing shops are closed in case a man enters.
- ❖ Women's hairdressers are closed for the same reason.
- ❖ Gynecologists must be female.
- ❖ Women shall not sit on chairs either in the market or in a shop.
- ❖ Shops must close at the time of prayers.
- ❖ Taxi drivers who take customers to a distant destination they have not asked for and then demand money to bring them back are considered to have acted "to disrupt the interests of the people" (apparently a common crime in Fallujah). The punishment is amputation or beheading.

There are many other crimes and prohibitions that Salem might have mentioned. Women who leave the house without being accompanied by a male relative are taken home by Isis officials and their husband is given 80 lashes.

When Isis declared on 29 June last year that it was reestablishing the caliphate, its opponents in the outside world hoped that its outlandish laws and their brutal application would provoke resistance. After all, what was being enforced went far beyond sharia or Saudi Wahhabism, so many of whose tenets are similar to those of Isis.

There was real anger in Mosul at the new subservient status of women and the destruction of famous mosques, like that of Younis (Jonah) in Mosul, which was deemed by Isis to be a shrine. But there is no sign of counter-revolution or even effective armed resistance against a movement that has mercilessly crushed all opponents such as the Albu Nimr tribe, which has seen 864 of its tribespeople slaughtered.

So far, those living within Isis territory who hate and fear it have reacted by fleeing rather than resisting.

The story of Salem, the barber of Fallujah, helps explain why this has happened. Isis monitors and restricts movement within its boundaries but he was able to pass through Isis checkpoints to Ramadi, explaining that he was going there to visit his brother. In the event, he stayed there only four days because of continuing air strikes and shelling in the days shortly before Isis captured the last governmentheld enclaves on 17 May. Salem says that many families were leaving Ramadi, but adds revealingly that "many preferred to stay, among whom was my brother. He says that, although they are living under bombs, Isis is far better than the Shia militia and the Iraqi army".

A similar point is made by Mahmoud Omar, a Sunni Arab photographer, whose parents were living in Ramadi. "Isis has shocked many people by its actions," says Mahmoud. "But instead of the government treating us better to win us over, they are treating us worse. "As an example, he cited a police station in the government-held enclave in Ramadi. He says: "The police go on arresting Sunni, torturing them and refusing to release them unless their families come up with a bribe. I know one man who was there for a week before his family paid the police $5,000 [£3,200] to get him released."

This is one of the strengths of Isis. For all its failings, Sunni Arabs in Iraq compare it with an arbitrary and dysfunctional Shia-dominated government in Baghdad. Asked to compare the situation in Ramadi before and after the Isis takeover, Salem says that under government rule, Ramadi had no electricity, no fuel, no internet and no clean water. The local hospital and medical centre were not working despite vain pleas to the government from local people.

"Under the rule of Isis," says Salem, who has no reason to like the group which beat him savagely and closed his business, "many big generators have been brought to Ramadi from Fallujah and Raqqa. In addition, they are repairing the power station at Khesab. As for the hospital, Isis brought in doctors, surgeons and nurses from Syria, so it is working again."

Monday, 29 June 2015

WHO IS STRONG ENOUGH TO FIGHT ISIS?

There are seven wars raging in Muslim countries between the borders of Pakistan in the east and Nigeria in the west. In all seven - Afghanistan, Iraq, Syria, Yemen, Libya, Somalia and north-east Nigeria - local versions of Isis are either already powerful or are gaining in influence. Key to the group's explosive expansion in Iraq and Syria since 2011 is its capability as a fighting machine, which stems from a combination of religious fanaticism, military expertise and extreme violence. In addition, its successes have been possible because it is opposed by feeble, corrupt or non-existent governments and armies.

The reach of the Isis was demonstrated last week by near simultaneous attacks in Tunisia, France, Kuwait and Kobani in Syria. The first three atrocities received blanket media coverage, but the fourth, and by far the biggest massacre, was at Kobani, where at least 220 Kurdish civilians, including women and children, were massacred last Thursday by Isis fighters.

Sadly, it was an event that has received only limited attention in the outside world, doubtless because the mass killing of civilians is seen as yet one more tragic but inevitable episode in the war in Syria and Iraq.

Such desensitivity to the ongoing slaughter in that conflict is not only morally wrong, but shows serious political blindness. What makes the killings in a suburb of Lyon, the beach at Sousse and the Imam al-Sadiq mosque in Kuwait so different from - and in some ways more menacing than - the 9/11 and 7/7 attacks is that today these crimes are promoted by a government, in the shape of the self-declared caliphate, which has a more powerful army and rules more people than most members of the UN.

The US and Western European governments are eager for their people to avoid focusing on this dangerous development because they do not want to highlight their own culpability in failing to weaken or even contain Isis.

Its strengths - as well as its opponents' weaknesses - help to explain its rapid rise and that of other al-Qa'ida-type movements in the Middle East and North Africa. But there is a further toxic ingredient which propels Isis forward: this is the exacerbation and exploitation of religious differences and hatreds, most crucially those between Sunni and Shia Muslim.

From the moment in the wake of the US invasion in 2003 that Abu Musab al-Zarqawi created the forerunner to AQI and Isis, its prime target was Shia Iraqis. Suicide bombers slaughtered Shia civilians as they prayed, sought work in the market places, or waited to catch a bus.

Much the same is now happening in Muslim countries across the world, and particularly in the seven convulsed by warfare. An example of this is Yemen, where one third of the 25 million population belong to the Shia Zaydi sect and the rest are Sunni, but where there has been little sectarian strife in the past.

In April this year, Isis announced its presence in Yemen by posting a video showing four government soldiers being beheaded and another 10 executed.

Compared to AQAP, Isis is a late-comer in Yemen but both groups flourish as Sunni-Shia hostility increases so they can present themselves as the shock troops and protectors of the Sunni community. Where Shia victims are unavailable, as in Libya, then Isis groups have ritually murdered Christian migrant workers from Egypt and Ethiopia.

The killing of Shia is not just an expression of hatred, but has a less obvious, though demonic, purpose behind it. An aim is to stir up the Shia into retaliating in kind, carrying out mass murders of Sunni in Baghdad in 2006 and 2007 so they were reduced to a few enclaves mostly in the west of the city. The aim of provoking the Shia is that the Sunni are left with no alternative but to turn to Isis or al-Qa'ida clones as defenders. The same calculation may now work in Yemen.

Because Isis publicises and boasts of its atrocities in order to spread fear, it masks the fact that official al-Qa'ida affiliates, such as Jabhat al-Nusra in Syria or AQAP in Yemen, are just as dangerous.

Their basic agenda is very similar to that of the self-declared caliphate, with al-Nusra carrying out the enforced conversion of Druze and the massacre of those who resist. This attempted rebranding of extreme but non-Isis Sunni jihadis is opportunistic and often directed at making them more palatable as proxies for Sunni states such as Turkey, Saudi Arabia and Qatar.

There has long been disagreement about the real strength of Isis and its ability to expand. Overall, the argument that Isis is more powerful than it looks has been borne out by events such as the capture of Mosul on 10 June 2014 and of Ramadi on 17 May this year. These Isis victories caught the world by surprise and were important in enabling it to claim success as being divinely inspired.

In reality, there are two crucial components to Isis expansion, one of which is the strength of the organisation itself, but equally important is the spectacular weaknesses of its opponents.

It is this weakness which has repeatedly exceeded expectations, leading not just to the Iraqi army taking flight at Mosul and Ramadi and the Iraqi Kurdish Peshmerga, supposedly a tougher force, disintegrating at equal speed last August. Adept though the militants may be at concealing the place and timing of its main assault, it is the feebleness of resistance that has determined the outcome.

The same pattern is repeated across the Muslim world and is presenting Isis and its al-Qa'ida equivalents with many opportunities.

Some countries have had no effective government in years - Somalia has had none since the overthrow of Siad Barre in 1991; but, after a spectacularly disastrous US intervention in the 1990s, foreign powers sought to contain rather than eliminate the threat. Somalia was written off as a bolt-hole for al-Qa'ida gunmen and pirates, but at least there were not many places in the world quite like it.

But "failed states" are more dangerous than they look because when central governments collapse, they create a vacuum easily filled by groups like Isis. Foreign military intervention has repeatedly been complicit in creating these conditions - in Iraq in 2003, but also in Libya in 2011 and in Yemen this year where a Saudi-led air campaign has been targeting the Yemeni army, the one institution that held the country together.

What might be called the "Somalianisation" of countries is becoming frequent and people in the rest of the world are learning that a "failed state" should be an object of fear rather than pity.

The beliefs of Isis are rightly seen as an offshoot of Saudi Wahhabism, both ideologies degrading the status of women, imposing fundamentalist Islamic norms and regarding Shia and Christians as heretics or pagans.

But though they have common features, they are not identical. What Isis believes and enforces is a sort of neo-Wahhabism, distinct from that variant of Islam which is prevalent in Saudi Arabia. In practice, the Saudi state does not try, as Isis does, to murder its two million-strong Shia minority, though it may discriminate against them.

A more accurate accusation against Saudi Arabia is that over the past half century it has successfully used its great wealth to bring mainstream Sunni Islam under the intolerant influence of Wahhabism, thus deepening religious antagonisms.

The violence and determination to expand its rule has brought Isis many enemies, but their disunity, rivalries and mutual suspicions are great. The US and Iran both fight the militants in Iraq and Syria, but do not want the other to emerge as the predominant foreign power.

Meanwhile, the US is hampered in fighting Isis, Jabhat al-Nusra and similar groups by a determination to do so without alienating Sunni states to which it is allied, and on whose support American power in the Middle East depends.

This has been the pattern since 9/11, when Washington wanted to punish the perpetrators, but carefully avoided linking the attack to Saudi Arabia, home country of Osama bin Laden, 15 out of the 19 hijackers, and of the private donors funding the operation. Isis is under pressure, but not enough to crush it or prevent its further expansion.

Tuesday, 14 July 2015

THE BATTLE FOR FALLUJAH

Tens of thousands of Shia militiamen are poised to join the battle for Fallujah, 40 miles west of Baghdad, in a bid to recapture it from Isis fighters who seized the city 18 months ago. The battle is likely to be one of the decisive military engagements of the Iraq war as Fallujah has been at the centre of the Sunni revolt in Iraq since the US invaded the country in 2003.

"Fallujah is surrounded, but we will take it little by little," Brigadier-General Ali Musleh, a senior commander of the Shia militia force known as the Hashid Shaabi, told *The Independent* yesterday as Iraqi armed forces pressed Fallujah on three sides. Iraqi forces say they are keeping open a corridor through which civilians can escape before ground fighting escalates.

In a brief statement, Iraq's Prime Minister, Haider al-Abadi, vowed to "take revenge from Daesh [Isis] criminals on the battlefield ... and their cowardly crimes against unarmed civilians will only increase our determination to chase them and to expel them from the land of Iraq".

The Hashid Shaabi is made up of volunteers who answered a call to arms by Grand Ayatollah Ali al-Sistani after Isis captured Mosul on 10 June 2014. The Iraqi government announced the beginning of the operation to retake the giant Sunni province of Anbar that is 85 per cent held by Isis yesterday. Hashid forces match Isis fighters in their fanatical willingness to fight to the death. They are numerous, inspired by religious faith and have been successful in fighting around Baghdad. But their failings include a lack of experienced commanders and training, leading to heavy casualties.

The Iraqi army was weakened and discredited when it unexpectedly lost Ramadi, the capital of Anbar province, to Isis fighters on 17 May this year. The Shia-dominated government badly needs a victory against Isis and has no alternative but to use Shia militia units.

In the build-up to the battle Hashid military leaders have been leaving the holy city of Karbala, site of two of the greatest Shia shrines, for the front line around Fallujah, 54 miles to the north.

"The fighting has already started and I have been told to be at the front by tomorrow morning," a Hashid member said late last night.

Fallujah was twice besieged by US Marines in 2004, their forces finally storming the city after prolonged bombardment by air strikes and heavy artillery. Isis has had a long time to plant IEDs and booby traps, which it has used to great effect in the past. Its tactics include well-trained snipers, mortar teams and suicide bombers, the latter deployed in large numbers and driving vehicles that have been specially armoured and packed with explosives.

The poor training of Hashid forces is confirmed by Colonel Salah Rajab, who was deputy commander of the Habib Battalion of the Ali Akbar Brigade, a 300-strong unit whose soldiers come from Karbala. He was so badly wounded by the blast from a mortar bomb on 3 July that his lower right leg has been amputated. Looking cheerful and resolute despite his injury, he explains that he is a 55-year-old military professional who was a colonel in the old Iraqi army from which he resigned in 1999. He says: "I joined the Hashid to defend my country against foreigners and I had been fighting in Baiji city for 16 days when a mortar bomb landed near me, leaving two of our men dead and four wounded."

Lying in bed in the Hussein Teaching Hospital in Karbala in a ward full of wounded Hashid fighters, Colonel Rajab lists the main weaknesses of his men. He says that "there is a lack of experienced commanders who know how to direct an attack, though they do ask advice from professional military officers and usually listen to us".

There is a general lack of training for the volunteers, making them less efficient and liable to suffer losses, Colonel Rajab says, adding that "they get a maximum of three months' training when they need six months". This lack of experience and training not only affects tactics, but security. He says that "Daesh [Isis] is continually hacking into our communications, finding out what we are doing and inflicting heavy losses".

These points are borne out by the stories of other wounded Hashid fighters in the hospital. OmarAbdullah, a thin-looking 18-year-old with a heavily bandaged broken arm and leg, says he had just 25 days' training before being committed to battle in Baiji. What happened next shows the sophistication of Isis's battlefield skills.

Mr Abdullah says: "We were shot at by snipers and we ran into a house to seek cover. There were 13 of us and we didn't realise that the house was full of explosives." No sooner had they fallen into the trap than Isis detonated the bombs in the house, killing nine and wounding four of the fighters. What did Mr Abdullah think of the short training period? He says: "It should be more, but we need to fight as soon as possible."

Isis has always relied heavily on IEDs, booby traps and suicide bombers to slow the advance of their enemies and cause casualties. Fadil Rashid is a bomb disposal expert from Nassiriya, south-east of Baghdad, who was on patrol north of Samara in Salahuddin province when he saw a suspicious looking bridge about 15 feet long over a canal. Before he could prevent him, one of his men put a foot on the bridge, detonating a bomb that killed four and wounded three men.

It seems likely that Isis will fight for Fallujah in a way that it did not fight for Tikrit, Saddam Hussein's home town, which fell on 1 April after a month's siege to an assault led by Shia militiamen. But Isis did not fight hard to hold it while preparing for a surprise counter-attack at Baiji and Ramadi.

Fallujah is more important because it was the first Iraqi city to be taken over by the militants, in January 2014. It is close to Baghdad and poses a threat to the capital. An early sign of the military weakness of the Iraqi government early last year was its inability to launch a successful counter-offensive to recapture Fallujah.

If Fallujah does fall then it will be a mixed blessing for the Iraqi government, which has only limited control over the Shia militias that are now its main fighting force. The regular army has only about between 10,000 and 12,000 reliable combat troops. These are, however, reported to be exhausted and fought-out by being rushed from crisis to crisis without rest.

An important feature in the battle for Fallujah will be the willingness of the US to use its air power to support the Hashid attack. At Tikrit and Ramadi the US insisted that its air power be used only to support regular Iraqi army troops. The US sees several of the Shia militias as being under the control of Iran, though there are others more closely allied to the government.

Yesterday, a delivery of 36 F-16 fighter jets purchased by the Iraqi government was reported to have arrived at Balad air base, north of Baghdad.

If Isis does fight for Fallujah street-by-street then the destruction may be greater even than it was in 2004 when the US used heavy artillery and air strikes on civilian areas. Isis is preventing civilians from leaving. Baghdad has postponed its bid to recapture Ramadi until after it has taken Fallujah but, if it fails to do so, there will be little long-term chance of defeating the "Islamic State" in Iraq.

Thursday, 16 July 2015

HOPES ADVANCE FOR A US-IRANIAN ALLIANCE

They are home to more than a million of Iraq's Shia Muslims, and contain the tombs of that faith's holiest figures. In recent months, they have provided thousands of fighters for the militias battling Isis, but watched in frustration as US air power has been deployed in support of the less effective Iraqi army.

But in the cities of Najaf and Karbala yesterday, there was an expectation that the nuclear deal struck on Tuesday between neighbouring Iran, the world's leading Shia nation, and the West may yet lead to closer US support for the Shia militias as they try to dislodge their Sunni jihadist foes from captured Iraqi cities.

"American air attacks are playing a role in the battle for Fallujah," admitted a divisional commander of the Iraqi paramilitary militia grudgingly, though he also listed the occasions when the US had failed to support Shia forces in previous battles against Isis.

The parallel but distinct wars against Isis pursued by the US and Iran in Iraq were converging even before this week's accord. Over the past year, the Iranians have mostly supported the militia forces, while the US air campaign and training has focused on backing the regular Iraqi army and the Kurdish Peshmerga fighters.

Shia religious leaders in Najaf and Karbala, whose shrines are venerated by Shia across the world, are uncertain what the nuclear accord will mean in practice. But some believe it will lead to greater military co-operation between the US and Iran against Isis. "It shows that diplomacy can work," said a senior clergyman in Najaf. "Now we need everybody to unite to destroy Isis as a threat to the whole world."

The capture of Ramadi by Isis on 17 May means that the Baghdad government now depends heavily on the Shia Hashid al-Shaabi, or Popular Mobilisation Units. Sheikh Karim Abdul Hussain, the commander of the 8,400-strong Imam Ali Division of five brigades from Najaf, puts the militias' total military strength at 120,000 men. He would not comment on how much impact any measure of détente between Iran and the US would directly have on the war.

A senior Shia clergyman called for the US to supply Iraq with modern weapons and to put pressure on Saudi Arabia, Turkey and Qatar to stop covert military aid to Isis and to rebel groups in Syria that are affiliated to al-Qa'ida.

Another demand of the Shia religious leaders is that neighbouring countries, notably Turkey, close their borders to volunteer fighters crossing into Iraq and Syria to join Isis.

Grand Ayatollah Ali al-Sistani and the senior Shia clergy, based in Najaf and Karbala, have always been influential in Iraqi politics. Two out of three of Iraq's 33 million population are Shia. But Iraqi government corruption, and its failure to stop Isis taking control of a third of the country, has discredited Iraqi politicians, including the Prime Minister, Hayder al-Abadi. The Iraqi army disintegrated in humiliating circumstances when it lost Mosul in June last year and was similarly defeated in Ramadi this May.

This puts the senior Shia clergy at the heart of the Iraqi war effort. The Hashid militia was created after Isis captured Mosul a year ago, when al-Sistani issued a fatwa calling for people to join military formations to fight Isis. The religious leaders say their call was to defend Iraq, not to set up sectarian Shia militia. However, the Hashid is overwhelmingly Shia and far outnumbers the combat ready strength of the Iraqi army, said by one Baghdad security official to number between 10,000 and 12,000 men.

The number of Hashid casualties is not known, but their training period is often as little as 25 days, leading to unnecessary losses, some say. Black banners with the names of those killed in the war are fastened to walls in prominent places, such as at crossroads, in Karbala.

The outcome of these battles against Isis in central Iraq may be affected by even a limited degree of rapprochement between Iran and the US. On the ground this would mean that the US would conduct air strikes in support of military action by the Hashid - nominally under the authority of Prime Minister Abadi and his national security adviser, Faleh al-Fayadh, and answerable to the Defence Ministry on operational matters.

In reality, Iranian control is predominant in some of the main militia units - though only three of them. "Would it surprise you to know that there are more American advisers in Iraq today than there are Iranian advisers?" said a senior cleric in Karbala, who played down Iranian influence. He added that Ramadi had only fallen because the Iraqi government, under pressure from the US and Sunni politicians, had rejected an offer of help from the Hashid.

Overall, the nuclear accord may not immediately translate into wide-ranging co-operation between Iran and the US against Isis. But over time it may encourage the US to do business with Iran's allies - the Shia militias in Iraq and the Syrian army in Syria - if it is to stop Isis winning more victories. Shia clerical leaders are cautious, but hope that the US will no longer automatically support the approach of Sunni states like Saudi Arabia and Qatar - its traditional allies, which have backed the Sunni dominated rebels in Syria.

AUTUMN 2015: BATTLING ISIS

ISIS flag near Azaz, Syria, 10 August 2015

Tuesday, 8 September 2015

THE GREAT FLIGHT

Thousands have become millions, as nation after nation succumbs to anarchy and fanaticism. It is an era of violence in the Middle East and North Africa, with nine civil wars now going on in Islamic countries between Pakistan and Nigeria. This is why there are so many refugees fleeing for their lives. Half of the 23 million population of Syria have been forced from their homes, with four million becoming refugees in other countries. Some 2.6 million Iraqis have been displaced by Isis offensives in the last year and squat in tents or half-finished buildings. Unnoticed by the outside world, some 1.5 million people have been displaced in South Sudan since fighting there resumed at the end of 2013.

Other parts of the world, notably south-east Asia, have become more peaceful over the last 50 years or so, but in the vast swathe of territory between the Hindu Kush mountains and the western side of the Sahara, religious, ethnic and separatist conflicts are tearing countries apart. Everywhere states are collapsing, weakening or are under attack; and, in many of these places, extreme Sunni Islamist insurgencies are on the rise which use terror against civilians in order to provoke mass flight.

Another feature of these wars is that none of them show any sign of ending, so people cannot go back to their homes. Most Syrian refugees who fled to Turkey, Lebanon and Jordan in 2011 and 2012, believed the war in Syria would soon be over and they could return. It is only in the last couple of years that they have realised that this is not going to happen and they must seek permanent sanctuary elsewhere. The very length of these wars means immense and irreversible destruction of all means of making a living, so refugees, who at first just sought safety, are also driven by economic necessity.

Such wars are currently being waged in Afghanistan, Iraq, Syria, south-east Turkey, Yemen, Libya, Somalia, Sudan and north-east Nigeria. A few of them began a long time ago, an example being Somalia, where the state collapsed in 1991 and has never been rebuilt, with warlords, extreme jihadis, rival parties and foreign soldiers controlling different parts of the country. But most of these wars started after 2001 and many after 2011. All-out civil war in Yemen only got under way last year, while the Turkish-Kurdish civil war, which has killed 40,000 people since 1984, resumed this July with airstrikes and guerrilla raids. It is escalating rapidly: a truckload of Turkish soldiers were blown up at the weekend by Kurdish PKK guerrillas.

When Somalia fell apart, a process which a disastrous US military intervention failed to reverse in 1992-94, it seemed to be a marginal event, insignificant for the rest of the world. The country became a "failed state", a phrase used in pitying or dismissive terms as it became the realm of pirates, kidnappers and al-Qa'ida bombers. But the rest of the world should regard such failed states with fear as well as contempt, because it is such places - Afghanistan in the 1990s and Iraq since 2003 - that have incubated movements like the Taliban, al-Qa'ida and Isis. All three combine fanatical religious belief with military expertise. Somalia once seemed to be an exceptional case but "Somalianisation" has turned out to be the fate of a whole series of countries, notably Libya, Iraq and Syria, where until recently people had enough food, education and healthcare.

All wars are dangerous, and civil wars have always been notoriously merciless, with religious wars the worst of all. These are what are now happening in the Middle East and North Africa, with Isis - and al-Qa'ida clones such as Jabhat al-Nusra or Ahrar al-Sham in Syria - ritually murdering their opponents and justifying their actions by pointing to the indiscriminate bombardment of civilian areas by the Assad government. What is a little different in these wars is that Isis deliberately publicises its atrocities against Shia, Yazidis or anybody else it deems its enemies. This means that people caught up in these conflicts, particularly since the declaration of Islamic State in June last year, suffer an extra charge of fear which makes it more likely that they will flee and not come back. This is as true for professors in Mosul University in Iraq as it is for villagers in Nigeria, Cameroon or Mali. Unsurprisingly, Isis's advances in Iraq have produced great waves of refugees who have all too good an idea of what will happen to them if they do not run away.

In Iraq and Syria, we are back to a period of drastic demographic change not seen in the region since the Palestinians were expelled or forced to flee by the Israelis in 1948, or when the Christians were exterminated or driven out of what is now modern Turkey in the decade after 1914. Multi-confessional societies in Iraq and Syria are splitting apart with horrendous consequences. Foreign powers either did not know or did not care what sectarian demons they were releasing in these countries by disrupting the old status quo. The former Iraqi National Security Advisor, Mowaffaq al-Rubaie, used to tell American political leaders, who glibly suggested that Iraq's communal problems could be solved by dividing up the country between Sunni, Shia and Kurds, that they should understand what a bloody process this would be, inevitably bringing about massacres and mass flight "similar to the Partition of India in 1947".

Why are so many of these states falling apart now and generating great floods of refugees? What internal flaws or unsustainable outside pressures do they have in common? Most of them achieved self-determination when imperial powers withdrew after the Second World War. By the late 1960s and early 1970s, they were ruled by military leaders who ran police states and justified their monopolies of power and wealth by claiming that they were necessary to establish public order, modernise their countries, gain control of natural resources and withstand fissiparous sectarian and ethnic pressures. These were generally nationalist and often socialist regimes whose outlook was overwhelmingly secular. Because these justifications for authoritarianism were usually hypocritical, self-interested and masked pervasive corruption by the ruling elite, it was often forgotten that countries like Iraq, Syria and Libya had powerful central governments for a reason - and would disintegrate without them.

It is these regimes that have been weakening and are collapsing across the Middle East and North Africa. Nationalism and socialism no longer provide the ideological glue to hold together secular states or to motivate people to fight for them to the last bullet, as believers do for the fanatical and violent brand of Sunni Islam espoused by Isis, Jabhat al-Nusra and Ahrar al-Sham. Iraqi officials admit that one of the reasons the Iraqi army disintegrated in 2014 and has never been successfully reconstituted is that "very few Iraqis are prepared to die for Iraq."

Sectarian groups like Isis deliberately carry out atrocities against Shia and others in the knowledge that it will provoke retaliation against the Sunni that will leave them with no alternative but to look to Isis as their defenders. Fostering communal hatred works in Isis's favour, and it is cross-infecting countries such as Yemen, where previously there was little consciousness of the sectarian divide, though one third of its 25 million population belong to the Shia Zaydi sect. The likelihood of mass flight becomes even greater. Earlier this year, when there were rumours of an Iraqi Army and Shia militia assault aimed at recapturing the overwhelming Sunni city of Mosul this spring, the World Health Organisation and the UN High Commission for Refugees began prepositioning food to feed another one million people who they expected to flee.

Europeans were jolted by pictures of the little drowned body of Alyan Kurdi lying on a beach in Turkey and half-starved Syrians crammed into Hungarian trains. But in the Middle East the new wretched diaspora of the powerless and the dispossessed has been evident for the last three or four years. In May, I was about to cross the Tigris River between Syria and Iraq in a boat with a Kurdish woman and her family when she and her children were ordered off because one letter spelling a name on her permit was incorrect. "But I've been waiting three days with my family on the river bank!" she screamed in despair. I was heading for Erbil, the Kurdish capital, which aspired until a year ago to be "the new Dubai" but is now full of refugees huddling in half-completed hotels, malls and luxury blocks.

What is to be done to stop these horrors? Perhaps the first question is how we can prevent them from getting worse, keeping in mind that five out of the nine wars have begun since 2011. There is a danger that by attributing mass flight to too many diverse causes, including climate change, political leaders responsible for these disasters get off the hook and are free of public pressure to act effectively to bring them to an end.

The present refugee crisis in Europe is very much the conflict in Syria having a real impact on the continent for the first time. True, the security vacuum in Libya has meant that the country is now the conduit for people from impoverished and war-torn countries on the edges of the Sahara. It is from Libya's 1,100-mile coastline that 114,000 refugees have made their way to Italy so far this year, not counting the several thousands who drowned on the way. Yet, bad though this is, the situation is not much different from last year, when 112,000 made their way to Italy by this route.

Very different is the war in Syria and Iraq which has seen the number of people trying to reach Greece by sea jump from 45,000 to 239,000 over the same period. For three decades Afghanistan has produced the greatest number of refugees, according to the UNHCR; but in the past year Syria has taken its place, and one new refugee in four worldwide is now a Syrian. A whole society has been destroyed, and the outside world has done very little to stop this happening. Despite a recent flurry of diplomatic activity, none of the many players in the Syrian crisis shows urgency in trying to end it.

Syria and Iraq are at the heart of the present crisis over refugees in another way, because it is there that Isis and al-Qa'ida-type groups control substantial territory and are able to spread their sectarian poison to the rest of the Islamic world. They energise gangs of killers who operate in much the same way whether they are in Nigeria, Pakistan, Yemen or Syria.

Where Syrian refugees are

Cumulative total since April 2011

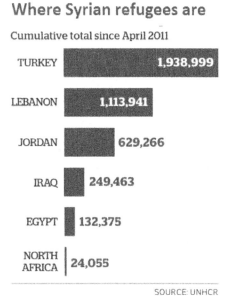

TURKEY	1,938,999
LEBANON	1,113,941
JORDAN	629,266
IRAQ	249,463
EGYPT	132,375
NORTH AFRICA	24,055

SOURCE: UNHCR

Wednesday, 23 September 2015

KOBANI A BEACON OF HOPE

Syrian Kurdish fighters won the greatest victory in Kurdish history in January when they defeated Isis - "Islamic State" - in the battle for the city of Kobani on the Syrian-Turkish border. One thousand YPG (People's Protection Unit) militiamen and several times that number of Isis militants were killed in the four-and-a-half-month siege. Some 70 per cent of Kobani city was destroyed, mostly by US air strikes that turned buildings held by Isis into fragments of pulverised concrete.

But in one important sense the siege of Kobani has never ended because the city is in the Kurdish region of Syria, known to the Kurds as Rojava, which has been deliberately isolated from the outside world. The border crossing to Turkey is closed to everybody, aside from two days a week when Kurdish refugees are allowed to return to Kobani from Turkey.

The KRG in northern Iraq also limits the flow of people and goods in and out of Rojava, the quasi-state which has developed out of the three Syrian Kurdish enclaves, of which Kobani is one, just south of the Turkish border.

Isis holds every other entry and exit point into Rojava, so the two million Kurds there are victims of a blockade on all sides which still claims its victims. Abdul Rahman Hamo, the general coordinator for Kobani's reconstruction, says that among those not allowed to enter Rojava from Turkey or KRG are desperately needed foreign de-mining experts with their specialised equipment. As Isis fighters retreated from Kobani City and the 380 villages around it, they left behind great numbers of mines and booby traps. "Some 48 of our people have been killed by mines in the last two months," says Mr Hamo.

"Many villages are still evacuated because they are full of mines that have not been defused." He estimates that there are 150,000 Kurds in Turkey who would like to come home "but they are scared of the mines". The YPG tried defusing the mines itself, but lacked the training and equipment necessary to do so without excessive risk. "We lost four of our men," says Mr Hamo. "Foreign NGOs have their own demining devices, but Turkey and the KRG does not allow them in."

The same blockade is preventing the entry of equipment needed to remove the great mounds of shattered concrete in Kobani. The streets we drove down were generally clear, but the buildings on either side of us had often been turned into giant concrete sandwiches as floors had concertinaed on top of each other. Mr Hamo said: "We have taken away 60,000 truck-loads of debris each weighing 20 tons, but that is only 40 per cent of the work".

Pockets of normal life continue in between individual buildings and blocks that are utterly devastated, with people running small shops or sitting on plastic chairs sipping tea. There is no electricity except what is provided by small generators and water comes from newly dug wells because Isis has cut off the water supply from the Euphrates. Local hospitals say they are short of almost everything they need, including simple medicines.

Despite this, 4,000 refugees are returning to Kobani every week from Turkey when the border crossing is briefly open. We found Aljin Bako who had returned from Turkey with her five sisters and four brothers on 25 May to their old house. She said that "the house suffered little damage, but the Isis fighters who were living there smashed everything before they left".

The Isis men appear to have spent a lot of their time trying to smash open an enormous safe they had found in the house, supposing it to be full of money. The Bako family all appeared to find this extremely funny because they said they had removed all documents and valuables from the safe before leaving. This did not quite explain why they needed such a large safe, but the fact that their father was in the money exchange business may have had something to do with it.

Aljin sounded unintimidated by the massacre that took place around her house, when between 80 and 100 Isis fighters disguised in YPG uniforms penetrated Kobani on 25 June. Over the next four days they slaughtered at least 223 civilians, men, women and children, before they were hunted down. "It started at 4.30am when we heard sounds of men shouting and we just stayed inside," she said.

Could Isis come back to Kobani? The commander of the YPJ (Women's Protection Units) in Kobani, Fidan Zinar, says that "we are not confident that they will not come back because they still have cells in the region and there are gaps in the line they could get through". She says this might be true of an Isis raid or suicide mission, but they could not launch a full military campaign to capture the city.

Though Kobani is mostly in ruins and the threat from Isis has not disappeared, its people are very conscious their city has become a symbol of Kurdish heroism and determination, the equivalent of Verdun in France or Stalingrad in Russia. "It was the first time that anybody had stopped Isis," says Idris Nassan, vice-minister of foreign affairs for Kobani Canton. "They took other cities like Mosul in a couple of hours."

There are already plans for a museum and a memorial hall for the fighters who died defending the city. In one corner of the civilian cemetery, there are three small tombs in grey marble where the drowned bodies of Aylan Kurdi, his five-year-old brother Galip and their mother Rehan are buried. They died trying to cross from Turkey to Greece this month.

But for all the fame of the battle of Kobani its future remains fragile, with a hostile Turkey closing the Kurds' border crossings that it kept open when Isis was in control. At Tal Abyad border crossing, captured by the YPG from Isis in June, the elaborate facilities are completely empty. Fawaz, the manager of the crossing, says that "many times we try to send ambulances with wounded people in them to the Turkish side, but they do not open the gates and many die".

The main problem for Kobani is the lack of any corridor to the outside world. Mr Hamo recalls bitterly that he attended a conference on reconstructing Kobani which was organised by the European Union in Brussels. He listened to speech after speech by government officials promising money and aid, but so far nothing has arrived. The siege of Kobani is not entirely over.

Friday, 25 September 2015

ISIS MUST BE OUR MAIN ENEMY

The overthrow of President Bashar al-Assad by Isis and rebel groups that are affiliated to al-Qa'ida would be a calamity for the world, says the Syrian Kurdish leader Saleh Muslim.

In an interview with *The Independent* he warned that "if the regime collapses because of the salafis [fundamentalist Islamic militants] it would be a disaster for everyone."

Mr Muslim said he was fully in favour of Mr Assad and his government being replaced by a more acceptable alternative. But he is concerned that Isis and other extreme Islamist groups are now close to Damascus on several sides, saying that "this is dangerous". During a recent Isis offensive in the north eastern city of Hasaka, the Kurdish YPG militia and the Syrian Army both came under attack from Isis, but Mr Muslim denied that there was any collaboration between the two.

The Syrian Kurds, previously marginalised and discriminated against by the Damascus government, have become crucial players in the country's civil war over the last year. In January, they defeated Isis at Kobani with the aid of US airstrikes after a four-and-a-half-month siege and their forces are still advancing. While Mr Muslim said that he wants an end to rule by Mr Assad, he makes clear that he considers Isis to be the main enemy.

"Our main goal is the defeat of Daesh [Isis]," he said. "We would not feel safe in our home so long as there is one Daesh left alive." The threat did not come from them alone, he said, but also from al-Qa'ida clones such as Jabhat al-Nusra and Ahrar al-Sham. "They all have the same mentality."

Mr Muslim is the president of the PYD that rules Rojava, as Kurds call the three Kurdish enclaves just south of the Turkish border. A stocky and affable man, aged 64, he apologised before the interview in the city of Ramalan for his broken English - though it turned out to be fluent, something explained by a year spent in Britain learning English and 12 years as an oil industry engineer in Saudi Arabia, where the working language was also English.

He says he is still surprised by the speed with which the Syrian Kurds have emerged from obscurity, since the withdrawal of the Syrian army from Kurdish enclaves in 2012, to become a major force in Syria. The highly-disciplined and committed YPG fighters have won victories over Isis this year at Kobani, Tal Abyad and Hasaka, at the same time that Isis was inflicting defeats on both the Iraqi and Syrian armies.

Mr Muslim and other PYD leaders now face an important decision about the future advance of YPG forces. Having retaken Kobani and 380 villages nearby, they are currently dug in on the east bank of the Euphrates River, close to Isis's last remaining border crossing to Turkey at Jarabulus and to a larger, strategically important, area north of Aleppo. Turkey is wary of the YPG and is eager to create a so-called "safe zone" which would be held by Syrian opposition groups under its influence - ostensibly to keep Isis from its borders but thus also preventing Kurdish forces from advancing westwards.

Mr Muslim says the present situation cannot continue in this area because Kurdish civilians there are being attacked by Isis. Only the previous day, he said, 300 Kurds had been forced out of their homes in the Isis-held town of Manbij, where Kurds make up 30 per cent of the population, and seven people had been killed. Another 150 Kurdish villages are under threat.

Mr Muslim stressed the YPG was acting to defend not only Kurds, but all Syrians under attack by Isis. He said that if people living in the zone west of the Euphrates and north of Aleppo were "to ask the YPG for help" they would most likely get it. In addition, the Kurds want to open a road to a third Kurdish enclave at Afrin, which is isolated and under threat.

Noting the US wants an Isis-free zone in this area, Mr Muslim said "the perfect way to do this is ground troops and air support". It is not entirely clear that the US will go along with this and give the YPG the air cover it may need, because it does not want to offend Turkey. However, the Syrian armed opposition is almost wholly dominated by Isis and its al-Qa'ida equivalents, so the US does not want to damage the successful collaboration between YPG ground troops and US air power.

How would Turkey respond to a further Kurdish advance? It is already alarmed by the rise of a Kurdish state-let in the form of Rojava on its southern frontier with Syria. It knows that the PYD is essentially the Syrian branch of the PKK against whom it has been fighting a guerrilla war since 1984. Mr Muslim said: "I do not think it is possible that Turkey will invade, but if it does it will be a big problem for Turkey."

Though the YPG is America's most effective military ally against Isis in both Iraq and Syria, Washington remains ambivalent about the extent of its co-operation with the Syrian Kurds. Mr Muslim says that "the Americans have not delivered any weapons or ammunition to the YPG".

They have reassured him their support for the Syrian Kurds will not be weakened by their agreement with Turkey, signed in July, for the US to use Incirlik airbase and for Turkey to join attacks against Isis. In the event, Turkey launched few air raids against Isis and many hundreds against the PKK in south-east Turkey and northern Iraq.

Mr Muslim says that since detachments of the PKK in northern Iraq are fighting Isis, the Turkish actions can only benefit the Islamic militants. He is only partially comforted by American reassurances, saying what worries him is "what has not been revealed" about the US-Turkish deal.

Throughout the interview Mr Muslim would periodically say the situation was confusing, but he is adept at seeking to conciliate rival powers. He had just returned from a meeting with President Masoud Barzani, who heads the KRG in northern Iraq and is himself wary of the sudden appearance of a rival Kurdish quasi-state in northern Syria. The KRG has been enforcing an intermittent embargo against Rojava, with some trucks kept waiting on the frontier. Mr Muslim said the border was opening and closing "according to the mood" of KRG authorities.

He is dubious about reports of Russian troops joining the war in Syria. He had been in Moscow last month and had been assured that the Russians "would not do that. [Russian special envoy for Syria Mikhail] Bogdanov said to me that they would not be involved in the fighting."

Though he is determined to fight Isis until it is defeated, Mr Muslim believes that the Syrian civil war must end in a compromise. "In the end there should be political solution," he says. "No side can finish off the other."

Saturday, 3 October 2015

THE WEST NEEDS A REALITY CHECK

Reaction to Russia's military intervention in Syria shows that the lack of knowledge of the Syrian political landscape on the part of Western political leaders and media is hindering the adoption of more constructive policies. During the past four years, oversimplifications and wishful thinking have prevented any realistic attempt to end the civil war, mitigate its effects or stop it from spreading to other countries.

Since 2011 the departure from power of President Bashar al-Assad has been prescribed as a quick way to bring an end to the conflict, although there is no reason to believe this. There are no quick or easy solutions: Syria is being torn apart by a genuine, multi-layered civil war with a multitude of self-interested players inside and outside the country. If Assad dropped dead tomorrow, Syrians in his corner would not stop fighting, knowing as they do that the success of an opposition movement dominated by Isis and al-Qa'ida clones such as Jabhat al-Nusra would mean death or flight for them and their families.

Today there are four million Syrian refugees, mostly from opposition areas being bombarded indiscriminately by government forces. But this figure could double if the more populous pro-government areas become too dangerous to live in.

In the past, this was not likely to happen because Assad always controlled at least 12 out of 14 Syrian provincial capitals. The Western rejection of any role for him in the future of Syria, even though he ruled most of its population, torpedoed negotiations before they could get off the ground. To say this is not to endorse Assad or the Baath party, who have always used gangster methods and extreme violence to stay in power, but to recognise that they were never offered terms they could accept and were only likely to go if they suffered complete military defeat.

Western governments have hitherto dealt with this problem by retreating into fantasy, lying or remaining willfully ignorant about the real situation on the ground. As long ago as August 2012 the Defence Intelligence Agency, the Pentagon's intelligence arm, said in a report first disclosed earlier this year that the "Salafists, the Muslim Brotherhood and AQI are the major forces driving the insurgency in Syria."

It noted that the opposition was supported by the West, Gulf countries and Turkey and forecast that Isis "could also declare an Islamic state through its union with other terrorist organisations in Iraq and Syria".

The influence at the time of this prescient DIA report is not known, but earlier this year there was a semi-public revolt by US intelligence analysts who said their conclusions that Isis was growing in strength were being diluted or disregarded by their superiors. Some 50 analysts working for the US military's Central Command were reported to have complained formally that their analyses were being manipulated to fit in with the administration's claim that Isis was weakening.

Centcom may have come to believe its own upbeat message because US generals were giving optimistic accounts of the success of their air campaign against Isis at the very moment in May when it captured the cities of Ramadi in Iraq and Palmyra in Syria.

From an early stage in the Syrian crisis, intelligence reports discounted or derided claims that moderate or secular forces were leading the opposition. In a moment of frankness in 2014, Vice-President Joe Biden gave a succinct account of what the administration really thought about what was happening in Syria. He said that Saudi Arabia, Turkey and the UAE "were so determined to take down Assad and essentially have a proxy Sunni-Shia war" they financed and armed anybody who would fight against Assad, "except that the people who were being supplied were al-Nusra and al-Qa'ida and the extremist elements coming from other parts of the world".

Mr Biden's summary of how the extreme Sunni sectarian jihadis came to dominate the armed opposition in Syria, marginalising or eliminating the "moderates", became accepted wisdom over the past year. The FSA - even at the height of its fame never more than an umbrella organisation - was considered dead and buried.

Anthony Cordesman of the Centre for Strategic and International Studies in Washington wrote that the time had come to stop pretending "that Syrian 'moderates' are strong enough to either affect the security situation or negotiate for Syria's real fighters".

But as news spread this week that the Russians had started bombing in Syria, the FSA and the "moderates" were disinterred in order to suggest that it was they and not Isis who were the targets of Russian air strikes.

One British newspaper claimed that the bombs "mainly appeared to hit less extreme groups fighting Bashar al-Assad's regime". David Cameron worried that if Russian action was "against the FSA in support of Assad the dictator, then obviously that is a retrograde step".

Television presenters spoke of anti-Assad forces being bombed in northern Syria, but seldom added that the most important of these were Jabhat al-Nusra and Ahrar al-Sham. More than 30 air strikes were against Jaysh al-Fateh, the Army of Conquest, which has seized much of Idlib province but is led by al-Nusra. The situation is genuinely complex, with between 20 and 30 opposition armed groups backed by Turkey, Saudi Arabia, Qatar and the UAE. But news reports had a strong whiff of Cold War propaganda when any fact could be distorted in order to demonise Moscow.

So many crises and confrontations have their central focus on the battlefields of Syria that any return to a unitary state is impossible. Conflicts include a popular uprising against Assad, Sunni against Shia, Iran against Saudi Arabia, Kurd against Turk, and now US against Russia.

But any solution or diminution of violence can only come if there is a realistic understanding by Western and regional powers of the destructive forces at work.

If political leaders, media reporters and think-tank specialists share a vision of Syria that is partisan, propagandist and over-simple, there is no chance of a solution to the great Syrian tragedy.

Monday, 12 October 2015

OMINOUS SIGNS IN TURKEY

Is Turkey joining the array of eight countries engulfed by violence in the Middle East and north Africa? The bombing of a rally in Ankara that killed 128 people on Saturday is an ominous sign that the same factors that have effectively destroyed Iraq and Syria as unitary countries are affecting Turkey.

It comes less than three weeks before the Turkish parliamentary election, when President Recep Tayyip Erdogan and the Justice and Development (AK) party will discover if they are going to maintain the monopoly of power that they have held since 2002.

The initial signs are not optimistic. People going to place flowers at the scene of the bomb attack were tear-gassed by police. Nobody has yet claimed responsibility for the suicide bombings, but it has all the hallmarks of "Islamic State".

The aim is obviously to increase polarisation between Kurds and Turks and between the government and its opponents. The bombing that killed 33 pro-Kurdish activists at Suruc in July led to retaliation by the PKK, whose insurgency has been at the centre of Turkish politics since 1984.

The general assumption is that Mr Erdogan aims to discredit, or even eliminate, the pro-Kurdish HDP party. It robbed the AK party of its parliamentary majority in June. The HDP's success came almost entirely because conservative and religious Kurds switched from the AK party. Nothing that Mr Erdogan or the AK have done since the last election is likely to woo these voters back in the coming election.

The PKK has now declared what amounts to a ceasefire, but the insurgents are militarily and politically stronger than they were previously, thanks to developments in Syria. Mr Erdogan has miscalculated at every stage of the Syrian crisis since 2011 and there is no sign of these missteps ending.

If he seeks to exploit the latest bombing in Ankara, almost certainly carried out by Isis, for his own political ends then he hands over to Isis the ability to shape the future direction of Turkish politics.

Saturday, 7 November 2015

HAS SISI CRUSHED TERRORISM IN EGYPT?

Isis has carried out revenge attacks against any state or group which fights against it. When the US started bombing its forces in Iraq and Syria last year, it decapitated American journalists and aid workers. When beheadings became the norm and lost their shock value, it burned to death a Jordanian pilot in a cage. And when it was defeated and driven from the city of Kobani by the Syrian Kurds, it sent suicide raiders to butcher over 200 Kurdish men, women and children.

The message in all cases was a show of strength and a demonstration that nobody can strike Isis with impunity.

These atrocities are not difficult to carry out as they are directed against civilians or prisoners who cannot defend themselves. The destruction of a Russian plane by a bomb is in keeping with Isis tactics. The fact that the group has not formally claimed responsibility is not a sign that it did not make the attack. It has not yet claimed two suicide bombings in Turkey, the first at Suruc in July, which killed 32 young Turks bringing aid to Kobani, and a second in Ankara on 10 October that killed 102 people demonstrating for peace. The attacks may have had the more subtle intention of deepening hostility between the Turkish state and the Kurdish minority.

The loss of the plane is damaging to both Egypt and Russia. President Abdel Fattah al-Sisi had wanted to show the outside world that he had crushed "terrorism" in his country since he came to power in 2013. His critics say that by persecuting the Muslim Brotherhood he is providing Isis supporters with a new constituency. The worst violence has been in Sinai, where there has been a slow burning insurgency for decades, and from which journalists have been excluded in order to sustain the fiction that order has been restored.

Few of the tourists visiting Sharm el-Sheikh will have taken on board that there is a fierce guerrilla war going on in other parts of Sinai, but these cannot be kept entirely separate from the sanitised tourist resorts of the Red Sea. On 1 July this year the Isis affiliate known as "Sinai Province" sent 300 to 400 armed fighters in a well organised attempt to take the town of Sheikh Zuwayed in North Sinai, using machine guns and rocket-propelled grenade launchers. The government announced that 241 jihadi fighters and 21 soldiers were killed in the clashes, but the number of civilian dead is unknown. Egyptian journalists who tried to investigate what was going on were arrested.

The planning and strength of the attack on Sheikh Zuwayed shows that Sinai Province can carry out sophisticated operations, which might include getting a bomb on board a Russian aircraft. Members of the group who have fought with the Syrian opposition will have had instruction in bomb making. The group was previously known as Ansar Beit al-Maqdis and swore allegiance to the self-declared caliphate in November 2014. In retaliation for attacks, the army launched an operation called "Martyr's Right" in which hundreds of people have been killed. According to Human Rights Watch the Egyptian military has destroyed 3,255 buildings and expelled thousands of people in North Sinai who now have nowhere to live. Most of the fighting is taking place 200 miles from Sharm el-Sheikh, but in 2004-2006 the resort towns on the Red Sea were hit by bomb attacks when 165 people were killed.

Several factors make the current insurgency more serious: it is plugged into the international Isis network and there are fighters who have been to Syria travelling via Libya, which has a long, porous border with Egypt, and have now returned to Sinai. There is also the question of how many former supporters of the deposed President Morsi and the Muslim Brotherhood are turning to the gun in their struggle with President Sisi.

Saturday, 14 November 2015

A SYMBOLIC SUCCESS

The assassination of Mohammed Emwazi by a US drone is a symbolic success for the US and Britain in a war that is full of symbols. The ritual murders of journalists and aid workers carried out by Emwazi were themselves intended to symbolise the ruthlessness and determination of Isis, and create fear among its enemies.

But his death, if confirmed, will not significantly weaken the group, which remains in command of a powerful army and state machine that rules an area the size of Great Britain. Unfortunately, it is a movement never likely to be short of executioners and in whose ideology martyrdom for the faith is a central feature. Nevertheless, part of the appeal of Isis to its followers is that it does not fail, that it wins divinely inspired victories against the odds, such as capturing Mosul last year when a few thousand of its fighters defeated 20,000 Iraqi troops.

Episodes like the killing of Emwazi show Isis as vulnerable and that its security can be penetrated by intelligence agencies. David Cameron exaggerated yesterday when he said that it was "a strike at the heart of Isis", though Isis will be worried that informers in Raqqa should be so well-informed.

State-sponsored assassinations by drone and special operations forces have a long history of failure. They depend on the assumption that the organisation targeted has a finite number of leaders who cannot be replaced if eliminated.

But the outcome of assassination campaigns has invariably been disappointing, if not counter-effective.

A US study of 200 cases in Iraq between June and October in 2007 found that, when a local insurgent leader was assassinated or captured, the number of IED attacks on US troops did not go down but increased - sometimes by up to 40 per cent. The dead leaders were being rapidly replaced by more violent and effective insurgents.

President Barack Obama's administration has much favoured the use of drones as a central element in its "War on Terror", notably in Yemen, where they have been used since 2002. The target has been AQAP, which has lost many of its leaders, but this has not prevented it expanding rapidly over the past year and playing an increasingly important role in the Yemeni civil war. In recent weeks it has been leading the struggle for control of Taiz, one of the country's largest cities.

The assassination of one individual in a guerrilla organisation such as Isis or Aqap is very difficult if the person is careful about their security. There is also the problem that drones, air strikes or killings by ground forces will eliminate an indeterminate number of innocent villagers, wedding parties or local gatherings. The temptation is then for those who carried out the attack to insist that the casualties all came from a "terrorist" group, but this has frequently been shown to be false.

Isis is coming under greater pressure from many sides, the killing of Emwazi being only one of them. It briefly cut but has now lost control of the only road into the government-held part of Aleppo after a counter-attack by the Syrian army, supported by Russian aircraft. The same forces have broken Isis's long siege of the Kweiris air base east of Aleppo and it is becoming less likely that Isis will be able to advance west to cut the main M-5 highway north of Damascus. In northern Syria, the Kurds have been pressing Isis back and could advance on Raqqa, or south from Hasaka City. In Iraq, Iraqi Kurdish forces backed by heavy US air strikes say they have captured Sinjar City, which Isis seized last year.

Cumulatively, these are serious territorial losses, but Isis is a guerrilla movement that does not necessarily fight for fixed positions and its retreats do not mean that it is anywhere near defeat.

Monday, 16 November 2015

THE ISIS BOMBERS WILL ALWAYS GET THROUGH

The "Islamic State", as Isis styles itself, will be pleased with the outcome of its attacks in Paris. It has shown that it can retaliate with its usual savagery against a country that is bombing its territory and is a power to be feared at a time when it is under serious military pressure. The actions of just eight Isis suicide bombers and gunmen are dominating the international news agenda for days on end.

There is not a lot that can be done about this. People are understandably eager to know the likelihood of their being machine-gunned the next time they sit in a restaurant or attend a concert in Paris or London.

But the apocalyptic tone of press coverage is exaggerated: the violence experienced hitherto in Paris is not comparable with Belfast and Beirut in the 1970s or Damascus and Baghdad today. Contrary to the hyperbole of wall-to-wall television coverage, the shock of living in a city being bombed soon wears off.

Predictions of Paris forever trembling in expectation of another attack play into the hands of Isis.

A further disadvantage flows from excessive rhetoric about the massacre: instead of the atrocities acting as an incentive for effective action, the angry words become a substitute for a real policy. After the Charlie Hebdo murders in January, 40 world leaders marched with linked arms through the streets of Paris proclaiming, among other things, that they would give priority to the defeat of Isis and its al-Qa'ida equivalents.

But, in practice, they did nothing of the sort. When Isis forces attacked Palmyra in eastern Syria in May, the US did not launch air strikes against it because the city was defended by the Syrian army and Washington was frightened of being accused of keeping President Bashar al-Assad in power.

In effect, the US handed Isis a military advantage which it promptly used to seize Palmyra, behead captured Syrian soldiers and blow up the ancient ruins.

The Turkish President Recep Tayyip Erdogan said at the G20 meeting in Turkey yesterday that "the time for talking is over" and there must be collective action against "terrorism".

This sounds like an impressive Turkish stand against Isis, but Mr Erdogan has explained that his definition of "terrorist" is wide-ranging and includes the Syrian Kurds and their paramilitary YPG whom the US has found to be its best military ally against Isis.

Mr Erdogan's enthusiasm for attacking Kurdish insurgents in Turkey and northern Iraq has turned out to be much stronger than his desire to attack Isis, Jabhat al-Nusra and Ahrar al-Sham.

There is little sign that the G20 leaders gathered in Turkey have understood the nature of the conflict in which they are engaged. Isis's military strategy is a unique combination of urban terrorism, guerrilla tactics and conventional warfare. In the past, many states have used terrorism against opponents, but, in the case of Isis, suicide squads focusing on soft civilian targets at home and abroad are an integral part of its war-making strategy.

When the YPG captured Isis's border crossing into Turkey at Tal Abyad in June, the group retaliated by sending fighters in disguise to the Kurdish city of Kobani where they slaughtered over 220 men, women and children.

When Russia started its air campaign against Isis and extreme jihadists on 30 September, Isis responded with a bomb planted on a Russian plane leaving Sharm el-Sheikh that killed 224 passengers.

Another mistake made by G20 leaders is to persistently underestimate Isis. David Cameron said it should not be dignified by the name "Islamic State", but unfortunately it is a real state and one which is more powerful than half the members of the UN, with an experienced army, conscription, taxation and control of all aspects of life within the vast area it rules.

So long as it exists, it will project its power through suicide operations like those we have just seen in Paris. Because the potential target is civilian populations as a whole, no amount of increased security checks or surveillance is going to be effective. The bomber will always get through.

The only real solution is the destruction of Isis: this can only be done by a US and Russian air campaign against it in partnership with those on the ground who are actually fighting it.

The US Air Force has done so effectively with the YPG, enabling them to defeat Isis at Kobani, and with the Iraqi Kurdish Peshmerga, who captured the city of Sinjar last week. But the US baulks at attacking Isis when it is fighting the Syrian army or the Shia militias in Iraq. Given that these are the two strongest military formations fighting Isis, America's military punch is being pulled where it would do most good.

Given the international sympathy for the French after the massacre in Paris, it is inevitable that there is almost no criticism of France's muddle-headed policy towards the Syrian conflict.

Earlier this year, in an interview with Aron Lund of the Carnegie Endowment for International Peace, one of the leading French experts on Syria, Fabrice Balanche, who is currently at the Washington Institute for Near East Policy, said that "in 2011-12 we suffered a kind of intellectual McCarthyism on the Syrian question: if you said that Assad was not about to fall within three months you could be suspected of being paid by the Syrian regime".

He noted that the French foreign ministry took up the cause of Syrian opposition, while the media refused to see the Syrian revolt as anything other than the continuation of revolutions in Tunisia and Egypt. They were blind to sectarian, political and social divisions which meant that there were always two sides to the Syrian civil war.

With the state bureaucracy, army general staff and security services packed with Alawites, it is almost impossible to get rid of Mr Assad and his regime, whose leaders come from the Alawite community, without the state collapsing, leaving a vacuum to be filled by Isis and its al-Qa'ida counterparts.

Despite the latest terrorist attacks, there is still no longterm policy to prevent it happening again.

Sunday, 29 November 2015

WHY ISIS IS SO PLEASED WITH ITSELF

David Cameron made a reasonable case last week for Britain going to war with Islamic State in Syria; what he did not do is explain how this war is going to be won by Britain or anybody else. Even now, 18 months after IS captured Mosul, there is a tendency by world leaders to underestimate its political and military strength.

Mr Cameron said that "military action [by the US, UK and others] seeks to degrade IS's capabilities, so that Iraqi security forces can effectively secure Iraq and moderate forces in Syria can defend the territory they control".

It would certainly be nice if that happened, except that the Iraqi state security forces are demoralised, dysfunctional and have had difficulty finding new recruits since they have been repeatedly defeated by Isis over the past two years. In Syria, we are to look to 70,000 "moderate" fighters whose existence Mr Cameron revealed to the House of Commons, but nobody in Syria has ever heard of.

Isis is not going to be defeated by these phantom armies which are to be Britain's allies in Iraq and Syria. It is the same weakness as in Iraq in 2003 and in Afghanistan a little later - in both cases, Britain was a junior partner in a US-led coalition that pretended to have local allies, but in practice these were too feeble to contribute much.

Does this matter much? After all, the British military contribution in Iraq has been small, some 360 air strikes out of a total of 5,432, and will be equally meagre in Syria. But this misses the point because, since the summer, Isis has extended its strategy of urban terrorism, so long used to slaughter non-Sunni Iraqis, to the rest of the world, as we have just seen in Ankara, Sharm el Sheikh, Beirut and Paris.

Isis is well pleased by the results since it has succeeded in showing its power to the world, by all reports. It is more than likely that it will retaliate against British citizens in response to Britain's joining the war in Syria. This consideration should not influence British decisions about what to do in Syria and Iraq, but such retaliation should not come as a surprise. Britain is still seen in the Middle East as a great power, whatever its actual status, and Isis is probably pleased that it has joined the roster of its enemies since it knows that British air strikes do not add much to the attack it is facing.

It is extraordinary how Isis has come to dictate the political agenda of a large part of the world. In Britain, its actions and British reaction to them have dominated the news since the killing of Mohammed Emwazi, nick-named "Jihadi John", on 12 November. This is quite intentional on the part of Isis, and one of the attractions of Paris as a target is that it is a news hub. The same would be true of London. In neither city is there any need for Isis to make videos of atrocities; it can be sure of wall-to-wall coverage by cameras from every television company in the world. It will also be pleased in Raqqa by the near hysterical tone of much of the reporting: bad as these mass murders are, they pose no existential threat to France, as the German invasions in 1914 and 1940 did.

The impact of Isis is measured not only in publicity, but in shaping relations between states. Poland and the Baltic states are alarmed to discover that the US and Western Europeans are becoming much more interested in finding a way of cooperating with Russia over Syria than in opposing its actions in Ukraine.

Whatever formal support there was in Nato for Turkey over the shooting down of a Russian aircraft, President Putin's denunciation of

Turkey's support for extreme jihadis over the past three years has struck home. If there are more Isis mass killings of civilians from Western Europe or the US, pressure for a closer alliance with Russia is bound to grow.

The crisis is increasingly centred on a small part of Syria where foreign powers and local proxies jostle each other. This is the north-west corner of Syria between the Euphrates and the Mediterranean, and south of the Syrian-Turkish border. It was here that the Russian plane was shot down by a Turkish jet on 19 November and where there has since been intense fighting. The Syrian army, backed by heavy Russian air strikes, has gained control of an important position known as the Turkmen mountain.

Some 10,000 Syrian soldiers are reportedly battling 6,000 Turk-men, the Army of Conquest, and the al-Qa'ida linked Nusra Front (underlining the problem with David Cameron's 70,000 moderate fighters: the Turkmen might be described as moderate, but they are fighting alongside the Syrian branch of al-Qa'ida). The Syrian armed opposition has always depended on the border with Syria being open and, if the Syrian army and the Russians begin to close it, they will have gone a long way towards winning an important victory in the war. Half of the 550-mile-long frontier is already held by the Syrian Kurds.

These parochial struggles are having international implications. It was one of the greatest diplomatic miscalculations in recent history to imagine that the Syrian war would not affect neighbouring states. In the past six months alone, developments in northern Syria have led to a renewed conflict between the Turkish state and the Kurds and to confrontation between Turkey and Russia. Isis will be pleased by both.

Despite all the furious rhetoric after the Paris killings, Isis does not look as if is going to be under pressure that it cannot withstand. Both Russia and Russia's critics have for different reasons portrayed Russia's military intervention as being on a larger scale than it really is. It has fewer than 100 fixed-wing aircraft and helicopters operating in support of the Syrian army. This may be enough to reverse the ad-vances by the Army of Conquest (mostly al-Nusra Front and Ahrar al-Sham) which, backed by Turkey, Saudi Arabia and Qatar happened in May. But it is not enough to give a depleted Syrian army the strength to win a decisive victory like the capture of the rebel-held half of

Aleppo. The Iranian role also tends to be exaggerated, both by Iran and its enemies. The Pentagon says that there are fewer than 2,000 Iranian troops in Syria and 1,000 in Iraq.

The politics of war in Syria are extraordinarily complicated, and it was probably inevitable that Britain would be sucked into this morass. Everybody agrees that there is no appetite today in Britain for sending ground troops, though this could change overnight if there were a repeat of the Paris massacre in London.

But, if there was such an intervention, Britain, the US and France, would all be hobbled militarily by their contradictory policy of trying to fight extreme Sunni jihadis like Isis and al-Nusra, while maintaining their alliance with powerful Sunni states like Saudi Arabia, Turkey and the Gulf monarchies. This has been the pattern since the US launched its "war on terror" after 9/11, but avoided confrontation with Saudi Arabia and Pakistan.

Monday, 30 November 2015

'SEAL THE BORDER WITH ISIS'

The US is demanding that Turkey close a 60-mile stretch of its border with Syria which is the sole remaining crossing point for Isis militants, including some of those involved in the massacre in Paris and other terrorist plots.

The complete closure of the 550-mile-long border would be a serious blow to Isis, which has brought tens of thousands of Islamist volunteers across the frontier over the past three years.

In the wake of the Isis attacks in Paris, Washington is making clear to Ankara that it will no longer accept Turkish claims that it is unable to cordon off the remaining short section of the border still used by Isis. "The game has changed. Enough is enough. The border needs to be sealed," a senior official in President Barack Obama's administration told The Wall Street Journal, describing the tough message that Washington has sent to the Turkish government. "This is an international threat, and it's coming out of Syria and it's coming through Turkish territory."

The US estimates some 30,000 Turkish troops would be needed to close the border between Jarabulus on the Euphrates and the town of Kilis, further west in Turkey, according to the paper. US intelligence agencies say that the stretch of frontier most commonly used by Isis is between Jarabulus, where the official border crossing has been closed, and the town of Cobanbey.

It has become of crucial importance ever since the YPG captured the border crossing at Tal Abyad, 60 miles north of Isis's capital of Raqqa in June. Turkey had kept that border crossing open while Isis was in control on the southern side, but immediately closed it when the YPG seized the crossing point. The Turkish authorities are refusing to allow even the bodies of YPG fighters, who are Turkish citizens and were killed fighting Isis, to be taken back across the border into Turkey.

The US move follows increasing international criticism of Turkey for what is seen as its long-term tolerance of, and possible complicity with, Isis and other extremist jihadi groups such as al-Qa'ida's branch in Syria, Jabhat al-Nusra and Ahrar al-Sham. Not only have thousands of foreign fighters passed through Turkey on their way to join Isis, but crude oil from oilfields seized by Isis in north-east Syria has been transported to Turkey for sale, providing much of the revenue of the self-declared Islamic State.

Last week a Turkish court jailed two prominent journalists for publishing pictures of a Turkish lorry delivering ammunition to opposition fighters in Syria. President Recep Tayyip Erdogan claimed that the weapons were destined for Turkmen paramilitaries allied to Turkey fighting in Syria, but this was denied by Turkish political leaders close to the Turkmen.

Turkey is now under heavy pressure from the US and Russia, with President Vladimir Putin directly accusing Ankara of aiding Isis and al-Qa'ida. In the wake of the shooting down of a Russian aircraft by a Turkish jet, Russia is launching heavy air strikes in support of the Syrian army's advance to control the western end of the Syrian-Turkish border.

The pro-opposition Syrian Observatory for Human Rights said a Russian air strike on the town of Ariha yesterday killed 18 people and wounded dozens more. Meanwhile Turkey said it had now received the body of the pilot killed when the plane was shot down and would repatriate it to Moscow.

The US demand that Turkey finally close the border west of Jarabulus could, if Turkey complies, prove more damaging to Isis than increased air strikes by the US, France and, possibly Britain. The YPG has closed half the Syrian frontier over the past year and defeated an Isis assault aimed at taking another border crossing at Kobani.

Syrian Kurdish leaders say they want to advance further west from their front line on the Euphrates and link up with a Kurdish enclave at Afrin. But Turkey insists that it will resist a further YPG advance with military force. Instead, it had proposed a protected zone on the southern side of the border from which Isis would be driven by moderate Syrian opposition fighters.

The US has opposed this proposal, suspecting that the Turkish definition of moderates includes those the US is targeting as terrorists. It also appears to be a ploy to stop the YPG, heavily supported by US air power, expanding its de facto state along Turkey's southern flank. US officials are quoted as saying that there could be "significant blowback" against Turkey by European states if it allows Isis militants to cross from Syria into Turkey and then carry out terrorist outrages in Europe.

Meanwhile in Iraq, officials said three more mass graves had been found in the northern town of Sinjar, which Kurdish forces backed by US-led air strikes recaptured from Isis earlier this month.

SUPPLY LINE TURKEY'S BORDER WITH ISIS

THE 500-MILE FRONT AGAINST ISIS

Isis blew up one of the last remaining bridges across the Euphrates at Ramadi this week as 300 of its fighters tried to hold on to the centre of the city, which has come under attack from Iraqi government forces supported by US air strikes. Here Isis is on the retreat, but in Syria it has recaptured the village of Mahein, south-east of Homs, from the Syrian army, which had seized it a few days earlier and had been expected to use the village to launch an attack to retake the city of Palmyra.

The recapture of a world famous city such as Palmyra, where Isis has publicly executed Syrian soldiers and blown up the ancient temples, would have been an important victory for President Bashar al-Assad. Failure to do so is a further sign that the Syrian army's multiple offensives against Isis and the Syrian armed opposition, which is backed by Russian air power, have so far failed to win any big successes that would tip the likely outcome of the war in Assad's favour.

It is a vast battlefield stretching 500 miles across Iraq and Syria from the outskirts of Baghdad to the mountains overlooking the Mediterranean. Every day there are skirmishes, bombings and battles, of which some are well publicised, but others are fought out in the semidesert of eastern Syria and get scarcely a mention in the local or international media.

Probably one of the most important military setbacks for Isis in recent weeks was the loss of al-Houl, a town captured by the YPG on 13 November. This attack threatens the road linking Isis's Syrian capital at Raqqa to Mosul and Isis's oilfields in eastern Syria.

On the same day, Kurdish forces in northern Iraq recaptured the small city of Sinjar which had been taken by Isis the previous year when it slaughtered or enslaved the Yazidi inhabitants. Unlike al-Houl, this success was broadcast around the world and there was speculation about whether or not the self-declared Islamic State was beginning to crumble. But it soon became clear that Isis had decided not to fight to the finish in Sinjar and had pulled out after two days' fighting against greatly superior numbers.

Western commentators hopefully predicted that the loss of Sinjar would cut Isis's supply lines between Raqqa and Mosul, and so it did for a week or more. The price of vegetables doubled in the markets of

Mosul, but soon fell when Isis hastily opened up a new route south of Sinjar and the trucks carrying vegetables started moving again. The war in Iraq and Syria over the past four years is full of military engagements that were claimed as decisive at the time by one side or the other. Most turned out to be no such thing. In the summer of 2014, the Syrian army was forecast to be close to sealing off the rebel-held parts of Aleppo, but it failed to do so. In May this year the Syrian armed opposition, including Isis, Jabhat al-Nusra and Ahrar al-Sham, won some important victories in Idlib province in the north and Palmyra in the east. This provoked Russian air intervention and greater involvement by Iran and Hezbollah of Lebanon, which collectively has had the effect of stabilising the Assad government. But the battle-lines have not moved that much and the biggest impact of the Russian action is to make it clear that Assad is not going to lose the war, if this was ever on the cards. Russia cannot afford to see an ally, for whom it has done so much, be defeated without serious damage to its international standing.

This does not mean that Assad is going to win. No doubt support from Russian fixed-wing aircraft, helicopters and missiles has helped the morale and military capacity of the Syrian army. But it has not transformed the battlefield because al-Nusra and the others were always going to fight hard and the Syrian army remains short of combat troops. If the opposition advance has been stemmed or in places reversed, the Syrian army has yet to regain Idlib city, Jisr al-Shughur or Palmyra. It is a long way from winning a decisive victory, such as the capture of the eastern opposition-held half of Aleppo.

The same is true, in Iraq, even if the Iraqi army and Shia militias succeed in regaining Ramadi. Isis is averse to defending easily identifiable fixed positions where it is an easy target for the US-led air campaign. It recalls that it lost 2,200 fighters failing to capture the Syrian Kurdish city of Kobani in a four-and-a-half-month siege that ended in January. Isis would probably defend Mosul, Fallujah and Raqqa to the last, but it might give up other places as not worth the heavy casualties it would suffer trying to cling on to them. Its best strategy is to use its strength as a mobile guerrilla force, seeking out its enemies' weak points and launching multiple attacks that catch the other side by surprise.

Contradicting this military approach is a political imperative that makes Isis different from al-Qa'ida and other extreme jihadi movements. The difference is that it is a genuine state with an administration, taxation, conscription and total control over the civilian population. This means that it will have to fight for some of its territory and this is where it is vulnerable to the massive air power - in the shape of the US and Russian air forces - arrayed against it. It has become conventional wisdom to say that air power alone does not win war, but continual pounding by hostile aircraft does limit the kind of operations that Isis can conduct successfully, and it shatters the infrastructure of roads, bridges, water and electricity supply used by soldiers and civilians alike.

Isis's cocktail of tactics such as mass use of suicide bombers in vehicles packed with explosives were highly effective last year and in the first half of this year. Some 30 such bombs were used in May to breach the defences of Ramadi, including 10 armoured dump trucks that overwhelmed the defenders. But anti-Isis fighters are now armed with an array of antitank weapons that stop most of these vehicles before they can do any damage. Isis cannot shock and terrify its enemies in the way it did at the time of the fall of Mosul.

Isis is being squeezed by growing military pressure from its many adversaries, but these remain disunited and hostile to each other so, for the moment, the overall stalemate continues.

THEATRE OF WAR **WHO CONTROLS WHAT**

● ISIS CONTROL ● ISIS FREE TO OPERATE ● KURDISH CONTROL

Sunday, 13 December 2015

SYRIA IN 2016 WILL BE LIKE THE BALKANS IN 1914

The CIA analyst is confident about what is likely to happen in Syria. He says that "Assad is playing his last major card to keep his regime in power". He believes that the Assad government will step up its efforts to prove that its enemies "are being manipulated by outsiders". The probable outcome is a split within Syria's ruling elite leading to Assad being ousted, though he admits that there is no obvious replacement for him.

The reasoning in the CIA special analysis, entitled "Syria: Assad's Prospects", is sensible and convincing, though overconfident that Assad's days are numbered. The extent of this overconfidence is highlighted by a glance at the date of the document, which is 17 March 1980, or 35 years ago, and the President Assad, whose imminent political demise is predicted as likely, is not Bashar al-Assad but his father, Hafez al-Assad, who died in 2000. The analysis was released by the CIA under the Freedom of Information Act in 2013.

The CIA paper is an interesting read, not least because it shows how many ingredients of the present crisis in Syria have been present for decades, but had not yet come together in the explosive mix which produced the present horrific war. In 1980, the writer assumed that Syrian politics revolved largely around the sectarian differences between the Alawites, the Muslim sect to which the Assads and Syria's rulers generally belong, and the Sunni Arab majority. The analysis is written in an upbeat tone as it forecasts that splits between the two communities may bring Assad down. The CIA certainly wanted Assad gone and had some ideas about how this might be achieved. "Army discipline may well collapse in the face of widespread riots," it says. "This could lead to bloody war between Sunni Muslim and Alawite units. The Alawites, however, may choose to topple Assad before such turmoil develops in order to keep their position secure."

This last sentence could have been written at any time since 2011 as a summary of what the US would have liked to happen in Syria: it has always wanted to get rid of Assad, but it does not intend to destroy or even weaken the Syrian state and thereby open the door to Isis and al-Qa'ida. Even superpowers sometimes learn from history, so the US and its Western allies today hope to avoid a repeat of the disastrous disintegration of Iraq state institutions in 2003 after the overthrow of

Saddam Hussein. Tragically, the unnamed CIA analyst eventually got the sectarian civil war he had half-hoped for, but Assad is still there and Syrian people have got the worst of all possible worlds.

US intelligence chiefs are far more outspoken these days than their counterparts in Britain about the calamitous consequences of US-led foreign interventions over the past 12 years. None more so than General Michael Flynn, recently retired head of the Defense Intelligence Agency, the Pentagon's intelligence arm, who says bluntly in an interview with the German magazine Der Spiegel that the Iraq war "was a huge error. As brutal as Saddam Hussein was, it was a mistake to just eliminate him. The same is true for Muammar Gaddafi and for Libya, which is now a failed state. The historic lesson is that it was a strategic failure to get into Iraq. History will not be and should not be kind to that decision."

Big players such as the US can more easily afford to admit mistakes than those, like Britain, which are smaller and lacking in confidence about their great-power status. But there is a price to be paid for remaining mute or in denial about past political, military and diplomatic errors. If it is admitted that anything went wrong for Britain in the Iraq, Afghan, Libyan and Syrian wars then it is only in the most general terms. A former diplomat at the Foreign Office says that it was striking how in the years following the Iraq invasion of 2003, he heard "almost nobody in the Foreign Office talk about the decision to go to war or what went wrong". This may have been because most officials privately opposed the war from the beginning as a bad idea, but did not want to say this publicly, or even within the office.

It is a natural British personal and institutional instinct to hush things up, but after four wars marked by British government blunders and misjudgements, it is curious that information from the intelligence services is not treated with greater scepticism. A recent sign of this was David Cameron justifying his unlikely claim that there are 70,000 moderate anti-Assad fighters in Syria by saying that this figure came from the Joint Intelligence Committee, as if this sourcing put its accuracy beyond doubt. It may be that endless harping on British success in breaking German codes in both world wars has combined with a diet of James Bond movies to exaggerate the reputation of British intelligence.

Foreign political leaders are often more dubious about what their intelligence services really know. Before the start of the Iraq war in

2003, President Jacques Chirac told a visitor that he did not believe that Saddam had any weapons of mass destruction. The visitor said: "Mr President, your own intelligence people think so." Chirac replied: "They intoxicate each other." In other words, intelligence services often become echo chambers for obsessive beliefs that are detached from reality.

The very secrecy with which they shroud themselves is useful when denying responsibility for failure. It also makes them vulnerable when governments or their own senior officers want to suppress or doctor politically inconvenient advice.

Early last year, President Barack Obama dismissed Isis, which was beginning to make spectacular advances, as being like a junior basketball team wanting to play in the big leagues. Soon after, it captured most of northern Iraq and eastern Syria. One of the reasons this may have happened was exposed this year when 50 intelligence analysts working for the Pentagon signed a joint letter of protest. They said that their intelligence findings that Isis was getting stronger and not weaker as the White House claimed, were being suppressed or doctored by their chiefs. This was par for the course. The personal or institutional interests of the heads of intelligence agencies or any other government department are seldom served by bringing bad or contradictory news to those who decide on budgets and promotions. Most of the time this does not matter but today it does, because the stakes are rising in the war in Syria and Iraq. Knowledge of what is happening on the ground should be at a premium.

Serious powers such as Russia and Turkey are being sucked in and have invested too much of their prestige and credibility to pull back or suffer a defeat. Their vital interests become plugged into obscure but violent local antagonisms, such as those between Russian-backed Kurds and Turkish backed Turkomans, through whose lands run the roads supplying Aleppo. The Syrian-Iraqi conflict has become to the 21st century what the Balkan wars were to the 20th. In terms of explosive violence on an international scale, 2016 could be our 1914.

WINTER 2016: A SAVAGE ENEMY

Saturday, 2 January 2016

FIVE YEARS AFTER THE ARAB SPRING

I was planning to visit Baghdad last summer and stay with my friend Ammar al-Shahbander, who ran the local office of the Institute for War and Peace Reporting. I had stayed with him for 10 days in June 2014, just after Isis forces had captured Mosul and Tikrit and were advancing with alarming speed on the capital.

Ammar was a good man to be with in a moment of crisis because he had strong nerves, an ebullient personality and was highly in-formed about all that was happening in Iraq. He was sceptical but not cynical, though refreshingly derisive as the Iraqi government claimed mythical victories as Isis fighters approached ever closer to the capi-tal. He did not believe that they could successfully storm Baghdad, but that did not mean they would not try - and one morning I found him handing over a Kalashnikov to somebody to have its sights readjusted.

We shared a fascination with the dangerous complexities of Iraqi life and politics and I had been looking forward to resuming our conversations in 2015. I was just about to send him a message saying that I was coming to Baghdad, when I heard that I was too late and he was dead. He was killed on 2 May by a car bomb that exploded as he left a café in the Karrada district, where he had been sitting with a friend after attending a concert. A piece of broken metal entered his heart and he died, along with 17 other people killed by Isis bombs in Baghdad that night.

All too many journalist friends have been killed in Iraq, Syria and Libya since 2011, but most were doing dangerous things when they died and knew the risks they were taking. Simply by living in Baghdad rather than London, Ammar knew that he was taking a risk but, high though the level of violence may be in the city, it is not a battle zone. He was not personally targeted so there was a greater element of ill-luck in his death than that of other journalists and people working in the media, making his murder feel all the more poignant and unnecessary.

His death made me think about how much more difficult it has become to be a foreign or local journalist in the Middle East and North Africa over the past few years. The overthrow of Saddam Hussein in 2003 and the Arab Spring in 2011 were meant to herald greater freedom of expression and an end to censorship and the persecution of journalists. In reality, just the opposite has happened with country after country becoming highly dangerous for foreign journalists to visit and independent local journalism being stamped out by authoritarian governments and murderous Islamist opposition movements.

Journeys I took in reasonable safety a few years ago are now impossibly dangerous. In 2003 I drove from Damascus to the city of al-Qamishli in north-east Syria in about 12 hours, passing through territory now divided up into hostile enclaves by the Syrian army, Isis, extreme Islamists and Syrian Kurds.

A year or so later, I went from Baghdad to Mosul and spent the night in Kirkuk before returning to the capital, a route that nobody would think of taking today.

In 2011, I travelled from Cairo to Benghazi in Libya without difficulty and later in the year, a little more problematically, from Tunisia to Tripoli, passing safely through territory now ruled by warring militias.

The figures for journalists killed in 2015 tell something of the story, with 110 reporters killed across the world over the year according to a report published last week by Reporters Without Borders. Unsurprisingly, the countries with the most journalistic fatalities are Syria, Iraq and Yemen. together with France - where the figure was boosted by the massacre of cartoonists, journalists and security staff on the Charlie Hebdo magazine. But the raw casualty figures do not really explain why so much of the wider Middle East and North Africa has fallen off the media map. Civil wars in Libya, Somalia, South Sudan and Yemen are barely reported because of the extreme danger of doing so and lack of interest in the rest of the world about what is happening there.

The fighting in Afghanistan has escalated sharply as the Taliban launch offensives across the country, but the foreign press corps in Kabul is very shrunken compared to a few years ago.

The war in Iraq and Syria is heavily covered by the international media, but much of the reporting is from other countries such as Lebanon or Turkey. Aside from a few brave exceptions, foreign journalists do not enter areas held by so-called Islamic State, deterred by the kidnapping and ritual decapitation of their colleagues. Areas controlled by non-Isis armed opposition have often proved equally dangerous.

Criminalisation is pervasive and local gangs know that a kidnapped foreign journalist is worth a lot of money because he or she can be held for ransom or sold on to Isis.

Even supposedly safe parts of Syria and Iraq are less risky only by comparison with the rest of the country.

In September, I was in the Kurdish held north-east corner of Syria that now extends from the Tigris to the Euphrates after a series of Syrian Kurdish victories against Isis. But front lines in this war are porous and it soon became clear that the threat from Isis had not wholly disappeared: in Tal Abyad, an important crossing point on the Syrian border captured from Isis in June, a local woman stopped our car to warn that a man dressed like an Isis fighter had just run through her courtyard. Police said there were still Isis sleeper cells around. In a Kurdish town, Ras al Ayn, there were two suicide bomb attacks in the brief period we were there.

The media-free zones that have opened up across the wider Middle East are worse than ever before because today both the region's governments and Islamist-dominated opposition are targeting journalists.

Saturday, 9 January 2016

A SPRING THAT BEGAN IN HOPE ENDED IN DESPAIR

Arab Spring was always a misleading phrase, suggesting that what we were seeing was a peaceful transition from authoritarianism to democracy similar to that from communism in Eastern Europe. The misnomer implied an oversimplified view of the political ingredients that produced the protests and uprisings of 2011 and over-optimistic expectations about their outcome. Five years later, it is clear that the result of the uprisings has been calamitous, leading to wars or increased repression in all but one of the six countries where the Arab Spring principally took place. Syria, Libya and Yemen are being torn apart by civil wars that show no sign of ending. In Egypt and Bahrain, autocracy is far greater and civil liberties far less than they were prior to 2011. Only in Tunisia, which started off the surge, do people have greater rights than they did before.

What went so disastrously wrong? Some failed because the other side was too strong, as in Bahrain, where demands for democratic rights by the Shia majority were crushed by the Sunni monarchy. Saudi Arabia sent in troops and Western protests at the repression were feeble. This was in sharp contrast to vocal Western denunciations of Bashar al-Assad's brutal suppression of the uprising by the Sunni Arab majority in Syria. The Syrian war had social, political and sectarian roots but it was the sectarian element that predominated. Why did intolerant and extreme Islam trump secular democracy? It did so because nationalism and socialism were discredited as the slogans of the old regimes, often military regimes that had transmuted into police states controlled by a single ruling family. Islamic movements were the main channel for dissent and opposition to the status quo, but they had little idea how to replace it. This became evident in Egypt, where the protesters never succeeded in taking over the state and the Muslim Brotherhood found that winning elections did not bring real power.

The protest movements at the beginning of 2011 presented themselves as progressive in terms of political and civil liberty and this belief was genuine. But there had been a real change in the balance of power in the Arab world over the previous 30 years, with Saudi Arabia and the Gulf monarchies taking over leadership from secular nationalist states. It was one of the paradoxes of the Arab Spring that rebels supposedly seeking to end dictatorship in Syria and Libya were supported by absolute monarchies from the Gulf.

The West played a role in supporting uprisings against leaders they wanted to see displaced such as Muammar Gaddafi and Assad. But they gave extraordinarily little thought to what would replace these regimes. They did not see that the civil war in Syria was bound to destabilise Iraq and lead to a resumption of the Sunni-Shia war there.

An even grosser miscalculation was not to see that the armed opposition in Syria and Iraq was becoming dominated by extreme jihadis. Washington and its allies long claimed that there was a moderate non-sectarian armed opposition in Syria though this was largely mythical. In areas where Isis and non-Isis rebels ruled, they were as brutal as the government in Damascus. The non-sectarian opposition fled abroad, fell silent or was killed and it was the most militarised and fanatical Islamic movements that flourished in conditions of permanent violence.

The Middle East as of 9 January 2016

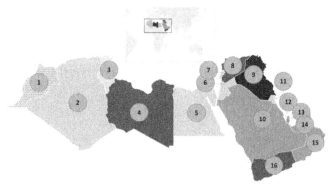

1. MOROCCO: Concessions by King Mohammed VI, including a referendum in July 2011 that led to changes in the constitution, helped ensure that protests fizzled out by end of 2012.

2. ALGERIA: Barely affected after an initial year-long state of emergency; some terrorist activity, including 2013 gas plant attack in which dozens of foreign hostages were killed.

3. TUNISIA: The birthplace of the Arab Spring is also its one success story. There were free elections in 2011 and 2013, and the country is largely peaceful - although up to 300 people died in the unrest that overthrew President Ben Ali in 2011. Terrorist attacks in 2015 have cast a shadow, and threaten to cause a disastrous fall in tourism.

4. LIBYA: Hopes raised by the Nato-aided overthrow of Colonel Muammar Gaddafi in August 2011 were bitterly disappointed. An elected parliament, the General National Congress, took power in August 2012 but was forced to withdraw to Tobruk as a rival government seized Tripoli. Much of the country is now under control of neither, with Isis established in some parts.

5. EGYPT: Up to 900 people were killed in protests that led to fall of President Hosni Mubarak in 2011. His successor, Mohamed Morsi of the Muslim Brotherhood, was ousted by the army in July 2013. Nearly 1,000 people were killed in the protests that followed. A new President, General Abdel Fattah el-Sisi, was elected in 2014; hundreds of Muslim Brotherhood members have since been sentenced to death.

6. JORDAN: Moderate protests led to modest reforms, and a few changes of government, by King Abdullah II. The main effect of the Spring has been the arrival of a least 600,000 Syrian refugees (and a similar number of Syrians who are not classified as refugees).

7. LEBANON: The country has taken in more than a million Syrian refugees as a result of the Spring. It is also at risk of violence spilling over from Syria. Sectarian violence in some cities, notably Tripoli.

8. SYRIA: A few weeks of hope in 2011. Since then, endless catastrophe, defined as a civil war by the UN since mid-2012. Up to 350,000 people have died, 4.4 million are refugees, swathes of the country are controlled by Isis, moderate rebels have been massacred, the Assad regime remains (partly) in place, and intervention by foreign powers - including Russia, Iran, the US, France and the UK - has not slowed the slaughter.

9. IRAQ: Minor protests in 2011 and major ones in 2012-13, aimed at corruption and anti-Shia discrimination. The electoral defeat of Nouri al-Maliki as Prime Minister in 2014 came too late to disperse the resentment; by then, Isis was running amok. Despite recent gains by the Iraqi army, large regions are under Isis control.

10. SAUDI ARABIA: Kept a lid on domestic discontent through a mix of authoritarianism and state largesse. Helped crush protest in Bahrain. Military intervention in Yemen has been bloody and inconclusive. Plummeting oil prices and a change of monarch have destabilised the regime.

11. KUWAIT: Protests in 2011-12 fizzled out after the fall of one government. The Al-Sabah family continues to rule.

12. BAHRAIN: Around 30 people died when protests against the ruling Khalifa family were suppressed, with Saudi help, in early 2011. Thousands have since been jailed in the crackdown by the Sunni regime on its majority Shia population.

13. QATAR: Largely unaffected by domestic protests but involved in upheavals elsewhere, notably by joining the Nato-led campaign that overthrew Colonel Gaddafi in Libya.

14. UAE: Calls for greater democracy fizzled out. Remains stable and, for now, prosperous.

15. OMAN: Protests in 2011 led to the creation of a Public Authority for Consumer Protection.

16. YEMEN: President Ali Abdullah Saleh was forced out of the country and office in, respectively, 2011 and 2012. An uprising by Shia rebels led by Abdul-Malik al-Houthi, which began in 2014, led to the flight of Saleh's successor, Abd Rabbuh Mansur Hadi, in 2015. The Iran-aligned Houthis now control the capital but are under attack from a Saudi-led Sunni coalition.

Wednesday, 13 January 2016

ISIS NO LONGER CAREFUL WITH TURKEY

Turkey is becoming a more dangerous place, but then so is the Middle East and North Africa and anywhere Isis can send its suicide squads.

The Turkish authorities say the bomber who killed at least 10 people, mostly German tourists, near the obelisk of Theodosius, not far from Hagia Sophia and the Blue Mosque in Istanbul, was a 28-year-old Saudi, making it likely, though not certain, that Isis ordered the attack.

If Isis was behind the bombing it is important to know if this is a one-off or the start of a new campaign. In July its suicide bombers killed 30 Turks going to help rebuild the Syrian Kurdish city of Kobani and in October they killed a further 100 peace demonstrators outside Ankara railway station. By doing so, Isis succeeded in setting the political agenda by provoking a resumption of hostilities between Turks and Kurds and setting the scene for President Recep Tayyip Erdogan's success in the parliamentary election on 1 November.

Isis targets civilians with such frequency that it is possible to read too much into a single explosion. It was presumably aimed at Turkey's $21 billion income from tourism with an implied threat of more to come. Turkey has been unenthusiastically sending planes to bomb Isis targets in Syria, under pressure from the US, and has arrested members of Isis cells inside Turkey.

The Government may not have done very much, but this is very different from the years when Isis volunteers were able to cross unimpeded the Turkish-Syrian border to reach territory controlled by Isis.

Much of this border has been closed on the Syrian side by the advances of the Syrian Kurdish forces that now control half the 550-mile-long frontier. The Turkish government has insisted that it will not allow Kurdish forces to advance west of the Euphrates, to close off the last 60-milelong stretch of territory which is Isis's last access and exit point with Turkey.

The US has been forcefully demanding that Turkey seal this border by stationing 30,000 soldiers on its side of the frontier, west of Jarabulus. This pressure has been growing since the Paris massacre on 13 November, in the light of evidence that the leader of the plot had been able to reach France from the territory controlled by Isis, by crossing easily into Turkey.

A possible motive for yesterday's bombing could be a warning that Isis will retaliate for any measures taken against it by the Turkish state. It certainly has the means to do so, because 1,000 or more of its fighters are Turks and it has pockets of committed support inside Turkey.

The violence emanating from the civil wars in Syria and Iraq has already affected Turkey. Low-level guerrilla warfare between the PKK and the Turkish army is spreading across Kurdish areas of south-east Turkey.

President Erdogan reinforced his power at home when his party won the parliamentary election. Turkey's influence in Syria is under threat, however, both from the Syrian Kurds, whose forces are backed by US airpower, and from Russia's extreme hostility to Turkey after Turkish jets shot down one of its aircraft in November, in what looks like a carefully prepared ambush.

Russian military engagement in Syria makes it more difficult for Turkey to threaten to act against the Kurds there.

Isis may be concluding that Turkey is no longer a place where it need tread carefully in order to preserve official tolerance of its activities. With no sign of the war in Syria ending, the latest Istanbul bomb could be the precursor of far worse carnage.

Friday, 29 January 2016

A CURIOUS MIX OF RUSSIAN-AMERICAN CO-OPERATION

The peace talks between Syrian government and opposition scheduled to begin today in Geneva were preceded by furious arguments about who should or should not attend. This did not augur well for ending or even de-escalating a war that has torn Syria apart and forced more than half its 22 million people to flee their homes.

Several of the most important parties taking part in the fighting will not be present in Geneva, including Isis, the al-Qa'ida affiliate Jabhat al-Nusra and the Syrian Kurds. Taken together, the groups control two-thirds of Syrian territory, though much of it is scantily populated.

Prospects for the Geneva talks are further hobbled because they are solely about Syria, though the war is taking place in both Syria and Iraq. Isis straddles the two countries, so the fighting cannot stop in one and continue in the other.

But the diplomatic chaos in the run-up to Geneva masks important changes on the battlefield and in the balance of power between the forces supporting the Syrian government and those opposing it. The most important development was the start of Russian air strikes in support of the Syrian army on 30 September, coming a year after the US began giving air support to the YPG to stop the Isis assault on Kobani.

The deployment of the world's two largest air forces, Russia in co-operation with the Syrian President Bashar al-Assad's armed forces, and the US with the YPG, gives these armies vastly increased firepower and military strength out of proportion to their numbers. Unsurprisingly, they have won victories against Isis and the non-Isis

Syrian armed opposition, the YPG supported by US air strikes capturing territory 250 miles long between the Tigris and Euphrates along Syria's border with Turkey. Arab fighters allied to the YPG are 30 miles north of Isis's Syrian capital, at Raqqa, while others have crossed the Euphrates at the Tishrin Dam and are close to sealing off Isis from Turkey and the outside world.

The Syrian army has been advancing under a Russian air umbrella in Latakia province in the north and in Deraa in the south, retaking towns and villages held by the rebels for two or three years, though it has not recaptured cities such as Idlib and Palmyra. Whatever the outcome of the war, few now expect Mr Assad to lose, even if his army is not strong enough to win a decisive victory.

The war in Syria and Iraq now has important common features: the Syrian army, the YPG, the Iraqi army and Iraqi Kurdish Peshmerga fighters advance on fixed positions held by Isis or other armed opposition. Ground forces identify targets, which are then obliterated by planes so the defenders suffer heavy casualties, if they decide to stand and fight, while the attackers, whose losses are small, mop up the survivors.

Such tactics are effective but they are not a sure-fire formula for complete victory, because those under air attack may disperse and resort to guerrilla warfare. Iraqi and Syrian infantry may take positions because of intense Russian or US air strikes, but they do not have the manpower to occupy permanently the ground they have taken. A year ago, the Iraqi army recaptured Tikrit from Isis and the Iraqi Prime Minister, Haider al-Abadi, visited his victorious soldiers in the city amid scenes of jubilation. But a week ago, in the Iraqi Kurdish capital of Irbil, an elderly man called Fadel Ali Shaher and his wife, Aida, who had returned to their home neighbourhood in Tikrit after the Iraqi army success, explained why they had had to flee a second time. "It was too dangerous to stay," Aida said. "The government is in the centre of Tikrit, but Daesh is in the villages around it and there was too much shooting between the two for us to stay."

Another feature of the fighting is the near-total destruction of cities because ground forces rely on calling in air strikes. Fadel and Aida said that during their return to Tikrit "we had to live in an empty house people found for us because our old neighbourhood was completely destroyed by bombing". Kobani, Sinjar and Ramadi have seen even greater levels of destruction than Tikrit.

Massive use of US and Russian air power is the decisive develop-ment in the war since the summer of 2014. This in turn has transformed the political landscape in a way that may not be obvious as rancorous Syrian parties, factions and militias along with their non-Syrian supporters denounce each other before and during the Geneva meeting. "The Syrian problem will be decided on the battlefield," says Fuad Hussein - the chief of staff of the Iraqi Kurdistan President, Ma-soud Barzani, one of several powerful players in the Syria-Iraq war not represented in Geneva - in an interview with *The Independent*.

But Mr Hussein notes that the politics of the war have changed since Russia and the US both became fully engaged. He says that the war in Syria has gone through three stages. The first was determined by local forces when the conflict began in 2011 and the second saw the dominance of regional players such as Turkey, Saudi Arabia, Qa-tar, Iran and Hezbollah of Lebanon. The third stage of the conflict is its internationalisation as the US and Russia increasingly take charge, something he sees as a hopeful development: "If the crisis is going to be solved, it will be by an agreement between Russia and the US."

Russian and American military and diplomatic action in Syria is a curious mix of cooperation and rivalry: an offensive by YPG proxy forces attacking Isis west of the Euphrates in recent weeks was sup-ported first by US and later by Russian air strikes. Farther west, in Idlib province, on the other hand, the US is supplying armed opposi-tion groups battling the Russian-backed Syrian army.

The military and political engagement of what used to be called the superpowers reduces the influence of regional Sunni states which stoked the Syrian war between 2011 and the fall of Mosul to Isis in June 2014. One UN negotiator said in frustration at the time that "the West seems to have subcontracted its policy on Syria to Saudi Arabia". But when Isis made spectacular advances, it became clear that the Sunni powers had no policy except the overthrow of Mr Assad, and this they were failing to achieve. At the same time, Turkey tolerated or was complicit in the growth of extreme Islamist terrorist move-ments such as Isis and al-Nusra.

The military balance in northern Syria could change again if Tur-key sends its army across the border. Mr Hussein believes that direct Turkish military intervention is now unlikely in the face of Russian air power and air defences. Others are less certain, the veteran Syrian Kurdish leader Omar Sheikhmous warning that "the PYD should not make the mistake of thinking that they are stronger than they are and that the Turks will not act".

Local powers in Syria and regional powers in the Middle East have failed to bring an end to the Syrian cataclysm either through war or diplomacy so real progress towards peace depends on action by the US and Russia.

Monday, 1 February 2016

ISIS CAN ONLY BE CRUSHED IN IRAQ IF DEFEATED IN SYRIA

Isis is losing ground in Iraq, but Kurdish leaders say its retreat is slow and do not expect to eliminate it unless it is also defeated in Syria. Real progress is limited, despite exaggerated claims by the Iraqi government that its soldiers have won decisive victories in cities such as Ramadi and Tikrit.

"The initial attack by Daesh in 2014 was like the Mongols, but they could not hold on to fixed positions," says Dr Najmaldin Karim, the Governor of Kirkuk province, in an interview with *The Independent.* "But this does not mean that they are being destroyed in Iraq and this will not happen until they lose in Syria."

He says that Kurdish Peshmerga in Kirkuk have pushed Isis fighters, which almost captured the city 18 months ago, some 10 to 20 miles further back but the front line is generally static.

The Iraqi government and the authorities in the KRG, which controls at least a quarter of Iraq, have boasted that they are defeating Isis by recapturing cities like Sinjar, west of Mosul and Ramadi, west of Baghdad. But these victories, won with the help of hundreds of air strikes by a US-led coalition, turned out to be less than decisive since Isis did not fight to the end in either place and withdrew in order to limit its losses.

"Isis is reverting to guerrilla warfare," says Dr Karim, a native of Kirkuk and formerly a brain surgeon in Washington DC, explaining that people displaced from cities that have supposedly been recaptured by the government are not going home because Isis is nearby or they fear sectarian persecution.

At Ramadi, for instance, once a Sunni Arab city with a population of 600,000, Isis killed 30 government soldiers on one day last week using snipers and suicide bombers. Isis even shot a video from a sniper's nest overlooking the city centre. An elderly couple from Tikrit, once Saddam Hussein's home town and retaken by the Iraqi army a year ago, told how they had fled to Irbil for the second time a week ago because of gun battles between progovernment forces and Isis.

Even if displaced people and refugees return they may not find much to live in because anti-Isis offensives rely on heavy bombing that, in the case of Ramadi, has destroyed 80 per cent of the city.

Isis was born out of the Islamic State of Iraq, which took advantage of the uprising against President Bashar al-Assad in 2011 to spread to Syria. But it has never been as strong in Syria as it is in Iraq, where it holds Mosul, a city of 1.5 million people, and Fallujah, just west of Baghdad. In Iraq it is the only substantial armed opposition movement while in Syria there are many others, though it is the largest and most powerful. In Syria, Isis faces the highly effective YPG and the Russian-backed Syrian army, which are threatening its positions in the north of the country.

Just to the west of the Kurdish capital Irbil, General Sirwan Barzani, who commands a force of 15,000 Peshmerga troops, says that though Isis has suffered losses it can still launch attacks. He told *The Independent*: "Daesh are getting weaker, but they have a front line of 3,700km [surrounding the self-declared Caliphate in eastern Syria and western Iraq] and they can always collect 500 fighters and 10 suicide bombers to make an attack."

He says that he has about 15,000 men, though not all are on duty at the same time, to defend a front that is about 120 kilometers long.

As in the rest of Iraq and Syria, the front lines are too long to be effectively manned and fortified, so each side can make a lunge forward but gains are difficult to hold. The Iraqi army and the Kurds have the great advantage of American air cover, but Isis takes refuge in elaborate tunnel systems and breaks up its forces into small units of eight to 10 men. Asked if Isis could be defeated, General Barzani points out that the US army in Iraq with 150,000 soldiers failed to defeat al-Qa'ida there.

It is not only that anti-Isis forces in Iraq are too weak to win a decisive victory, but they are divided. Speaking about an assault on Mosul, which Isis has held since June 2014, General Barzani says that Peshmerga would not try to capture it alone and there are no Iraqi army soldiers in the region capable of doing so. He says that at Ramadi "between 60 and 65 per cent of the fighting was done by the Hashid al-Shaabi [the Shia militias] but we are told they will not take part in the battle for Mosul."

This is different from the usual account of the fighting for Ramadi, where the ground forces in the centre of the city were drawn from Iraqi Special Forces. The US opposes the use of Shia militias in Sunni areas on the grounds that the Sunni inhabitants would fear a sectarian bloodbath.

Claims in Washington and London that Isis is buckling under attacks by the Iraqi army and the Peshmerga look like wishful thinking on the plains around Kirkuk and Irbil. There have been significant successes but Isis fighters have not lost any of their core regions from which they began to attack two years ago.

Thursday, 25 February 2016

THE SAVAGE RULE OF ISIS

People in Mosul call it "the Biter" or "Clipper" - a metal instrument newly introduced by Isis officials to punish women whose clothes they claim do not completely conceal their body. A former school director, who fled from the city earlier this month, describes the tool as causing agonising pain by clipping off pieces of flesh.

Fatima, a 22-year-old housewife who does not want to give her full name, said she had finally escaped from Mosul after several failed attempts because her children were starving and Isis had become more violent and sadistic compared with a year ago, especially towards women.

"The Biter has become a nightmare for us," Fatima said after reaching safety in Mabrouka Camp for displaced people near Ras al-Ayn in Kurdish-controlled north-east Syria. "My sister was punished so harshly last month because she had forgotten her gloves and left them at home."

Isis insists that women be fully veiled, wear loose or baggy trousers, socks and gloves, and be accompanied by a male relative whenever they step outside their homes.

Fatima said that a month after the use of this metal tool to punish her sister "the bruises and scars are still visible on her arm." She quoted her sister as saying that "the biting punishment is more painful than labour pains".

Other witnesses describe the Biter as operating like an animal trap, or a metal jaw with teeth that cut into the flesh.

It is difficult and dangerous to escape from Mosul, which Isis has held since capturing it from the Iraqi army in June 2014. But people from the city, who have had themselves smuggled across the border to Syria and then to Kurdish-controlled territory known as Rojava in the past two months, all confirm that living conditions have deteriorated sharply. There are serious shortages of almost everything including food, fuel, water and electricity.

Isis was violent from the start of its rule 20 months ago, but public whippings and executions have become far more common in recent months. Mosul residents say that Saudi and Libyan volunteers, who have joined Isis, are the most likely to impose penalties for minor infringements of regulations in the self-declared caliphate.

It is as if Isis fighters and officials are compensating for setbacks in the war by showing that they still have power over the population under their control.

Ibraham, a 26-year-old pharmacist who left Mosul on 16 January, said that there was little food and only a limited supply of medicine left in the city. "My pharmacy became half empty," he said. Pharmaceutical factories around Mosul have stopped production and there are fewer medicines being imported from Syria. Simple painkillers like Panadol that cost $1 (70p) for a bottle last year now cost $8, according to Ibrahim.

There is a shortage of food and what is available is very costly. The "caliphate" is increasingly cut off from supplies from Turkey and the rest of Syria. It also has less money to spend because of air attacks on its exports of crude oil, combined with the fall in the price of oil.

The Baghdad government continued to pay the salaries of public servants in Mosul even after Isis took over, but Ibrahim said that money stopped coming through nine months ago. "I have spent almost all my savings," he said. "Last year, $500 a month was enough for a family to live on, but now even $1,000 is not enough because prices are twice or even five times what they used to be."

Refugees speak of starvation spreading throughout the city under the impact of this economic siege. "For me, I could stand the bad treatment and lack of food, but when my toddler of 11 months began to starve it became impossible to stay," said Fatima.

Baby milk has not been available for six months and other food-stuffs are prohibitively expensive. Rice costs $10 a kilo. Nor are these problems confined to Mosul. Farmers are leaving their fields because "there is no electricity to pump water so they cannot irrigate their crops", according to Ghanem, 25, an unemployed plumber who is now in north-east Syria.

He insists that the main reason he fled Mosul was not the bad living conditions, but Isis "poking their noses into the details of people's daily lives with their arbitrary fines and punishments". He speaks of the increasingly harsh treatment of women, with the Biter being used as a punishment "on women deemed to have shown too much skin".

Popular revulsion against Isis within the "caliphate" does not necessarily translate into resistance or mean that its rule is fatally undermined, however. There have been few anti-Isis armed attacks in Mosul and Isis uses its well organised and merciless security arm to target real and imagined opponents. Where tribes have risen up against Isis in Iraq and Syria their members have been hunted down and slaughtered in hundreds. Whatever the shortages affecting the ordinary population in Isis-held territory, officials and fighters will not go without food or fuel - though falling revenues does mean that their salaries have been cut in half.

The "caliphate" is under heavy attack from its numerous though disunited enemies, the most important of which are the Syrian and Iraqi armies, the Iraqi Kurdish Peshmerga and the YPG. These armies are not very large, but their fire power is greatly multiplied by the close support they receive from US and Russian air strikes. This makes it impossible for Isis to hold fixed and identifiable positions without suffering serious casualties.

But Isis can still act as a skilled and experienced guerrilla force, attacking vulnerable roads such as that linking Syrian government-held Homs and Aleppo, which the group cut this week.

Even so, there are clear signs of growing corruption and disorganisation within Isis. The very fact that so many people have escaped from Mosul, despite strict rules against leaving, shows that Isis is less capable of enforcing its regulations than previously, for all the terror that it still inspires. The former school director, who does not want to give his name, says: "They threaten to kill us if we go outside Mosul." Smugglers commonly charge between $400 and $500 to secretly transport someone to safety, though some of this may go straight to Isis which is desperate for money.

Ghanem said he was frightened at first as he left Mosul for Syria, but a smuggler reassured him saying: "Don't worry. Money makes everything possible and they [Isis] will take their share."

Isis was always a paranoid organisation, seeing traitors and spies everywhere, and this is growing worse. Anything can be grounds for suspicion: one woman, who eventually reached safety in Irbil, mentioned casually that her brother-in-law had been arrested and executed because he had once been a member of a police unit that specialised in protecting the oilfields.

Wisam, a 19-year-old student, had worked in a minor capacity as a photo editor in the local TV station and for news agencies, an activity he thought might put him at risk. "I spent more than a year working in the bazaar selling vegetables," he said. "I could not work online because the internet is heavily monitored by Isis."

Mosul is returning to a premodern era without electricity or drinking water, say its former inhabitants. During the first year of its "caliphate", Isis made great efforts to ensure that public services worked as well as, or better than, under the Iraqi government, but it appears to have abandoned the attempt.

"We only get drinking water once a week," said Wisam. "Pipes are broken and need repair, but the administration in Mosul has become careless and confused over the past five months."

The main electricity supply has likewise almost stopped and people rely on private generators, either their own or those owned by local businessmen who sell the power. This can be too expensive for many families. Fatima said that "most areas of the city are dark and Mosul has become like a ghost town".

Dependence on generators means reliance on locally produced fuel, which is of poor quality since US air strikes have destroyed the refineries in Syria that were controlled by Isis. The fuel cannot be used in cars and damages the motors in generators, which often stop working. Isis tried a coupon system to ration fuel but later abandoned it. Ghanem said that "we feel we are living in the Stone Age: no mobiles, no TV, no cars, even no lighting".

The pressure of war on many fronts, combined with the tightening economic blockade, has undermined the caliphate's attempt to show Sunni Arabs that it is better able to administer a state than the

Iraqi or Syrian governments. When its fighters captured Ramadi in May last year they got credit from local people for swiftly reopening the local hospital, something the Iraqi government had failed to do, by bringing in doctors from Syria.

They also brought in large generators to provide electricity. In much of eastern Syria, Isis's draconian regulations were preferable to the criminality and insecurity which had flourished previously under other armed opposition movements.

The testimony of refugees is inevitably biased against those who forced them to abandon their homes and flee and, while the accounts of their suffering are undoubtedly true, they cannot speak for those who stayed behind. Isis still has fanatical supporters and there is no mass exodus of deserters from its ranks, even though they are being bombed by the two largest air forces in the world. Isis was always infamous for relating to the rest of the world solely through violence and, as the tide turns against it on the battlefield, it is not surprising that this violence is becoming steadily even more extreme.

Sunday, 28 February 2016

ISIS RAGES LIKE WOUNDED BEAST

In fighting in the outskirts of Ramadi a week ago, Zaman Hussein, a member of the Hashd al-Shaabi Shia militia, was trying to repel an attack by several Islamic State suicide bombers wearing vests packed with explosives. He says: "We killed all of them except one who had hidden himself behind an oil tanker. We were searching for him when he suddenly appeared and blew himself up." The blast seriously wounded Zaman, who is now in the Al-Hussein hospital in the Shia holy city of Karbala with a badly broken leg, injured hand and shrapnel wounds.

Suleiman Haydar Abbas, a 20-year-old member of the Hashd al-Shaabi, was spending his first days in the front line on 18 February in a position on Makhoul Mountain north of al-Baiji refinery, which has been the scene of prolonged battles between Isis and Iraqi government forces over the past 18 months. "I was scouting for targets 300 metres from the Isis trenches, along with three other fighters, when an IS sniper hit me," he recalls. The bullet shattered his thigh and he is waiting for the second of three operations needed to repair the damage.

The type of injuries inflicted on Hashd al-Shaabi militiamen re-covering in the Al-Hussein hospital reflects the kind of warfare being waged by Isis. Although its fighters are generally outnumbered and outgunned, they rely on tactics and weapons that a dozen years of fighting have shown to be effective. Even during the present military stalemate in Iraq, Isis continues to cause its enemies losses by using snipers, suicide bombers, IEDs, booby traps and mortars.

The attrition rate may not be high, but it is continuous. Isis is skilled at laying minefields full of pressure mines and booby traps. Hayder Daoud Abdullah, at 44 older than most of the other Hashd al-Shaabi fighters, had entered such an area in Ramadi in a vehicle to start defusing mines. But as soon as his mine disposal team left their vehicle and started walking, one of the men detonated a mine that ex-ploded, killing two of them and wounding another two. Mustafa Hashem, a soldier from the 17th division of the Iraqi army, who was in a hospital bed nearby after being wounded by a mortar bomb at Fallujah, is sure that Isis is weaker than before - "they have lost a lot of cities" - but their decline is gradual and there are few deserters or prisoners.

Nevertheless, Isis has lost Ramadi, the capture of which was their biggest victory last year, as well as Tikrit, Baiji and Sinjar. Road traffic is once again flowing freely along the main highway between Baghdad and the Kurdish north of the country. "I would say the road has be-come 90 per cent safe over the last year," said Ali Karim, a professional driver, which was less than reassuring but clearly an improvement on the days when Isis had cut the country in two. Traffic diminishes at night time, and drivers are nervous, but it is a long time since the last serious attack. "IS don't initiate fighting like they used to do," says Shaikh Maythan Zayd, the civilian director of the Al-Abbas Division, a Hashd al-Shaabi unit formed by the Imam Hussein shrine in Karbala. He says that the division has 5,000 combatants and can draw on an-other 35,000 volunteers.

What keeps Isis in business is as much the divisions of its enemies as its own strength. The Hashd al-Shaabi were created in the panicky atmosphere after Isis captured Mosul and were advancing on Bagh-dad in June 2014. Grand Ayatollah Ali al-Sistani issued a fatwa calling on people to aid the defeated Iraqi security forces. Out of this grew an organised militia force made up in part of volunteers who joined up at the time of the fatwa and in part on well established Shia paramilitary units such as the Badr Organisation, Kataeb Hezbollah and Asaib Ahl al-Haq, all of which are deemed to be under Iranian influence. The Hashd al-Shaabi claim to be 100,000 strong but a more realistic figure is probably between 35,000 and 50,000 combatants, though they can draw on a much larger reservoir of volunteers.

Since the fall of Mosul, the Hashd al-Shaabi have become one more power centre in Iraq, paid for by the Iraqi state but not quite under its control. The Iraqi army has never recovered from the defeats of 2014, though it does have a limited number of elite combat units which can call in air strikes by the US-led coalition, giving it devastating fire power. Where Isis makes a stand it is pulverised by bombs and missiles, enabling the Iraqi army or Iraqi Kurdish Peshmerga to act as a mopping-up force. The US is wary of Hashd, which it views as a Shia sectarian and pro-Iranian force, while Shia leaders denounce conspiracies by the US to marginalise the Hashd in the war. A senior religious official said that the US and Iraq leaders fear the power of the militia, "but all conspiracies against the Hashd will fail".

Quarrels dividing Isis's opponents in Iraq have visibly contributed to the present military stalemate. I visited a Hashd detachment from the Al-Abbas division that is taking part alongside the Kurdish Peshmerga in the siege of Bashir, a small town held by Isis south-west of Kirkuk. Blown up bridges and wrecked buildings on the main road north from Baghdad are evidence of fierce fighting when Isis was at the height of its power. Colonel Karim Hassan says: "IS only has 100 men in Bashir and is encircled on all sides except the west by ourselves and the Peshmerga." The Isis fighters have little artillery and rely on IEDs and suicide bombers, while the Hashd proudly show off their 122mm and 130mm artillery, firing shells into Bashir from 10 kilometres away. So why hasn't Bashir fallen? Colonel Hassan says: "We have been waiting for four or five months for the order to take Bashir, but the order has never come."

Driving up from Baghdad, we passed a long column of armoured vehicles belonging to an Iraqi army division heading north to take up positions east of Mosul. It was the capture of this city that launched Isis on its 100 days of conquest in the summer of 2014 when it seized much of western Iraq and eastern Syria. But Isis is today very much at bay, facing pressure on every front.

Iraqi politicians and parties know that exactly who is on top when Isis is defeated - Iraqi army, Hashd, Peshmerga - will go far to determine who holds power in Iraq in the future. The central government is restraining the Hashd and the Peshmerga from taking Bashir and other Isis strongholds because it does not want them to fill the vacuum left by the ousting of Isis before it can do so itself.

Monday, 27 March 2016

US GROUND TROOPS RETURN TO IRAQ

It was suddenly announced last week that the Iraqi army was taking territory from Islamic State forces in what was presented as the first steps in an offensive to recapture the city of Mosul. It sounded as if the self-declared Caliphate was crumbling and was particularly welcome news since it coincided with the Isis suicide bombings in Brussels. The message was that Isis might be able to slaughter civilians in Europe, but was being defeated on its home turf in Iraq and Syria.

I was particularly interested in the attack because two months ago I had been with the Iraqi Kurdish Peshmerga in Makhmour, the town in the front line between Mosul and the Kurdish capital Erbil, where the offensive by the 15 Division of the Iraqi Army was said to have taken place. At that time, local Kurdish commanders said that there was little fighting and they did not expect an offensive to recapture Mosul, which Isis had captured in June 2014, to happen any time soon.

Several weeks later in February, I was travelling on the main road between Baghdad and Kirkuk when I was held up by a large convoy of military vehicles moving north. I asked what was happening and was told that this was the 15 Division heading for Makhmour with the long term intention of joining an Iraqi army-Kurdish Peshmerga assault on Mosul. It did not appear that this was imminent since I did not see any tanks and most of the divisions vehicles were soft-skinned or lightly armoured Humvees.

Back in Baghdad, I asked several senior officials about recapturing Mosul and they all downplayed the idea that this would take place before the end of 2016. It may have been that they knew more than they were saying about what had happened to the 15 Division, said to be 4,500-strong and to be one of the better units in the Iraqi army, in the days immediately after I had seen it on the road.

What had really occurred at Makhmour is significant because it shows the continuing weakness of the Iraqi military as well as the extent to which US military troops are returning to the battlefield in Iraq in far greater numbers than the US administration has been willing to admit.

The 15 Division had indeed established a base near Makhmour where its arrival was greeted by the Iraqi Defence Minister Khalid al-Obaidi. But Nancy Youssef writing in The Daily Beast cites three US defence officials as saying that the Iraqi soldiers had then come under sustained attack from Isis fighters and had fled into the mountains, largely abandoning their base. One of the officials is quoted as saying that "they dispersed into the mountains out of an abundance of caution." Only a few headquarters units stayed behind dug in at the base.

At this point, the US military took an important decision to send its own troops to prop up the Iraqi forces in and around Makhmour. Without any pubic admission or even telling the families of the US soldiers involved, they sent 200 Marines from the Marine Expeditionary Unit with four artillery units to the by now largely abandoned base. Their arrival was wholly contrary to the impression the Pentagon had previously given that US soldiers in Iraq are limited in number and not engaged in front line combat duties. Though the Marines were within rocket range of Isis ten miles away, they were not added to the official US roster of 3,870 troops in Iraq because they were supposedly there on a temporary assignment.

The US public may not have known that their soldiers were back in Iraq defending a fire base, but Isis certainly had observed the arrival of the Marines and the artillery. They began firing rockets at the base, one of which hit a bunker on 19 March, killing Master Sergeant Louis Cardin, a 27-year-old Marine from California, and injuring eight other Marines, three of them seriously. Two days later they made a ground attack in which two Isis fighters were killed. At this point, the Pentagon was forced to become more open about where Sergeant Cardin had been when he died and admit that Marines were not just acting in support of the Iraqi Army and Peshmerga.

The purpose of sending the Marine unit into such a dangerous place was to revive the morale of the 15 Division and to some extent this was successful. Though US defence officials spoke of the Iraqi troops fleeing into the mountains, they may mean the ridge of steep hills behind Makhmour and not the mountains further north. Last

Thursday Iraqi troops supported by the Marine artillery and air-strikes by the US-led coalition captured three abandoned villages in the front line after an advance of less than a mile.

The episode does not bode well for a successful attack to retake Mosul this year. The Iraqi army has never really come together again since its defeat by Isis in northern and western Iraq in 2014. Though it recaptured Ramadi, the capital of Anbar province, which it lost last May the city is largely in ruins with 5,700 buildings destroyed or damaged by airstrikes. The Iraqi ground forces involved were limited in number and largely acted as a mopping up force.

This is an ominous sign for any future attack on Mosul, since Isis is likely to fight for it to the last man and could only be defeated if all the buildings in the city were systematically destroyed by US airpower as happened a year ago in Kobani.

The story of the 200 US Marines at Makhmour and the flight of the 15 Division illustrates more than just the fragility of the Iraqi armed forces. It underlines the degree to which the US already has combat troops in Iraq, while all the while claiming that there are no "boots on the ground". Sergeant Cardin was not officially even in Iraq when he died because he was one of 1,470 US service personnel only temporarily in the country. Taken together with the 3,870 officially there and 1,100 contractors working for the Pentagon in Iraq who are US citizens this brings the total to over 6,400.

The US military have been crowing over how their special forces killed the Isis finance director Haji Iman last week and there is no doubt Isis is under extreme pressure in Iraq. In Syria, the Syrian army backed by Russian airstrikes is close to recapturing Palmyra, while the Syrian Kurds have been pushing south in Hasakah province in the north east of the country.

All this looks more impressive on a small scale map than when one travels for hours skirting the Isis front line in Iraq and Syria which one Peshmerga general put at 3,700 kilometres long. Claims of Isis losing control of important roads and supply routes are less significant than appears because Middle East truckers are adept at using makeshift tracks to bypass obstacles.

The speed with which Isis responded to the arrival of the 15 Iraqi Division and the US Marines at Makhmour shows that they are by no means a spent force, their enemies are weaker than they look and the Caliphate is still far from final defeat.

SPRING 2016: AGE OF JIHAD

Saturday, 9 April 2016

CORRUPTION PAVED THE WAY FOR THE RISE OF ISIS

"Who shall doubt 'the secret hid
Under Cheops' pyramid
Was that the contractor did
Cheops out of several millions?"

The message of Rudyard Kipling's poem is that corruption is always with us and has not changed much down the ages. There is some truth in this, but degrees of corruption matter, as Cheops would have found to his cost if he tried to build his pyramid in modern Iraq instead of ancient Egypt. The project would cost him billions rather than millions - and he would be more likely to end up with a hole in the ground than anything resembling a pyramid.

Three years ago I was in Baghdad after it had rained heavily, driving for miles through streets that had disappeared under grey-coloured floodwater combined with raw sewage. Later, I asked Shirouk Abayachi, an adviser to the Ministry of Water Resources, why this was happening and she said that "since 2003, $7 billion (£5 billion) has been spent to build a new sewage system for Baghdad, but either the sewers weren't built or they were built very badly". She concluded that "corruption is the key to all this".

Anybody discussing the Panama Papers and the practices of the law firm Mossack Fonseca should think about the ultimate destination of the $7 billion not spent on the Baghdad drainage system. There will be many go-betweens and middle men protecting those who profited from this huge theft, but a proportion of it will have ended up in offshore financial centres where money is hidden and can be turned into legally held assets.

There is no obvious link between the revelations in the Panama Papers, the rise of Isis and the wars tearing apart at least nine countries in the Middle East and North Africa. But these three developments are intimately connected as ruling elites, who syphon off wealth into tax havens and foreign property, lose political credibility. No ordinary Afghans, Iraqis and Syrians will fight and die for rulers they detest as swindlers. Crucial to the rise of Isis, al-Qa'ida and the Taliban in Iraq, Syria and Afghanistan is not their own strength and popularity, but the weakness and unpopularity of the governments to which they are opposed.

Kipling was right in believing that there has always been corruption, but since the early 1990s corrupt states have often mutated into kleptocracies. Ruling families and the narrow coteries around them have taken a larger and larger share of the economic cake. From the turn of the century in Syria, for instance, the rural population and the urban poor no longer enjoyed the limited benefits they had previously received under an equally harsh but more egalitarian regime. By 2011, President Bashar al-Assad's first cousin Rami Makhlouf was reported to be a dominant player in 60 per cent of the Syrian economy and to have a personal worth of $5 billion. In Iraq earlier this year, a financial specialist, who wished to remain anonymous, said that the government of the Prime Minister Haider al-Abadi held files on corrupt individuals, including "one politician who has amassed a fortune of $6 billion through corrupt dealings".

The danger of citing extreme examples of corruption from exotic and war-ravaged countries like Iraq, Afghanistan and Syria is that these may sound like events happening on another planet. But the political and economic systems in Iraq and Afghanistan were devised under the tutelage of the US and allies such as Britain. They were proponents of free market economics which in the West may increase inequality and benefit the wealthy, but in Kabul and Baghdad were a licence to steal by anybody with power.

Neo-liberal economists have a lot to answer for. A few days after Isis had captured Mosul in 2014, I was in Baghdad and asked a recently retired four-star Iraqi general why the much larger and better-equipped Iraqi army had been defeated so swiftly and humiliatingly. He replied that the explanation was: "Corruption! Corruption! Corruption!" He added that this was pervasive and had begun when the US was building a new Iraqi military after the overthrow of Saddam Hussein in 2003. The American commanders had insisted on outsourcing food and other supplies to contractors. These businessmen and the army officers soon determined that, if the Iraqi government was paying money to feed and equip a battalion of 600 men, but its real strength was only 150, they could pocket the difference. So profitable was this arrangement that by 2014 all officers' jobs were for sale and it cost $200,000 to become a colonel and up to $2 million to purchase the position of a general in charge of a division.

Blatant corruption at the top in Kabul and Baghdad has been frequently reported over the years, though nothing much seems to change. But it is a mistake to imagine that this was simply the outcome of a culture of corruption specific to Afghanistan and Iraq. The most corrupt ministers were appointed and the most crooked contracts signed when US officials were the real decision-makers in Baghdad. For example, the entire military procurement budget of $1.2 billion was effectively stolen in 2004-5 when the defence ministry was substantially under US control. It seems implausible that US officers and officials were not complicit in the theft.

The use of offshore financial centres by the moneyed elite in the oil states and much of the rest of the world is not to avoid taxes, which they would not pay if they kept the money at home, but firstly to conceal what they have stolen and later to launder it legally. Some of this can be done by buying property in places such as Baghdad, which explains why property prices in that dangerous city are as high as London. But it is safer and better to buy property in London itself, something that will ultimately require the services of a company such as Mossack Fonseca.

The Panama Papers give insight into the names and mechanisms through which globalised elites hide their wealth and avoid paying tax on it. Commentators now predict that popular disgust with political establishments will benefit radical leaders like Bernie Sanders in the US and Jeremy Corbyn in the UK. What they do not see is that the way in which the detachment of financial interests of elites from the countries they rule has already produced states that have failed or are failing or are racked by conflict and war.

Saturday, 16 April 2016

AL-QA'IDA NOW HAS A MINI STATE IN YEMEN

They have done it again. The US, Britain and regional allies led by Saudi Arabia have come together to intervene in another country with calamitous results. Instead of achieving their aims, they have produced chaos, ruining the lives of millions of people and creating ideal conditions for salafi-jihadi movements like al-Qa'ida and Islamic State.

The latest self-inflicted failure in the "war on terror" is in Yemen, where Saudi Arabia and a coalition of Sunni states intervened on one side in a civil war in March 2015. Their aim was to defeat the Houthis - labelled somewhat inaccurately as Shia and pro-Iranian - who had seized most of the country in alliance with the former President Ali Abdullah Saleh, who retained the loyalty of much of the Yemeni army. Yemeni politics is exceptionally complicated and often violent, but violence has traditionally been followed by compromise between warring parties.

The Saudi intervention, supported in practice by the US and Britain, has made a bad situation far worse. A year-long campaign of air strikes was supposed to re-impose the rule of former president Abd Rabbo Mansour Hadi, whose dysfunctional and unelected government had fled to Saudi Arabia. Relentless bombing had some success and the forces fighting in President Hadi's name advanced north, but were unable to retake the capital Sanaa. Over the last week there has been a shaky truce.

The real winners in this war are AQAP which has taken advantage of the collapse of central government to create its own ministate. This now stretches for 340 miles - longer than the distance from

London to Edinburgh - along the south coast of Yemen. AQAP, which the CIA once described as the most dangerous protagonist of "global jihad" in the world, today has an organised administration with its own tax revenues.

Unnoticed by the outside world, AQAP has been swiftly expanding its own statelet in Yemen in 2015/16, just as Isis did in western Iraq and eastern Syria in 2013/14. Early last year, President Obama contemptuously described Isis as being like a junior basketball team that would never play in the big leagues. Likewise in Yemen, the American and British governments misjudged the degree to which AQAP would benefit from Operation Decisive Storm, the ill-chosen Saudi name for its military intervention that has proved predictably indecisive.

The Saudi intervention turned a crisis into a catastrophe. Some 6,427 people are known to have been killed in the fighting, but these are only the figures for casualties known to the health authorities. Since the UN says that 14.1 million Yemenis, 54 per cent of the population, have no access to health care, this is likely to be an underestimate. Even before the war, Yemen was the poorest Arab nation and its people are now starving or malnourished. OXFAM estimates that 82 per cent of Yemen's 21 million people are in need of humanitarian assistance.

The disaster is not only humanitarian, but political, and does not only affect Yemen. As in Iraq, Libya, Syria and Afghanistan, foreign intervention energises and internationalises local difference as factions become the proxies of outside powers.

Yemen has always had Shia and Sunni, but it is only recently that sectarian hatred has begun to get anywhere near the level of Syria and Iraq. Saudi Arabia portrays the Houthis as pawns of Iran, though there is little evidence for this, so Yemen is drawn into the regional confrontation between Saudi Arabia and Iran.

A point seldom given sufficient weight is that AQAP is expanding so fast, not because of its own strength, but because its opponents are so weak. The Saudi-and Gulf-financed media often refer to pro-President Hadi forces as taking territory, but in reality the government-in exile remains in Saudi Arabia. It recaptured the port city of Aden last summer, but its few officials who are there dare not leave their heavily-defended compound except by helicopter.

Even where Saudi-backed fighters advance, they leave anarchy behind them, conditions in which the arrival of disciplined AQAP forces may be welcomed by local people.

I have been struck, ever since the US and British invasion of Iraq in 2003, by the extent to which their whole strategy depends on wishful thinking about the strength and popularity of their local ally who usually, on the contrary, is feared and hated. I seldom spoke to Afghans who truly supported the Taliban, but I was always impressed by the number who detested the Afghan government. Yet when one UN official stated publicly that the foreign powers fighting the Taliban, supposedly in support of the government, had "no local partner", he was promptly fired.

There was the same lethal pretence by Western powers in Libya and Syria that the rebels they backed represented the mass of the population and were capable of taking over from existing regimes. In reality, the weakening or destruction of central government created a power vacuum promptly filled by extreme jihadi groups.

The dire consequences of the Saudi intervention and the rise of AQAP has been largely ignored by Western governments and media. Contrary to their grim-faced declarations about combating terrorism, the US and UK have opened the door to an al-Qa'ida mini-state.

This will have an impact far beyond the Middle East because what makes the atrocities orchestrated by Isis in Paris and Brussels so difficult to stop is that they are organised and funded by a real administrative apparatus controlling its own territory. If one terrorist cell, local leader or bomb expert is eliminated, they can be replaced.

As has happened repeatedly since 9/11, the US and countries like Britain fail to combat terrorism because they give priority to retaining their alliance with Saudi Arabia and the Gulf monarchies, even when their policies - as in Yemen - wreck a whole country and enable al Qa'ida and Isis to use the chaos to establish safe havens.

Saturday, 7 May 2016

ISIS ON ITS BACK FOOT IN SYRIA AND IRAQ

Carnage alternates with ceasefires as the Syrian air force pounds the rebel-held eastern side of Aleppo in a bid to drive out the remaining civilians. Rebel artillery replies in kind against government areas in the west of the city, but cannot match the firepower used against its enclave. Air strikes on Thursday killed at least 28 people in a refugee camp close to the Turkish border.

The purpose of the Syrian government's air and artillery attacks has remained the same over the past five years and is to separate opposition fighters from the civilian population. "This is the same classic counter-insurgency strategy that was used by the French in Algeria and the US in Vietnam," says Fabrice Balanche, an expert on Syria at the Washington Institute for Near East Policy. Syrian government forces target rebel-held zones and essential infrastructure such as hospitals and markets so whole districts of cities like Damascus and Homs are reduced to rubble.

In Iraq, the US-led coalition is more careful about avoiding civilian casualties, but even so 70 per cent of Ramadi, the capital of Anbar province, has been destroyed and surviving houses have been turned into death traps by booby traps and IEDs planted by Isis. In both Syria and Iraq, inadequate numbers of ground troops - Syrian army, Syrian Kurds, Iraqi Kurds, Iraqi army - claim great victories but in reality act as mopping up forces that can only advance after a devastating aerial bombardment.

The Syrian, Russian and US-led air campaigns have all had their successes, but they have their limitations. Dr Balanche says that the population of opposition-held east Aleppo may be down to as low as 100,000 because of air strikes, while the much safer government-controlled west of the city still has a population of two million. The US and the coalition have carried out 8,067 air strikes in Iraq and 3,809 in Syria, which have inflicted heavy casualties on Isis and interrupted its communications. But strict rules of engagement, intended to avoid civilian casualties, mean that Isis and al-Nusra fighters can stay safe by taking over one floor in a five-storey building and leaving the other four floors occupied by families. While the term "human shield" is much abused, the armed opposition in places like Mosul, Raqqa and Eastern Ghouta forbid civilians from leaving, so terrified people must balance the possibility of being killed by air strikes against that of being murdered or detained by salafi-jihadi checkpoints.

Bombs and drones weaken Isis, but probably not as much as is hoped in Washington and European capitals. Isis fighters have generally not been fighting to the last man for cities like Ramadi and Palmyra, but pulling back and resorting to guerrilla warfare. In the past few days they claim to have captured the important Shaer gas field in the desert not far from Palmyra. Isis's and al-Nusra's many enemies are divided and pursue different goals. The US and its allies want to defeat Isis, but do not want the Syrian army or the Iraqi Shia militias to be the instruments which inflict that defeat. Syrian and Iraqi Kurdish leaders detest each other, but they are at one in fearing that their value to the West will lapse once Isis is defeated and they will be left to the mercy of Turkey and resurgent regimes in Baghdad and Damascus.

This probably won't happen for some time. The US is pressing for a swift attack on Mosul and may be deceiving itself about the real military strength of the Iraqi Kurds and the Iraqi army with the result that US special forces get sucked into the fighting when their local ally falters. US military aid is now very extensive. The Pentagon recently announced that "US artillery will support the Iraqi ground offensive against Mosul and the United States will provide up to $415m to the Kurdish Peshmerga". There is a small but politically significant trickle of US casualties, including a Navy Seal killed by Isis fighters in a surprise attack north of Mosul last week.

Isis is battered and on the retreat, but is unlikely to be defeated this year. It is losing territory but it is important to keep in mind that much of this is desert or semi-desert. More important is its progressive loss of access to the Turkish border, which has been largely sealed off by the advance of the Syrian Kurdish YPG militia assisted by a US air umbrella. The increasingly narrow corridor between Aleppo and the Euphrates that links the self-declared Caliphate to Turkey is under threat from the YPG and their Arab proxies in the east and the Syrian army in the west. If this gap is closed then Isis will have great difficulty receiving foreign volunteers or dispatching terrorists to carry out attacks abroad.

If Isis and al-Nusra are defeated, what will be the impact on the political geography of this part of the Middle East? Sunni Arabs in Iraq make up 20 per cent of the population and 60 per cent in Syria but there is really only one battlefield, so, if the salafi-jihadis lose, so too will the Sunni Arabs as a whole in the band of territory between the Iranian border and the Mediterranean. "In Iraq the war is destroying the Sunni population," says Professor Joshua Landis who heads the Centre for Middle East Studies at Oklahoma University, pointing out that most of those displaced in the fighting in Iraq over the past two years are Sunni Arabs and the Sunni had already been driven out of much of Baghdad in the sectarian slaughter of 2006-7. A prolonged struggle for Mosul would reduce the last great Sunni stronghold in the country to ruins. "We Sunni in Iraq are going to end up like the Palestinians," predicted a Sunni Arab from Ramadi last year, before the city was partly destroyed.

President Bashar al-Assad said last week that he would fight on to recapture all of Syria and he might go a long way to achieving this. But it would be the triumph of a minority government that could only maintain its authority by terror and military force. It would resemble Saddam Hussein's Sunni-dominated regime in Iraq after he had crushed the rebellions of the Shia and Kurds, together with 80 per cent of the population, in 1991.

It may not come to this. Not all the news is bad. The most hopeful sign in Syria is that Russia and the US are on occasion acting in unison and have been able for the first time in five years to prod their allies into agreeing to ceasefires, however shaky and short-term. The lesson of the past five years in Syria and the past 13 years in Iraq is that it is very difficult for any single army, government, militia, party, sect or ethnic group to fight successfully for a long period without the support of a foreign power or powers. They may not want to compromise but they may be forced to do so if the alternative is the loss of this essential outside backing. Given that the Assad and anti-Assad forces hate each other, want to kill each other and have no intention of sharing power in the future, such compromises are likely to be grudging and short term.

The real test over the coming months will be the extent to which the US and Russia have the desire and capability to enforce a ceasefire or at least a de-escalation of the fighting. A state of permanent war has suited both the government in Damascus and its extreme fundamentalist enemies, because many Syrians who do not like Assad feel that the only alternative to his regime, as the French Algerians used to say, is "the suitcase or the coffin". Anti-Assad Syrians are likewise faced with a black-or-white choice between a murderous government and murderous Islamists.

Only a de-militarisation of Syrian politics might open the way to other alternatives and a distant prospect of permanent peace.

Tuesday, 24 May 2016

THE BATTLE FOR FALLUJAH

Isis execution squads have appeared in the streets of Fallujah, a city 40 miles west of Baghdad, with orders to kill anybody trying to flee or surrender as government forces advance towards the Isis stronghold. "Groups of Isis fighters are saying they will kill anybody in Fallujah who leaves their house or waves a white flag," says Ahmed al-Dulaimi, a political activist who spoke by phone to relatives and friends in the city. Iraqi army units started an offensive east of Fallujah yesterday morning after heavy shelling and airstrikes overnight. Mr Dulaimi said that Shia militias known as the Hashd al-Shaabi were joining in the bombardment with a homemade-rocket called the "Nimr", named after the leader of the Saudi Shia minority, Sheikh Nimr al-Nimr, who was executed by the Saudi authorities in January this year.

The loss of Fallujah, a Sunni commercial hub on the main road to Jordan, would be a serious blow to Isis. Its capture of the city so close to Baghdad at the beginning of 2014 was the extremist Sunni movement's first spectacular military victory. An interesting development yesterday was a report that three Isis gunmen were killed inside Fallujah, which would be a first sign of armed resistance by local people to Isis.

The Iraqi Prime Minister Haidar al-Abadi claimed a "big success" by his troops within hours of the start of the operation. Wearing the black uniform of Iraq's counter-terrorism forces he said that it had already achieved "more than was planned" as he met with commanders of the Fallujah Operational Command. Earlier in a television address on Sunday night, he pledged to "tear up the black banners of strangers who usurped the city".

Mr Abadi is under intense popular pressure in Baghdad to drive Isis out of Fallujah after bomb attacks on civilian targets earlier in the month that killed at least 200 people. "Rightly or wrongly people in Baghdad believe these bombs are coming out of Fallujah and they want the city taken," says a retired senior Iraqi official. The failure of government forces to expel Isis from a city so close to the capital for over two years has for long discredited its claims that it is defeating Isis.

The Iraqi armed forces are short of combat-ready soldiers and they are reliant on two brigades of well-trained and experienced counter-terrorist troops numbering about 5,000 men. In addition, there are two divisions of the regular army able to fight, but military success over the last year has been dependent on support from the US-led air coalition which destroys Isis positions while Iraqi troops act as a mopping up force,

Fallujah has already suffered badly from prolonged fighting and lack of food supplies. Local sources estimate that its population is down to between 50,000 and 60,000 people compared to 350,000 in 2011 before Iraq slid back into a full-scale war. An Iraqi observer with contacts in the city said that "people have been starving there over the last six months because there is little food coming in. A 50kg bag of flour costs 800,000 Iraqi dinars (£470)." He added that many in Fallujah were trying to supplement their diet by fishing in the Euphrates river, but they "only catch a few small fish".

Fallujah is not entirely surrounded on all sides and there is one desert road open to the north through which comes a trickle of food supplies, but these are monopolised by Isis fighters for their own use. Other sides of the city are besieged, with the Iraqi army and Shia militia to the east, anti- Isis Sunni tribal militia to the south and more government forces, backed by US troops, around Habbaniyah to the west. The main attack on Monday was being directed towards the agricultural town of Garma where Isis has lost some ground in farming areas.

People in Fallujah are reported by refugees to be terrified of Isis, but equally so of the Shia militias, which they say refer on their social media to "Terrorist Fallujah". Isis withdrew from other cities like Ramadi, Hit and Rutba without fighting to the last man, but their fighters might put up such a stand for Fallujah because of its military and political importance. In 2004 it was the target of two famous sieges by the US Marines that left much of it in ruins. Ramadi, the capital of Anbar province, once had a population of 400,000, but 70 per cent of it was destroyed by US airstrikes and only about 15 per cent of its people have been able to return. Fallujah may well suffer the same fate.

The Iraqi government will have to recapture Fallujah at some point because of the threat it poses to Baghdad and its importance as a sign that Isis is undefeated. But previous government offensives have been marked by stops and starts because of divisions between the US, the Iraqi government, Shia militias and Kurds.

Mr Abadi may also want to assert his patriotic credentials after protesters demanding an end to corruption and appointment of a technocratic cabinet burst into the Green Zone two days ago. They were driven out by security forces firing live rounds as well as tear gas, and two protesters were killed and 60 wounded. Mr Abadi claims that the counter-offensive against Fallujah has been delayed by political divisions in Baghdad.

The so-called Islamic State is showing signs of weakening but its many opponents also have their weaknesses. The US has been pushing for ground offensives against Mosul and Raqqa, but ground forces in Iraq and Syria may not be capable of taking them this year. "There is no real plan about what to do after they have fallen," says Hiwa Osman, an independent political analyst based in Irbil. "Only the Sunni Arabs can really put an end to Isis and until they do so it will never be really finished."

Saturday, 28 May 2016

IS IT REALLY NECESSARY TO DESTROY A CITY TO SAVE IT?

"They make a desert and they call it peace," is the bitter line Tacitus attributed to the British tribal leader Calgacus speaking 2,000 years ago of the devastation inflicted by the Roman army on the rebellious British. The denunciation has echoed down the centuries and been applied to many pacification campaigns, but it is peculiarly appropriate to what is now happening in Iraq.

Some 20,000 Iraqi soldiers, special forces, federal police and Shia paramilitaries are advancing on Fallujah, a Sunni Arab city held by Isis since early 2014. They are backed by the destructive might of the US-led coalition of air forces that have carried out 8,503 air strikes in Iraq and 3,450 in Syria over the last two years. Without such close air support, the anti-Isis forces in Iraq and Syria would not have had their recent successes.

"I think they [government forces] will take Fallujah but the city will be destroyed in the process," said Najmaldin Karim, the governor of Kirkuk to the north east of Fallujah in an interview with *The Independent*. "If they don't have air strikes they probably won't be able to take the city."

The precedents are ominous. The Iraqi army backed by Coalition airpower recaptured the city of Ramadi from Isis last December, but more than 70 per cent of its buildings are in ruins and the great majority of its 400,000 people are still displaced. "The destruction the team has found in Ramadi is worse than any other part of Iraq. It is staggering," said Lise Grande, the UN's humanitarian coordinator in Iraq.

Soon after government forces had taken the city five months ago, Ibrahim al-Osej, a member of the Ramadi district council, said that "all water, electricity, sewage and other infrastructure - such as bridges, government facilities, hospitals and schools - have suffered some degree of damage."

This included no less than 64 bridges destroyed.

Some of the destruction was caused by Isis mining buildings, but most was the result of 600 Coalition air strikes and Iraqi army artillery fire. US air commanders congratulate themselves on the pinpoint accuracy of their bombardment (so unlike Vietnam or earlier wars) but, if this is so, why was it necessary to destroy Ramadi?

The same is true of other victories over Isis in Iraq and Syria. Last year I was in the Syrian Kurdish city of Kobani that Isis tried to capture in a siege lasting four-and-a-half months until they were driven out by Syrian Kurdish fighters and 700 US airstrikes that pulverised three-quarters of the buildings. Everywhere I looked there was a jumble of smashed concrete and broken metal reinforcement bars sticking out of the heaps of rubble. Only in the enclave the Syrian Kurds had clung onto were buildings still standing.

Fallujah may now share the same fate. There are some 900 Isis fighters defending well-prepared fighting positions above ground and a warren of tunnels underneath it. They are experienced in inflicting maximum casualties on their enemies by sniping, IEDs, booby traps, mortars and suicide bombers.

In places like Tikrit, Ramadi and Sinjar they slipped away at the last moment, but in Fallujah they may fight to the end because it is close to Baghdad, and because it is a symbol of Sunni resistance to the US occupation ever since it was twice besieged by US marines in 2004. It can be argued that there is no alternative to the massive use of airpower if fanatical and battle-hardened Isis fighters are to be defeated. But, as with so much in the war in Iraq and Syria, the type of warfare being waged is determined by political priorities.

In the case of Fallujah, and previously Ramadi, the US acts in support of regular Iraqi government forces and politically acceptable
allies such as the Sunni tribal militias. It does not want to give air support to the heavily armed and more numerous Shia paramilitaries in
the Hashd al-Shaabi or Popular Mobilisation Units which it sees as being sectarian and under the influence of Iran.

The problem is that the combat-effective Iraqi security forces are
limited in number, amounting to two brigades or 5,000 soldiers by
one account in addition to two divisions in the regular army. But many
of these units have to be held back in Baghdad or elsewhere in the long
front line and cannot be committed to the assault on Fallujah which
may therefore take a long time even with Coalition air strikes. The assault force that finally took Ramadi numbered only 750 Iraqi special
forces, which acted as a mopping force after Isis fighters had been targeted from the air.

The strategy of using a limited number of highly skilled ground
forces - in which US specialists are intermingled - able to call in air
attacks against any point of resistance makes sense militarily.

It is also noticeable that that there are no international protests
as the Sunni cities and population centres of Iraq are systematically
destroyed. The notorious remark of a US officer about the town of Ben
Tre in Vietnam 50 years ago - that "it became necessary to destroy the
town to save it" - could equally be applied to Ramadi.

This does not happen because the present bombing campaign is
being justified as is customary in air wars, by its perpetrators saying
it is of pinpoint accuracy and designed to keep civilian casualties to a
minimum. But there is also a widespread feeling that any means are
justifiable when used to defeat a movement of such monstrous cruelty
and savagery as Isis. The present assault on Fallujah is partly motivated by the slaughter of 200 civilians in Baghdad by Isis bombers
earlier this month.

What happens in the next few months in Fallujah is of significance because it may tell us what will happen if there is an attempt by
the Iraqi government, the Kurdish Peshmerga and the Coalition to recapture Mosul which may still have a population of two million
people. Isis is not letting anybody out of the city and will fight hard for
it because the capture of Mosul in June 2014 was what enabled it to
declare the "Caliphate".

The US would like to recapture the city this year. Mr Karim believes that President Obama "is desperately trying to get Isis out of Mosul before the end of his term". This is scarcely surprising since its loss and the rise of Isis was perhaps the greatest miscalculation of his eight years in office.

But, even if it does fall, the war will not end because the five million Sunni Arabs in Iraq are being given no alternative to Isis other than submission to Shia and Kurdish rule.

The US and allies like Britain insist that the government in Baghdad should be more inclusive of people formerly living under the control of Isis, but inclusion will not make much difference if the places where they lived are heaps of ruins.

Tuesday, 31 May 2016

CITY ON EDGE AS ANTI-ISIS FORCES CLOSE IN

In the past few days somebody has been painting the initial letter of the Arabic word for "resistance" - muqawama - on walls in Mosul. Some 15 Isis members have been assassinated by a group calling itself Ketaib Mosul, which is evidently well-informed about who it targets.

There are repeated air strikes by the US-led coalition on Isis personnel and facilities, and there has long been an expectation among the estimated 1.5 million people still in Mosul that there would be an assault on the city by the Iraqi army, Kurdish Peshmerga and Sunni tribal militias backed by the massive firepower of coalition aircraft and drones.

The anti-Isis forces began what they said were the first stages of this attack on Sunday. To avoid being caught up in what may be the climactic battle for the war in Iraq and Syria, some 4,000 people from Mosul have paid up to $600 (£410) a head to have themselves smuggled into Syria over the past month according to the UN High Commission for Refugees.

"People don't feel safe," says Ahmed, 40, a villager who visited his two brothers in Mosul two weeks ago. "There is pressure all the time. Nobody knows when he will die or be punished for something small like smoking a cigarette."

Salem, 29, a former teacher of English who gave up his job when Isis introduced their own curriculum, agrees that punishments are arbitrary. He recalls that last year he received six lashes from a whip on his back because he had shaved his upper cheeks in a way that Isis militants considered un-Islamic, though he had retained his long beard. "I was lucky," he says. "I have friend who received 20 lashes for exactly the same thing."

Hatred there may be against Isis in Mosul, but there is not much people can do about it as they are unarmed and Isis responds ferociously to any sign of dissent. Last August it posted on the wall of the main morgue a list of 2,070 people it had executed since June 2014 when it captured the city.

Many were former policemen, army officers, journalists and political activists who had disappeared and whose fate was unknown. Salem says that he "had a friend who had taken a picture on his phone of himself in military uniform, though it was an act of bravado and he was never in the army, but Isis found it and shot him in the head".

The feelings of people in Mosul are important because it is almost exactly two years ago since Isis captured the city and declared its "Caliphate". Only a few months earlier President Obama had compared the movement to a minor league baseball team that was never going to get anywhere.

By seizing Mosul, the second largest city in Iraq, Isis proved him wrong and began a campaign in which it overran western Iraq and eastern Syria, showing the world that there was a new and terrifying player in the Middle East.

Isis today may be battered by attacks by its many enemies, and it has lost many population centres in Iraq and Syria such as Ramadi, Tikrit, Baiji, Sinjar and Palmyra. But Mosul is far more important than any of these because of its size, making up between a quarter and a third of the five or six million people living under the rule of Isis. The loss of the city would be a calamitous psychological blow to Isis's prestige, just as its capture in 2014 by several hundred fighters opposed by a garrison of 20,000, was claimed by Isis as a sign that it had divine assistance.

Mosul is the last big city held by Isis in the civil war being waged across Iraq and Syria. Isis's Syrian capital Raqqa is small by comparison. Mosul has kept most of its population and is largely undamaged, while Ramadi, which once had a population of 400,000, is 70 per cent destroyed, Fallujah may soon go the same way and in Aleppo the rebel-held half of the city may now have only a population of 200,000, because of indiscriminate barrel bombing and artillery fire by government forces.

Mosul still has its population because it is very difficult to get out of. All the eyewitnesses cited in this article, none of whom want their real names published, escaped by paying smugglers or had visited the city briefly from their villages that were then captured by the Iraqi army.

Ahmed says that "Isis stops most people from permanently leaving Mosul by confiscating their ID card so they have nothing to show their identity when they reach Kurdish forces who suspect they are Isis agents."

Salem paid $2,000 (£1,400) to smugglers for himself, his wife and his small daughter, though he was terrified that Isis would discover them as they walked for hours through overgrown fields. He says that most people in Mosul would leave if they could but, though Isis may be weaker than it was, it is still fully in control and capable of terrifying potential opponents who chose silence or flight rather than resistance.

Fadel, who was in the Iraqi army at the time of the fall of Mosul, says he did not leave his house in a village close to the Tigris River west of Mosul because he had been in the Iraqi army and feared being stopped at a checkpoint. One day last month he was in his house when his small nephew whispered to him that "Daesh have come and are looking for you." He fled out the back of the house and eventually made his way to the Kurdish frontline.

Living conditions have got tougher in Mosul over the last year because of the cutting by the Peshmerga of the main road link to Syria, from which most imports used to come under Isis rule.

Tinned food, oil and gas still get through but are expensive and the crudely refined oil is poor quality and can only be used in generators and not in vehicles. Fresh vegetables are expensive, but meat is cheap at 5,000 dinars or £3 a kilo because the farmers cannot send it to other parts of Iraq as they did in the past. Even so, many in Mosul are jobless and cannot afford it.

Fresh water, which used to be in short supply, is now more plentiful because people have been digging wells. Significantly, Isis is still able to give a ration of flour, so a family of seven will get a 50kg sack every month, showing that the group's administrative base has not broken down even though it may be under strain. Even Salem, who detests Isis rule and hopes for their defeat, admits that they repair the roads and keep them cleaner than the Baghdad government ever did. Life under Isis, though difficult and dangerous, is still sustainable.

A problem in assessing what people in Mosul really think about Isis is that those fleeing the city are partial witnesses with every reason to emphasise the horrors they have escaped. Information from the Kurdish authorities and the US-led coalition tends to be propagandistic and unreliable.

There is strong evidence that Isis is opposed by the majority in Mosul for its extreme violence, the catastrophic decline in living standards, the destruction of revered mosques and monuments and the reduction of women to servile status. But the movement can still find volunteers to be fighters and suicide bombers, despite heavy losses.

It is very seldom possible to get convincing testimony from committed Isis supporters about their recruitment and willingness to die in battle. But an Iraqi correspondent for the Berlin-based website NIQASH recently obtained a rare insight into how and why a 15-year-old in Mosul decided to become a suicide bomber. He was interviewed in a Mosul hospital where he had been sent after he became seriously ill, and before he could go on a suicide mission. His story is worth quoting at length because it shows how Isis attracts recruits and turns them into fanatical fighters.

He describes how one day he saw a crowd of people gathered around screens in a small house built by Isis at the entrance to his neighbourhood. He says that "everyone was watching a film of a battle between the Caliphate's soldiers and the Iraqi army. There were suicide bombers and mortars going off. The scene peaked with Daesh's occupation of the area they were fighting for and the raising of Daesh's flag on buildings and around the streets. It was an action movie! There was so much excitement. But it was all real." He went to more films and, enthused by what he saw, eventually volunteered to become an Isis fighter.

He was taken with two other boys of his own age to the cellar of a house where 24 boys aged between 12 and 17 were living. "I was pretty scared there," he says. "And I was confused. I didn't talk to anybody in the basement and my hands were shaking. I remember saying to myself: Why are you here, you crazy idiot?" But after half an hour an older man with a long grey beard arrived and spoke to him kindly, introducing himself as Ali Abdullah who had once spent 10 years in Saddam Hussein's Republican Guard. He spent a month with the boys teaching them about religion and holy war for eight hours a day. "Around him we all felt like we were strong men, confident. He used to tell us how we would fight for the Islamic State's victory and how we would go to heaven where we would find delicious food, beautiful women and wine and 'everything you crave'."

The recruits received rigorous military training supervised by Ali Abdullah, going to woodland around Mosul to be taught how to use weapons, explosive belts and bombs, as well as how to drive cars and motorbikes. Back in the cellar of the house, which had once belonged to a Christian family, they were permanently hungry, living on a handful of dates, bread and water in what was evidently a toughening up process. "During the three months we were there, we only washed properly three times. We all smelled like rats," the 15-year-old says.

Because of the unsanitary conditions in the cellar, the young man got a serious kidney and stomach infection and ended up in Mosul hospital, where he was interviewed. He is still intending to become a suicide bomber when he gets well, and says he will follow his friends to paradise.

SUMMER 2016: ROLLING BACK ISIS

Wednesday, 1 June 2016

ISIS NO LONGER THE CONQUERING FORCE IT ONCE WAS

Isis is under attack in and around the last three big cities it holds in Iraq and Syria: Fallujah, Mosul and Raqqa. It is likely to lose these battles because its lightly armed, if fanatical, infantry fighting from fixed positions cannot withstand air strikes called in by specialised ground forces. They must choose between retreating and reverting to guerrilla war, or suffering devastating losses.

It is two years since Isis launched itself on the world by capturing Mosul, the second largest city in Iraq, though it had already taken Fallujah, 40 miles west of Baghdad, at the start of 2014. In its first campaigns, its ability to achieve surprise by using mobile columns of vehicles packed with experienced fighters was astonishingly effective. It had developed these military techniques in the years of warfare that followed the US invasion of Iraq in 2003, first fighting the Americans and later, the Iraqi army.

Its menu of tactics combined ideological fanaticism with a high degree of expertise and rigorous training and was distinguished by the mass use of suicide bombers, snipers, IEDs, booby traps and mortars. Atrocities highly publicised through the internet terrified and demoralised opponents even before Isis fighters appeared and go a long way to explaining why an Iraqi army, far superior to Isis in numbers and equipment, broke up and fled when Isis attacked it in Mosul in 2014.

But these tactics no longer work as well as they did. All the armies battling Isis are trained to eliminate suicide bombers before they get close enough to kill. Isis can still recruit young men - and occasionally women - willing to die, but these days they seldom inflict mass casualties among enemy soldiers as they used to do. Last weekend, six suicide bombers attacked the front line between Mosul and the Kurdish capital (Irbil), but although they all died blowing themselves up or were killed before doing so, they succeeded only in wounding a single Kurdish Peshmerga fighter. Like the Japanese kamikaze pilots who attacked US and British ships in 1944-45, suicide bombers are achieving diminishing returns against better prepared defences.

Peshmerga advancing towards Mosul in the past few days have been accompanied by excavators to dig trenches immediately in front of their forces as soon as possible, so that bombers cannot reach them with vehicles full of explosives. Unfortunately, suicide bombers are still able to slaughter civilians in great numbers by attacking undefended targets such as markets, pilgrimages, checkpoints and hospitals.

Isis is not the all-conquering military force it once was, but the war in Iraq and Syria is as much about politics as military success. At issue for all involved in the conflict in its present phase is not only the breaking of Isis control of territory, but determining who will rule there in place of Isis. So if the Shia paramilitaries of the Hashd al-Shaabi, whom the US says are under Iranian influence, play the leading role in capturing Fallujah, this will help to secure their long-term power and prestige in Iraq. It will be seen as a success for Iran rather than for the US and its allies. Equally important in shaping the future political geography of the Middle East will be the relative roles of the Kurdish Peshmerga, the Iraqi army and the US in driving Isis from Mosul or, in Syria, of the Syrian Kurds, their Arab allies, the US and the Syrian Army in taking Raqqa from Isis.

"It all depends on who liberates Fallujah, how it is liberated and when it is liberated," says Fuad Hussein, the chief of staff to the Kurdish President, Massoud Barzani. He believes that the balance of power has shifted decisively against Isis compared to a year ago, but warns that nobody should imagine that the fall of Isis will bring peace and stability to the region.

He notes that Isis is suffering defeats but has also shown great powers of revival and reorganisation, citing as an example a recent attack by 400 Isis fighters and 20 armoured vehicles in which they penetrated the Peshmerga front line at an abandoned Christian village called Teleskof, 14 miles north of Mosul. What is different today, compared with last year, is that they were not able to exploit their local success before they came under air attack and lost between 200 and 250 fighters.

Mr Hussein says that if the selfstyled Islamic caliphate falls, "Isis will transform from a terrorist state into a terrorist movement". It will be weakened by not having secure bases for training, but it will neither evaporate nor be replaced by the moderate Arab Sunni politicians who claim great influence on their own communities and are well-financed by foreign powers.

In Syria, a more likely successor to Isis would be the Syrian branch of al-Qa'ida, Jabhat al-Nusra, which has been growing in popularity among Sunni Arabs. Though ideologically similar to Isis in its Salafi-jihadi fundamentalist beliefs, Nusra is presenting itself as a less maniacal alternative to Isis and one that can probably count on a measure of support from Turkey and Saudi Arabia.

Sunni Arabs as a whole have every reason to feel under threat. The great majority of the five million Syrian refugees come from Sunni Arab opposition areas. In Iraq, they were reduced to holding a few enclaves in Baghdad in the 2006-7 sectarian bloodbath - "islands of fear" in the words of a US diplomat at the time, a description that now fits almost every Sunni population centre in the country.

The governor of Kirkuk, Najmaldin Karim, says there are 500,000 internally displaced Iraqis (IDPs), mostly Sunni Arabs who have sought refuge in his province. He ticks off why they cannot go home: they are banned from Diyala province north-east of Baghdad for sectarian reasons by the authorities there, from mixed communities in Salahudin province (though they can go to districts that are wholly Sunni), while Anbar is still too dangerous. It may be that the enemies of Isis are dividing the lion's skin before checking that it is truly dead or close to dying. The territorial losses of Isis may look impressive on a small-scale map of Iraq and Syria, but what is impressive when driving outside the borders of the caliphate is how big it remains. It has the advantage that its enemies are wholly disunited and detest each other almost as much as they hate Isis, if not more so. Turkey has failed to close Isis's last access to the outside world west of the Euphrates and has prevented the Syrian Kurds from doing so. Isis may be weakened but its opponents are also fragile.

The latest limited offensive by the Kurds to take back villages on the Nineveh Plain east of Mosul showed that these days they have the upper hand, but in reality the attack was delayed by several days because some of the troops taking part had not been paid their salaries. The economy of the KRG area is in ruins.

Isis is good at selecting vulnerable targets, in this case rebel groups backed by the US and Turkey in the north Aleppo province who control the towns through which the rebel side of Aleppo used to be supplied. Isis fighters have been driving them backwards in recent days, gaining control over a larger section of the border and reinforcing their hold on the fertile and heavily populated countryside of north Aleppo province.

The Syrian army does not look as strong as it did when it was getting greater support from Russian airstrikes and drove Isis out of Palmyra. Isis has been fighting back, capturing an important gas field and targeting civilians in cities famous for their loyalty to President Bashar al-Assad on Syria's Mediterranean coast.

In both Iraq and Syria, Isis is responding to military pressure by the mass slaughter of civilians, killing 148 in the Syrian coastal cities of Tartus and Jableh and another 198 in a week of bombings in Baghdad. The purpose of these massacres is to show that Isis has not lost its strength and can still strike anywhere, while at the same time hoping to force Syrian and Iraqi regular forces to leave the front lines to defend their civilian populations. It is an effective strategy which has generally worked in the past.

One of the many problems about ending the war is that many of the players have an interest in seeing it continue. Why, for instance, are there offensives against Isis by the Kurdish authorities and the Baghdad government this week? There are many reasons, but one important motive is the President Barzani and Iraq's prime minister,

Haider al-Abadi, are presenting themselves as fighting Isis while their local political opponents are demanding reform of corrupt and dysfunctional governments.

"The main reason people here in Kurdistan are quiet and not protesting about the collapse of the economy and in their standard of living is that they are afraid of Daesh," said a Kurdish businessman this week. President Assad benefits from having an enemy so monstrous as to rule it out as an alternative to himself and therefore secures him in power. Isis is a very convenient enemy for many of those fighting it, which may be one reason why it is so difficult to defeat.

Thursday, 2 June 2016

OFFENSIVE AIMS TO CUT ISIS OFF FROM OUTSIDE WORLD

US-backed forces are threatening to cut the last link Isis has to the outside world by launching an offensive against the town of Manbij west of the Euphrates.

The Syrian Democratic Forces (SDF) -a Kurdish-led group supported by US airstrikes -has launched the attack on the town close to the Turkish border in an attempt to cut Isis off from an area it uses to move weapons and fighters across the border.

US airstrikes have destroyed bridges between Manbij and the Turkish border showing that the US is backing the attack despite Turkey's past objections to the Syrian Kurds extending their control of northern Syria just south of the Turkish frontier.

An SDF commander told a Kurdistan24 television correspondent embedded with the SDF operation against Manbij that their forces had already crossed the Euphrates and were close to the town. He said that "our forces reached the outskirts of Manbij and are now holding a series of hills about 15 kilometres from it. We can see its grain silos from the top of the hills." Isis has retreated from some 20 villages in the area.

The SDF includes Sunni Arab tribal units as well as Turkman and Christians but its military strength depends on the YPG. In the last few days, they have started a multi-pronged attack against Isis along the Euphrates between its de facto Syrian capital Raqqa and Jarabulus on the Turkish border.

One axis of attack is directed at Syria's largest dam and hydroe-lectric power station at Tabqa to the west of Raqqa. This is an industrial town, once largely inhabited by Allawites and Baathists who got jobs there because of their loyalty to the Syrian regime, though they have long since fled. Isis captured Tabqa airbase in 2014 and massacred 160 captured government soldiers.

Isis is likely to fight hard to retain control of the territory linking Raqqa and north Aleppo province which is fertile, heavily populated and has access to the Turkish border. Turkey originally forbade the Syrian Kurds or the SDF from crossing the Euphrates and, when they did so five months ago, warned them not to take Manbij.

The US was wary of offending Turkey and did not bomb in sup-port of the SDF advance at that time, but now appears to have changed its policy. The US has long urged Turkey to deploy 30,000 troops to block Isis members from entering Turkey via a 60-mile-long section of the Syrian-Turkish frontier held by Isis. The US may have been wor-ried by recent Isis military successes in this area against US and Turkish backed Syrian armed opposition groups.

Isis is also under intense pressure at Fallujah in Iraq where its forces are hemmed into the beleaguered city where they are greatly outnumbered by the Iraqi security forces and the Shia paramilitaries. The Iraqi army has in theory opened humanitarian corridors for the 50,000 civilians trapped in Fallujah to escape, but they have been de-taining men leaving the city to see if they are Isis members. Given that the government will suspect anybody who has remained in Fallujah long after the majority of its 300,000 people have fled of having Isis sympathies or connections, many now being detained may be held for a long time.

Thursday, 2 June 2016
'I THOUGHT THEY WERE REAL MUSLIMS, BUT I WAS WRONG

When Isis first arrived in her village two years ago, Ameena, a 51-year-old Sunni Arab widow with three sons, was happy when they told people to pray. "I thought that they were real Muslims," she re-calls. "But after a few months they started poking their noses into all the details of people's lives." Ameena, who comes from the village of Fatisah, north of Isis's de facto Syrian capital Raqqa, says it was not only Isis's emphasis on religion that explains their initial popularity, but the fact that they were seen as part of the revolution against President Bashar al-Assad.

"When people in Syria started talking about toppling the regime, we were happy with any force trying to do this," she says. "But when those so-called saviours turned out to be criminals who killed people for any silly reason, we started to feel nostalgic for the old regime." She has a strong personal reason for her anger against Isis: she accuses them of brainwashing her 15-year-old son and persuading him to join them. She has not seen him since he left home and does not know what has happened to him.

Ameena was speaking after Fatisah had been liberated by the SDF, a grouping strongly backed by the US which brings together Sunni Arab, Turkman and Christian paramilitaries - although its real military punching power comes from the YPG. Isis may have gone from Fatisah but it has left many mines and booby traps so Ameena is going to seek safety in the mixed Kurdish-Arab province of Hasaka in the country's north-east.

The SDF, supported by some 250 US troops who specialise in logistics and calling in air strikes, started an operation a week ago with the aim of moving south from Ain Issa to take over the fertile cotton and grain growing land in the north of Raqqa province. This will bring them very close to Raqqa city on the Euphrates River, which Isis seized from other Syrian rebel groups in August 2013. An agricultural and transport centre with a population of 200,000, the city had the advantage of being a road hub centrally placed within the "caliphate" that gave Isis a direct link to Mosul to the east, the Turkish border to the north and Aleppo to the west. Down-river from two big dams and hydroelectric power stations on the Euphrates - Tishrin and al-Tabaqa - it was at first well supplied with electricity, although the SDF took Tishrin earlier in the year and its columns are now advancing on al-Tabaqa.

So far there has been limited fighting as Isis conserves its forces and pulls back from the hundreds of villages in north Raqqa. The Syrian Observatory for Human Rights says Isis has lost 61 fighters in the past week including a French commander and 24 children known as "the Caliphate's Cubs". Isis's strategy in Syria and Iraq is evidently to trade territory for time and prepare for a long guerrilla war without exposing its experienced fighters to the devastating firepower of the

US-led coalition of air forces. But military logic is not the only consideration here, because it would be politically damaging for Isis to give up too easily the last three big cities - Raqqa, Fallujah and Mosul - it holds in Syria and Iraq. In any case, people in the north Raqqa countryside are taking no chances and are leaving their villages to avoid the fighting. In Raqqa city they do not have this option: Isis is preventing them fleeing in the hope of forcing the coalition - overwhelmingly American in the case of Syria, where the US has carried out all but 235 of 3,715 air strikes - to limit its bombardment to avoid civilian casualties.

People in villages liberated by the SDF give graphic descriptions of what it was like to live under Isis rule for the past two and a half years. For reasons that Ameena came to understand all too well, many were worried that their teenage sons would be lured by Isis propaganda into volunteering to fight and die for the "caliphate". Jasem al-Ahmad, 42, a Sunni Arab from Hesha, a village north of Raqqa, was so concerned about his 15-year-old son that last year he sent him to relatives in Hasaka. He says that "it was not permitted for anybody to leave the region under Isis rule, but I got a smuggler to take him out of the village".

Isis gave priority to indoctrinating young people. Mr Ahmad says the previous educational curriculum was cancelled and replaced by religious courses which were obligatory for children and teenagers and were held in special centres in the villages and in Raqqa. "When they join the religious courses, they are called Lions of the Caliphate," Mr Ahmad says. "In general, people were not happy with these courses so they tried to keep their children at home."

As elsewhere in the so-called Islamic State, personal behaviour and appearance was regulated by severe punishments, starting with fines but rapidly graduating for repeat offenders to whipping. For un-Islamic shaving practices the penalty was a $25 (£17) to $30 fine, 30 lashes and attendance at a religious course for 45 days. The whip used was either an electrical cable or a thin slice from a car tyre with a metal wire inside it.

Mr Ahmad's experience is worth quoting at length because it gives a frightening insight into life lived under the constant threat of physical punishment. "Once I was caught smoking," he says. "They asked me to pay $10 and I answered that I did not have it. They decided to give me 30 lashes with a whip. I had the punishment and with the 20th lash I fainted. My cousin took me to the clinic and I stayed there for more than two weeks, suffering from the pain and the wounds."

Isis began its rule in this well-irrigated agricultural area by offering a range of services to farmers such as fertilisers, pesticides and veterinary assistance. But as Isis's income from oil sales fell, it increased taxes and fees, particularly over the past eight months. It demanded that people pay in US dollars as the Syrian pound fell sharply in value. Control of the big dams meant that electricity was widely available, but Isis charged high prices for it.

A feature of Isis's control, which makes outright opposition difficult and dangerous, is that it is merciless towards any type of individual or communal resistance. Six months ago people in a village described as being near Hutteen state farm, 12 miles north of Raqqa, tried to prevent Isis men taking away a local man for punishment. Isis called for reinforcements who besieged the village and eventually arrested 235 people - most of its population. Some were detained for a month and freed, while others are in jail.

A further intriguing development is that villagers say that in recent days there have been differences and even clashes between local and foreign members of Isis over how to respond to the SDF offensive. The local Isis fighters generally want to withdraw, possibly because they do not want to see their villages destroyed, while the foreigners, who are described as being mostly Saudi and Libyan, want to stay and fight.

Isis is being pressed back on many different fronts but it can still counterattack briskly and effectively, as it showed in recent fighting north of Aleppo. It has defeated armed opposition groups backed by the US and Turkey and expanded the section of the Turkish border it controls - giving it greater access to the outside world, although not on the scale it enjoyed two years ago. It wants to maintain its rule in heavily populated and fertile areas of north Aleppo province, which has a population of about 700,000, from which it can draw supplies and manpower. But its overall position is deteriorating sharply as it loses more and more of the Euphrates valley that used to be the spinal column of the "caliphate" stretching from Fallujah, west of Baghdad, in the south to Jarabulus on the Syrian-Turkish border. It also faces a more active front with the Syrian army, backed by the Russians, which at one stage appeared capable of pressing east from Palmyra towards

Raqqa and seizing it before the SDF. Overall, Isis commanders can still counter-attack but they have not found a new set of tactics to replace those made obsolete by coalition and Russian airpower.

Isis's position is weakening, but reports from displaced or recently liberated Syrians and Iraqis complaining about their grim life under Isis rule must be taken with a pinch of salt and can be misleading about the real state of public opinion. People escaping from Isis and wishing to persuade suspicious new hosts that they are not Isis secret agents have every incentive to stress the degree to which they and their neighbours have always detested it. Most importantly, all those in authority, in all parts of Syria and Iraq, are highly unpopular with their own people, to whom they have brought only violence and ruin. This is true of Isis, but it is also true of the Iraqi, Syrian and Kurdish governments. Their people only support them - in so far as they do - because they fear that the alternative will be even more dangerous to themselves, their families and their communities.

Friday, 3 June2016

CAUGHT BETWEEN TWO HELLS

Iraq is breaking up into competing centres of power and truck drivers are among those who can best describe the miseries of trying to travel from one fragment of the country to another. "Our life is horrible," says Mohammed Oday, a driver sitting with seven or eight others in the shade of a road bridge beside a parking lot filled with trucks on the outskirts of the oil city of Kirkuk.

All the drivers bar one were Sunni Arabs from Ramadi in Anbar province, a city that was 80 per cent destroyed by US airstrikes and Iraqi army artillery when they besieged it last year. "One room in my house is not as badly damaged as the others, so maybe my family could live in it," said one of the drivers, but he added that there was not much chance of this happening because the road to Anbar is too dangerous.

The furthest west he and the other truckers dared go on the road to Anbar was a checkpoint called Bzeybiz beyond which the road is controlled by much-feared Shia paramilitaries like Ketaeb Hezbollah and Asaib Ahl al-Haq. "They question us to see if we have Sunni names like Baqr, Othman, Omar or Muawiya," says Mr Oday. "And, if they don't arrest us, they charge between $800 (£555) and $1,000 per truck to let us through."

Levying charges on vehicles passing through the frequent check-points on the roads is one of Iraq's most remunerative rackets. Nothing moves without paying up and a good security reason can al-ways be given for imposing endless delays while the real purpose is to extract the maximum bribe. Police and army officers pay heavily to be given charge of checkpoints on well-used routes and paramilitary groups use them as a regular source of revenue. The drivers in Kirkuk spoke of paying $500 at smaller checkpoints or up to $5,000 if they are carrying perishable goods like chicken or eggs to the markets in Baghdad.

"It is not we drivers who pay the bribes but whoever owns the goods we are carrying," said one the drivers, only a few of whom own their own trucks. "Then the owner adds the cost of the payoffs to the price of goods when they are sold in the shops or the markets in Bagh-dad."

They agree that this helps explain why everything for sale in Iraq is so expensive, with a frozen chicken that costs $1 in Turkey costing $4 in Iraq and a pair of jeans made in a Turkish factory for $4 or $5 being sold in Irbil for $40. Iraq produces almost nothing itself apart from oil and gas, so everything needed by 33 million Iraqis has to be imported by road. Even the tomatoes sold in street stalls in Baghdad come from Iran.

The drivers accept these bribes as more like customs tariffs that are an inevitable fact of life, but they are angered by the extraordinary length of time they may have to wait - up to a month - to get through checkpoints where they should stay only a few minutes. They com-plain they are continually mistreated by officials and there is nothing they can do about it. "An officer killed a driver who lost his temper at a checkpoint on the road into Baghdad," says Mustafa Ali, a driver who came from Mosul two years ago.

Mr Ali's journey illustrates the extraordinary difficulties and dan-gers Iraqis face moving quite short distances within their own country. Unemployed in Mosul after it was captured by Isis in 2014, he went first to Syria, then to Turkey and finally to Irbil in the KRG area where he was arrested to make sure he was not an Isis agent.

Cleared of this, Mr Ali was sent to Kirkuk, which is controlled by Kurds but outside the KRG and told not to come back. This restriction limits his ability to earn a living because he cannot pass through the KRG to pick up goods from Turkey. "I wish I had stayed in Mosul despite Daesh," he says bitterly. "At least then I would be able to see my wife and children."

The life of these drivers is hard when they are working and harder still when they are not, because it is too dangerous for them to return to their homes. "Where are you living?" we asked and they replied in chorus: "Under this bridge. This is our address." Up to four months ago they got the occasional load to take to Basra in the far south in Iraq, but this is no longer happening, probably because of the cost of bribing checkpoints or the danger of being identified as a Sunni in Shia provinces. Trucking companies frequently switch between Sunni, Shia and Kurdish drivers so they will be driving through an area where their own community is in control.

The degree of danger for drivers varies greatly from one part of Iraq to another. For instance, a businessman involved in the freight forwarding business in Baghdad, who wished to remain anonymous, says that it costs about $7,000 in bribes to get a truck to al-Asad air base in Anbar province where US troops are stationed alongside the Iraqi army. The fees are often paid in advance through an intermediary in return for an unofficial permit and they increase the closer the vehicle gets to the base. He says that each of the big Shia paramilitary groups have their own territory, usually retaken from Isis, in which they can extract illicit revenues from the transport industry or through kidnapping individuals: Ketaeb Hezbollah dominates in eastern Anbar, Asaib Ahl al-Haq on the Samarra to Tikrit road and Badr in Diyala province to the north-east of Baghdad.

The drivers are angry at having to live a life in which they are at the mercy of predatory and sectarian checkpoints that treat them with contempt. "We are back to the Stone Age," says Mohammed Oday, describing how he sleeps on the open ground or in his truck, cannot go back to Ramadi or drive through Isis-held areas.

They probably thought that anything to do with Isis was too dangerous to talk about, though Mustafa Ali said that "we live between two hells: Daesh accuses us of being apostates and the government suspects that we are Daesh terrorists".

Iraq and Syria are both infested with checkpoints that are meant to provide security and detect Isis suicide bombers, but in practice this seldom happens. One reason may be that those manning the checkpoint are well aware that if they do detect a suicide bomber he will blow himself up immediately and they will be killed.

But another reason why the bombers get through so easily is that that those manning checkpoints see them primarily as a way of making money and an Isis bomber who pays a small sum will be waved through without being searched. "They must have bribed their way through a checkpoint," an intelligence official in Baghdad told *The Independent* in February when dozens of Isis gunmen and bombers launched a fierce attack at Abu Ghraib.

Long columns of stationary trucks, often stretching for miles, have been a frequent sight on Iraqi roads for years. The reason may be elaborate security checks or the Turkish border being closed or some more complicated reason, though a common feature of these stoppages is that those responsible for them do not care what happens to the drivers.

Last week I drove past a five-mile long immobile line of well over a thousand trucks loaded with sacks of grain outside of the town of Makhmour west of Irbil. I was surprised because I did not know that the KRG produced so much grain and in this I may have been right. Further enquiries revealed that Kurdish farmers were eager to get their heavily subsidised grain to a Baghdad government controlled silo near Makhmour and get paid. But the federal ministry of trade was causing delays because it suspects the farmers are engaged in a massive scam at its expense.

The ministry pays three times the market price for the grain so the KRG farmers purchase cheap grain from Iran and Turkey and sell it to the state at the inflated subsidised price as their own production. The ministry is in the future going to insist on more documentation to show where the grain really comes from, so the farmers are eager to off-load all the foreign grain they have imported while they still can.

Iraq is unlikely to disintegrate because all parts of the country are too dependent on the oil revenues from the oil fields concentrated in the southern provinces around Basra. Outside powers, who have done so much to weaken the central state by supporting their chosen proxies, do not want Iraq to formally cease to exist.

Its break-up would not be bloodless, but would be more like the Partition of India in 1947. To a substantial degree this is already happening, and three million Iraqis have already been displaced from their homes. Communities under threat have responded to danger by consolidating their control over a compact piece of territory and evicting everyone else.

South of Kirkuk, in Tuz Khurmatu, the Kurds and the Shia Turkman have split the town down the middle and neither side ventures into the others' domain. Even street cleaners working for the municipality have to come from the right sect and ethnicity. It is one more tricky disputed area through which Iraqi truck drivers will have to make their way.

Tuesday, 14 June 2016

TRUMPED UP LINKS TO ISIS ONLY PLAY INTO THE HANDS OF TERRORISTS

Isis will benefit from the slaughter carried out by Omar Mateen in Orlando regardless of how far it was involved in the massacre. It will do so because Isis has always committed very public atrocities which dominate the news agenda, spread fear and show its strength and defiance.

So far there is strong evidence that Isis motivated Mr Mateen in his attack, but not that it played a role in organising it as it did in the killings in Brussels and Paris. Isis's Albayan radio station based in Iraq, is saying that "God allowed Omar Mateen, one of the soldiers of the caliphate in America, to carry out an attack entering a crusader gathering in a night club...in Orlando, killing and wounding more than 100 of them." The FBI says that he made an emergency call just before he started shooting claiming allegiance to Isis.

Western media are likely to emphasise the Isis angle because it feeds into popular fear of a vast Isis-led conspiracy that menaces every home in the US and Europe. This is scarcely surprising since it is the worst terrorist attack in the US since 9/11, but it is worth keeping in mind that the casualties in Orlando are much less than the 200 killed last month by Isis suicide bombers in and around Baghdad over a four-day period and a further 150 in the Syrian cities of Tartous and Jableh on 23 May.

These massacres were barely reported by the Western media which tends to under-cover or overcover Isis actions, depending on whether Americans or Europeans are among the dead. This gives a distorted picture of the degree of danger posed by Isis, which at times appears to be on the wane and at others is exaggerated by round-the-clock news coverage to seem like a threat to our very existence.

These exaggerations play into the hands of Isis, a prime example being the infamous tweet from Donald Trump about the Orlando killings asking if President Obama is "going to finally mention the words radical Islamic terrorism? If he doesn't he should immediately resign in disgrace!" This is the sort of hysterical and divisive response that Isis likes to provoke and Mr Trump is being rightly castigated for making such a comment. But recall that David Cameron did much the same last December before the House of Commons vote on extending British airstrikes to Syria by warning MPs not to vote with "Jeremy Corbyn and a bunch of terrorist sympathisers."

An all-too-successful motive for Isis atrocities, whether they are carried out around Baghdad or the boulevards of Paris, is to provoke communal punishment whether it is against Sunni Arabs in Iraq or Muslims in general in the US or Europe. All sense of proportion is lost in what politicians in Northern Ireland forty years ago used to call "the politics of the last atrocity." Isis gains because excessive and all-embracing retaliation becomes the unwitting recruiting sergeant for the very movement it is supposedly trying to suppress.

Much of what Salafi-jihadi movements such as Isis and al-Nusra believe about gays, women, Shia Muslims and Christians comes out of Wahhabism, the extreme variant of Islam that is effectively the state religion of Saudi Arabia. The Saudis likewise punish homosexuality and transgenderism with death, whipping and imprisonment. In 2014, for instance, a man in Saudi Arabia was reportedly sentenced to three years in prison and 450 lashes for using Twitter to arrange dates with other men.

Wahhabi beliefs are close to the Salafi-jihadi ideology and over the last fifty years Wahhabism has become an increasing influence over mainstream Sunni Islam. Sunni who once saw Shia merely as a different type of Muslims now often view them as heretics who are outside Islam. Supported by the vast oil wealth of Saudi Arabia and the Gulf those trained to preach and oversee mosques have become increasingly extreme and, while they may not support terrorist attacks, their beliefs provide fertile soil for those who do.

Here we touch on the reasons why Western leaders in the US, France and Britain have so entirely failed to win "the War in Terror" which they have supposedly been fighting at vast expense since 9/11.

Few wars have been quite so demonstrably unsuccessful given that in 2001 al-Qa'ida had only a few hundred fighters at most in camps in Afghanistan and Pakistan, while today their militants rule millions in swathes of territory across the Middle East.

This has happened because the US and EU states have not wanted to acknowledge the link between the terrorism and their strategic Sunni allies such as Saudi Arabia, the Gulf monarchies, Turkey and Pakistan.

Fabrice Balanche of the Washington Institute for Near East Policy writes that "the jihadists who hit Paris and then Brussels on 22 March, 2016, had been indoctrinated in the Salafi ideology sponsored by Saudi funded mosques, indirectly financed by private donors in the Gulf, and tolerated by Turkey - the country through which they pass to Europe."

A further sign of the extent to which Western security services are wedded to their alliance with Saudi Arabia came this week when the CIA director John Brennan went out of his way to deny that the Saudi government or senior Saudi officials were involved in the 9/11 attack and that the 28 redacted pages of the 9/11 Commission report did not implicate them. Saudi Arabia has repeatedly denied any involvement.

The link between a mentally unstable security guard in Orlando and Isis may be limited, but it is still there and such attacks will continue to be inspired or organised by Isis so long as it exists. As has been the case since 9/11, Western states are refusing to confront their Sunni allies in the Middle East whose well-funded ideology creates the conditions in which terrorism flourishes.

Until they do, Orlando will only be the latest in a string of atrocities."

Saturday, 18 June 2016

ENDING TWO YEAR ISIS OCCUPATION OF FALLUJAH

Iraqi security forces are driving out Isis fighters from the government compound in the centre of Fallujah, the city 40 miles west of Baghdad that Isis has held for two-and-a-half years.

Heavily armed Interior Ministry police units say they raised the Iraqi flag over the main government buildings yesterday, including the police station and court houses, in the latest stage of an attack that began on 23 May.

Clouds of smoke were rising from the centre of Fallujah as it was hit by air strikes and artillery fire, while Isis snipers in the General Teaching Hospital tried to pick off advancing government troops.

After a week of heavy fighting on the outskirts of the city, a government spokesman said that Isis resistance had weakened. The offensive is led by elite federal police and Counter-Terrorism Service troops advancing along Baghdad Street that bisects the city which had a population of 300,000 before it was seized by Isis in January 2014. The number of the government forces has been put at 20,000, the majority of whom belonging to the Shia Hashd al-Shaabi.

Some 90,000 civilians remained at the start of the present assault of whom 68,000 have fled, many of them over the past 24 hours because Isis reversed its previous policy of forbidding anybody to leave on pain of death. Witnesses say that Isis was announcing by loudspeakers that everybody could leave, leading 6,000 families to depart on Thursday alone. Two bridges over the Euphrates River were opened allowing people to get away from the city centre.

But displacement camps have been overwhelmed. The former mayor of Fallujah before the Isis takeover, Issa al-Issawi, who now resides outside the city said: "we don't know how to deal with this large number of civilians".

The exodus of people from the city was also enabled by Isis fighters suddenly retreating from important checkpoints inside Fallujah witnesses told the Norwegian Refugee Council. The nature of this retreat is important because it could mean that Isis leaders have decided not to risk suffering devastating casualties among their experienced fighters by resisting to the last man in the face of an attack backed by US-led airstrikes which was bound to win in the end.

Isis pursued similar tactics in Ramadi, Sinjar and Tikrit of using snipers, mines and booby traps but fading away at the last minute, often using elaborate networks of tunnels in which to hide and later escape.

Nevertheless, the capture of Fallujah by Iraqi government forces, though still continuing and incomplete, is the most serious defeat suffered by Isis in Iraq. Its loss is so significant because the city is close to Baghdad and it has an historic significance for Sunni Arabs as a place always sympathetic to fundamentalist Islam which resisted the US in two famous sieges in 2004.

The Sunni Arabs make up a fifth of Iraq's 33 million population and their whole community is under pressure as their population centres are captured by the Iraqi security forces and Shia paramilitaries. Many people who once lived in Fallujah have fled to Iraqi Kurdistan because they cannot take refuge in Shia-dominated Baghdad where Shia often suspect displaced Sunni civilians of being Isis infiltrators. Men of all ages leaving Fallujah were being detained yesterday amid claims that some had been murdered and tortured earlier in the week by Shia paramilitaries.

It is unclear how badly Fallujah has been damaged by air strikes and shellfire, but Ramadi, the capital of Anbar province, was 70 per cent destroyed by artillery and bombing in the second half of last year at the end of which it was recaptured. Most of its population has yet to go home. Human rights organisations report that men from the city were confined in conditions so cramped that they could not lie down for days at a time.

Iraqi commanders say that Isis is at its last gasp but this is an exaggeration and in other parts of Iraq it has been able to make limited counter-attacks, killing 24 policemen at Tuz Kharmatu south of Kirkuk. Isis is likely to fight much harder for Mosul, which, with a population that once numbered two million, is by far the largest city held by Isis.

Saturday, 18 June 2016

CIA'S RELATIONSHIP WITH SAUDI ARABIA UNDERMINES THE FIGHT AGAINST ISIS

In 1996 the CIA set up a special unit called Alec Station with the aim of targeting Osama bin Laden and the al-Qa'ida network. It was headed by Michael Scheuer, who found the Saudis less than cooperative. "When we set up the unit in 1996 we asked the Saudis for some basic material on bin Laden, like his birth certificate, his financial records - obvious stuff," recalled Mr Scheuer many years later. "We got nothing."

The CIA unit pursuing bin Laden kept on requesting this mundane but necessary information about their target from the Saudis for the next three years but got no reply. "Finally, in 1999, we get a message from the [CIA] station chief in Riyadh, a Mr John Brennan," Mr Scheuer said in an interview published in *Kill Chain: Drones and the Rise of High-Tech Assassins* by my brother Andrew Cockburn. "He said we should stop sending these requests as it was 'upsetting the Saudis'."

The story is important because John Brennan has been director of the CIA since he replaced David Petraeus in 2013 and he was once again avoiding any upset to the Saudis last week by telling the Saudi-owned al-Arabiya television station that the 28 pages in the 9/11 Congressional Inquiry relating to Saudi Arabia that have never been released contain "no evidence to indicate that the Saudi government as an institution - or as senior Saudi officials individually - had supported the 9/11 attacks."

This is not the impression of others who have read the report and dodges the question of indirect Saudi support for or tolerance of al-Qa'ida in the past. But the important point is that in the 20 years between 1996 and 2016, the CIA and British security and foreign policy agencies have consistently given priority to maintaining their partnership with powerful Sunni states such as Saudi Arabia, the Gulf monarchies, Turkey and Pakistan over the elimination of terrorist organisations such as al-Qa'ida, al-Nusra, Isis and the Taliban.

This contradiction between what is required to destroy the Salafi-jihadi Sunni fundamentalist networks and the need to maintain the alliance with these Sunni states goes a long way to explain the failure of the vastly expensive "War on Terror". Commentators focus their criticism on Saudi Arabia and with good reason, but it was Pakistan that was crucial to the rise of the Taliban and Turkey to that of the extreme Islamists in Syria.

Mr Brennan does not take responsibility for this calamitous failure but he did admit its extent in revealing evidence to the Senate Intelligence Committee on Thursday. "Our efforts have not reduced the group's terrorism capability," he said. "The group would have to suffer even heavier losses of territory, manpower and money for its terrorist capacity to decline significantly."

Isis is certainly weaker than it once was at its apogee as its divided but numerous enemies press forward on multiple fronts in Iraq and Syria. Its call for "lone wolf" attacks by Isis militants in their own countries is because it is more difficult for them to pass to and fro across the Turkish border, which has been progressively sealed off by the advance of the Syrian Kurds backed by US air power. But Isis leaders are all too aware that an atrocity like the one committed in Orlando - as in Brussels in March, and Paris last November - propels their movement to the top of the news agenda for weeks at a time and, for all the obloquy they receive, augments their strength and acts as a recruiting tool.

Isis is transmuting into more of a terrorist movement using guerrilla tactics as the onslaught against the self-declared Caliphate grinds slowly forward. The slaughter of civilians abroad is designed to mask a real weakening of the de facto Isis state compared to a year ago when it was still capable of launching offensives that captured Ramadi and Palmyra. President Obama is much more realistic than his critics allow in his claim that his campaign against Isis is showing real gains.

Unfortunately, the credibility of his administration in convincing people of this is undermined by past exaggerations about victories over Isis that were swiftly contradicted by events.

What makes the current wave of terrorism different is that it is backed by the resources of a de facto state which, even in its current battered condition, can mobilise money, expertise, equipment and communications. The possession of territory with its own well-organised administration makes a great difference to the punching power of Isis when it comes to either terrorism or war.

It is helped also by its enemies' divisions, which are graphically on display at the moment in the battle for Aleppo where the CIA and the Pentagon pursue radically different policies. The Pentagon holds that its prime aim is to fight and defeat Isis, while the CIA maintains that Isis can be only be eliminated by first overthrowing President Bashar al-Assad and his regime. "The defeat of Assad is a necessary precondition to ultimately defeat [Isis]," a US intelligence official told Nancy Youssef of the Daily Beast. "As long as there is a failed leader in Damascus and a failed state in Syria, Isis will have a place to operate from." This makes the dubious assumption that there would be less of a failed state in Damascus after Assad than there was before his fall.

Much the same argument is made by 51 US State Department diplomats in an internal memo calling for military strikes against Assad's forces to compel him to abide by a ceasefire. It says that the Syrian government's barrel bombing of civilians is the "root cause of the instability that continues to grip Syria and the broader region". It calls for "a judicious use of stand-off and air weapons, which would undergird and drive a more focused and hard-nosed US diplomacy". The mid-level diplomats, taking advantage of a State Department channel for officials to diverge from official policy without damaging their careers, say that at present Assad feels under no pressure to agree to a ceasefire, known as a "cessation of hostilities", which excludes Isis and al-Nusra.

The diplomats' demand for air strikes appears extraordinarily naïve and ill-considered since the last thing that Syria needs is yet more violence. Their protest avoids the problem that the Syrian armed opposition is dominated by Isis, al-Nusra and Ahrar al-Sham. It is understandable that the diplomats should denounce Assad for carrying out atrocities, but they should also accept that the only alternative to his rule is the Islamists. The US has found to its cost over the last few years that there is no moderate armed opposition fighting Assad which it can support aside from the Syrian Kurdish paramilitary army and some Arab units under Kurdish control.

The dissident US diplomats may genuinely believe that peace will be brought closer by adding a US-Syrian government war to the cat's cradle of existing wars in Syria and Iraq. The CIA has a long dismal history since Afghanistan of being manipulated by jihadi groups and their Sunni government backers in Saudi Arabia and Pakistan. Before anybody talks of starting new conflicts, the priority should be the complete destruction of Isis."

Sunday, 17 July 2016

ISIS REIGN OF TERROR SPREADING

It was near inevitable that Isis should organise or inspire another atrocity in Western Europe after a string of defeats culminating in the loss of Fallujah to Iraqi government forces. Isis has always used acts of mass terrorism directed against civilians as a way of showing its strength and dominating the news agenda. It is part of its repertoire of tactics at all times, but particularly when it is suffering losses and hopes are rising that it is not only retreating but has gone into irreversible decline.

Isis had already reacted to defeat at Fallujah by sending a vehicle packed with explosives into the Karada district of Baghdad, where it exploded, killing 292 people. This happened just as the Iraqi government was congratulating itself on taking the city which people in the Iraqi capital believed was the source of many of bombs that have slaughtered them over the last three years.

Isis now claims that Mohammed Lahouaiej Bouhlel, who drove his truck through crowds of people in Nice, was one of their "soldiers". It is possible that they did not know what was going to happen until it was over, but the attack has all the hallmarks of an Isis mass killing: it was directed against civilians in a very public place and its savagery was so extreme that it inevitably instils fear and dominates the world news agenda for days on end. All that was needed to carry it out was a fanatical perpetrator willing to be killed as a proof of his faith.

This was the tactic of al-Qa'ida, shown most famously on 9/11, but Isis has used it on a greater scale and, even when it is on the retreat in Iraq and Syria, it can mobilise bombers swiftly and effectively.

The Isis attack on Ataturk Istanbul International Airport was carried out by gunmen and bombers from Central Asia, whom Turkish security had not identified as a threat because it supposed they were committed to overthrowing President Bashar al-Assad and his regime in Syria. What gives Isis' terrorism its relentless quality is that it is backed by a well-organised, if battered, state machine in the form of the socalled caliphate, that can mobilise men, equipment, expertise and money.

Isis is under pressure on almost every front in Iraq and Syria. It cannot withstand ground attacks backed by precision bombing from the US-led air armada and the same is true of the Syrian army supported by Russian bombers. This may weaken Isis, but does not put it permanently out of business because it can revert to guerrilla warfare and wait for its numerous enemies to fall out, as they invariably do. The Iraqi and Syrian governments are short of good combat troops and have difficulty occupying the territory they have taken.

It is often said that there can be no peace in Iraq without conciliating the Sunni Arabs, the community from which Isis draws its strength, but this is to underestimate the sectarian and ethnic cleansing now being carried out by all sides in the civil war engulfing Iraq and Syria. An increasing number of the Sunni Arab community in both countries - one-fifth of the population in Iraq and three-fifths in Syria - are being permanently displaced and are unlikely to go home.

The sectarian map of this part of the Middle East is being permanently redrawn, which can only intensify the fighting. Isis is a long way from total defeat, but it is giving up population centres and has not made a successful counter-attack for over a year. It will seek to spread its networks of militants to other countries and make sure that its retreats are masked by further atrocities like the ones in Baghdad and Nice."

AFTERWORD

Turkish president Recep Tayyip Erdogan, 23 May 2016

Tuesday, 23 July 2016

A NIGHTMARE SCENARIO IN ISTANBUL

The failed military coup is a disaster for Turkey, but its success would have been a far greater calamity. If the plotters had killed or captured President Recep Tayyip Erdogan then other parts of the armed forces might have joined them, but a civil war would have been inevitable as the security forces split and Erdogan's supporters fought back.

The disaster is that it will now be much more difficult for Turks to resist Erdogan establishing a monopoly of power. By resisting the coup as the leader of a democratically elected government, he has enhanced his legitimacy. Moreover, all opposition to his rule can be labelled as support for terrorism and punished as such.

"Human rights and democracy will be weaker and they were already in a bad way before the coup," says a critic of Erdogan, who does not want his name published, adding that it is difficult for him to criticise Erdogan today while he is under threat from military conspirators. He has no doubt that the attempted putsch was carried out by the followers of Fethullah Gulen, who has lived in the US since 1999. Leaving aside the confessions of the plotters, which may have been forced, only the Gulenists had a network of adherents capable of staging an uprising in so many units of the security forces.

"Fethullah did not help us, he killed us," says the Turkish commentator bitterly. "He left us totally in the hands of Erdogan."

He says that the Gulenists operate in two different ways: they have a moderate public face with schools, universities, media and business associations, but they also have always had a secret organisation devoted to taking positions of power within the military, police and security services. As long ago as 1987, the movement was being investigated for infiltrating military colleges. It is now being compared to the Roman Catholic organisation Opus Dei, notorious for its links to Franco and other rightwing governments, though a better analogy might be a secretive cult with a charismatic leader.

The coup went off half-cock. It was staged prematurely because of fear of an imminent purge of Gulenists in the military. Analysts have been explaining how badly organised the attempt was and how it could never have succeeded.

But the initial response of the government to the putsch was equally cack-handed, with Erdogan saying that he first heard something was amiss from his brother-in-law who phoned him between 4pm and 4.30pm on 15 July to say that soldiers were stopping cars next to the Beylerbeyi Palace in Istanbul.

Erdogan's account of what happened next is worth quoting in order to convey the atmosphere of confusion in the first hours of the abortive takeover. He says his brother-in-law "was telling me that soldiers were actually cutting off streets, and they were not allowing cars to proceed to take to the bridge. When I got the news, initially I did not believe that this was happening and I called the head of national security, the head of national intelligence, I could not reach him. I called the Chief-of-Staff of the armed forces, I could not reach him, they were not in a position to be able to answer their phones. Then I tried to contact the Prime Minister, and although with some difficulty, we were able to get into contact."

It was only almost four hours later, at 8 pm, that Erdogan made plans to act by contacting the media - quite long enough for the pro-coup forces to have eliminated him. If victory goes to the side that makes the fewest mistakes, then it was a close run thing. Aside from their organisational failings, the plotters made a miscalculation in im-agining that, because Turks are deeply divided between supporters and opponents of Erdogan, the latter might side with anybody trying to get rid of him by physical force.

In the event, the plotters found no support because people felt, as one Kurdish activist was quoted as saying, that "the worst politician is better than the best general".

Much now depends on the extent to which Erdogan sees the fail-ure of the coup as a heaven-sent excuse to remove all who do not obey him. The temptation is clearly there: some 60,000 soldiers, judges, prosecutors, civil servants and teachers have been detained, arrested or sacked.

All 3.3 million civil servants in Turkey have been told to stay in their jobs, presumably so they can be investigated. The crackdown un-der the State of Emergency appears to be spreading well beyond the circle of those implicated in the coup or connected to the Gulenists.

Overreaction by the state may be deliberately contrived in order to benefit from the crisis, but there is also real fear mixed with para-noia that the coup is not over.

Supporters of the government tweeted yesterday that there might be a second attempt and some military units have been con-fined to their bases. Meanwhile, the coup is being presented as a symbol of evil, as was Guy Fawkes' Gunpowder Plot of 1605 in English political tradition. Public demonstrations of anticoup feeling are being demanded by the state, with people asked to attend daily demonstra-tions and actors in Istanbul being asked to produce an anti-coup video.

The next few weeks will tell if Erdogan is going to target all dis-sent and further divide a deeply divided country. He may have difficulty in pursuing the war against Kurdish guerrillas in south-east Turkey and, at the same time, purging the Second Army that is meant to be fighting them and whose commanding general is under arrest. It might be sensible to conciliate the Kurds, with whom Erdogan was negotiating not so long ago, but his combative political instincts are more likely to lead him to opt for confrontation.

Isis will benefit from the new political landscape because security forces will be tracking Gulenist sleepers rather than Isis cells. Isis will gain from the anti-American mood in Turkey post-coup because the government and much of the population are convinced that the US was implicated in the attempt. Turks are convinced of a US role, citing as evidence Gulen's long presence outside Philadelphia. Isis will seek the support of a widening anti-US constituency in Turkey. Relations between Ankara and Washington were not good before; they are about to get worse. Erdogan emerges politically stronger from the crisis, but he rules a weakened Turkish state. The army and state institutions are being hollowed out by purges and loyalty, not competence, becomes the test for advancement. Turkish involvement in Syria has produced only failure: sectarian and ethnic warfare between Sunni and Shia, Kurd and non-Kurd, is infecting Turkey.

Saturday, 30 July 2016

NOW TURKEY?

Coup and purge are tearing Turkey apart. The Turkish armed forces, for long the backbone of the state, are in a state of turmoil. Around 40 per cent of its generals and admirals have been detained or dismissed, including senior army commanders. They are suspected of launching the abortive military takeover on 15-16 July, in which at least 246 people died, parliament and various security headquarters were bombed and a near successful bid took place to kill or capture President Recep Tayyip Erdogan.

In response, Mr Erdogan and his government are carrying out a purge of everybody from soldiers to teachers connected in any way to the movement of the US-based cleric Fethullah Gulen which is accused of organising the coup. Among media outlets closed in the last few days are 45 newspapers, 16 TV channels - including a children's channel - and 23 radio stations. People fearful of being implicated in the plot have been hurriedly disposing of Gulenist books and papers by burning them, throwing them into rivers or stuffing them into rubbish bins.

Five years ago Turkey looked like the most stable and successful country in the Middle East and an example that its neighbours might like to follow. But instead of Iraq and Syria becoming more like Turkey, it has become more like them in terms of political, ethnic and sectarian division.

Mr Erdogan's personal authority is being enhanced by his bravery and vigour in defeating the coup and by the removal of remaining obstacles to his rule. But the failed putsch was also a sign that Turkey, a nation of 80 million people with an army 600,000 strong, is becoming weaker and more unstable. Its leaders will be absorbed in the immediate future in conducting an internal purge and deciding who is loyal and who is not. While this is going on, the country faces pressures on many fronts, notably the war with Kurdish guerrillas in the south-east, terror attacks by Isis and diplomatic isolation stemming from disastrous Turkish involvement in the war in Syria.

The security organisations, never very assiduous in pursuing salafi-jihadi rebels, will be devoting most of their efforts to hunting down Gulenists. Isis and al-Qaeda type movements such as the Nusra Front will benefit from the anti-American atmosphere in Turkey, where most believe that the US supported the coup.

The Turkish armed forces used to be seen as a guarantee of Turkey's stability inside and outside the country. But the failed coup led to their breaking apart in a manner that will be very difficult to reverse. No less than 149 out of a total of 358 generals and admirals have been detained or dishonourably discharged. Those arrested include the army commander who was fighting the Kurdish insurrection in south-east Turkey and the former chief of staff of the air force.

Many Turks have taken time to wake up to the seriousness of what has happened. But it is becoming clear that the attempted putsch was not just the work of a small clique of dissatisfied officers. It was rather the product of a vast conspiracy to take over the Turkish state that was decades in the making and might well have succeeded. At the height of the uprising, the plotters had captured the army chief of staff and the commanders of land, sea and air forces.

They were able to do so through the connivance of guards, private secretaries and aides who occupied crucial posts. The Interior Minister complains that he knew nothing about the coup attempt until a very late stage because the intelligence arm reporting to him was manned by coup supporters. Mr Erdogan gave a near comical account of how the first inkling he had that anything was amiss came between 4pm and 4.30pm on the day of the coup from his brother-in-law who had seen soldiers blocking off streets in Istanbul. The President then spent four hours vainly trying to contact the head of the national intelligence agency, the chief of staff and the Prime Minister, none of whom could be found. Mr Erdogan apparently escaped from his holiday hotel on the Aegean with 45 minutes to spare before the arrival of an elite squad of soldiers with orders to seize or kill him.

There is little question left that the followers of Fethullah Gulen were behind the coup, despite his repeated denials. "I don't have any doubt that the brain and backbone of the coup were the Gulenists," says the journalist Kadri Gursel, who is usually a critic of the government. He adds that he is astonished by the degree to which the Gulenists were able to infiltrate and subvert the armed forces, judiciary and civil service. He says that the closest analogy he can think of to recent events is in the famous 1950s film Invasion of the Body Snatchers, in which aliens take over an American town without anybody noticing until it is almost too late.

The coup was so unexpected that Turkey today is full of people asking questions about their future and that of their country to which there are no clear answers. Will Mr Erdogan exploit the opportunity offered by the failed coup to demonise all opponents and not just Gulenists as terrorists? Around 15,000 people have been detained, of whom 10,000 are soldiers. The presidential guard has been stood down. One third of the judiciary has been sacked. So far most of the journalists and media outlets targeted have some connection with the Gulenists, but few believe that the clampdown on dissent will end there. "Erdogan's lust for power is too great for him to show restraint in stifling opposition in general," predicts one intellectual in Istanbul who, like many interviewed for this article, did not want his name published. When one small circulation satirical magazine published a cartoon mildly critical of the government last week, police went from shop to shop confiscating copies.

For the moment, Mr Erdogan is benefiting from a degree of national solidarity against the conspirators. Many Turks, and not just his supporters, criticise foreign governments and media for making only token condemnations of the coup before demanding restraint in the conduct of the post-coup purge. They point out that if the coup had been that little bit more successful, then Turkey would have faced a full-blown military dictatorship or a civil war or both. Mr Erdogan said in an interview that foreign leaders who now counsel moderation would have danced for joy if he had been killed by the conspirators.

Sabiha Senyucel, the research director of the Public Policy and Democracy Studies think-tank in Istanbul says that the evening of the coup "was the worst of my life". She complains that foreign commentators did not take on board that "this was a battle between a democratically elected government and a military coup." She has co-authored a report citing biased foreign reporting hostile to Mr Erdogan and only mildly critical of the coup-makers. She quotes a tweet from an MSNBC reporter at the height of the coup attempt, saying that "a US military source tells NBC News that Erdogan, refused landing rights in Istanbul, is reported to be seeking asylum in Germany."

Turkey is deeply divided between those who adore and those who hate Mr Erdogan. Ms Senyucel says that "there are two parts of society that live side by side but have no contact with each other". But, even so, it is difficult to find anybody on the left or right who does not suspect that at some level the US was complicit in the coup. Mr Erdogan is probably convinced of this himself, despite US denials, and this will shape his foreign policy in the future. "The lip-service support Erdogan got from Western states during and immediately after the coup shows his international isolation," said one observer. The Turkish leader is off to see President Vladimir Putin on 9 August, though it is doubtful if an alliance with Russia and Iran is really an alternative to Turkey's long-standing membership of Nato.

Mr Erdogan can claim that the alternative to him is a bloody minded collection of brigadier generals who showed no restraint in killing civilians and bombing parliament. But the strength and reputation of the Turkish state is being damaged by revelations about the degree to which it has been systematically colonised since the 1980s by members of a secret society. Gulenist candidates for jobs in the foreign ministry were supplied with the answers to questions before they took exams, regardless of their abilities. The diplomatic service, once highly regarded internationally, received an influx of monoglot Turkish-speaking diplomats according to the Foreign Minister.

"The state is collapsing," says one commentator, but adds that much will depend on what Mr Erdogan will do next. In the past he has shown a pragmatic as well as a messianic strain accompanied by an unceasing appetite for political combat and more power. His meeting last week with other party leaders, with the notable exception of the Kurds, may be a sign that he will be forced to ally himself with secularists. He will need to replace the ousted Gulenist officers in the army and many of these will be secularist victims of past purges by the Gulenists.

Turkey is paying a heavy price for Mr Erdogan's past alliances and misalliances. Many chickens are coming home to roost. The Gulenists were able to penetrate the armed forces and state institutions so easily because between 2002 and 2013 they were closely allied to him and his ruling Justice and Development Party in opposition to the secularists. Isis has been able to set up a network of cells in Turkey because until recently the Turkish security forces turned a blind eye to salafi-jihadis using Turkey as a rear base for the war in Syria. Mr Erdogan arguably resumed confrontation and war with the Kurdistan Workers' Party as an electoral ploy to garner nationalist support after his failure to win the general election on 7 June last year.

PHOTO CAPTIONS AND COPYRIGHTS

ALSO AVAILABLE FROM THE INDEPENDENT

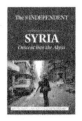

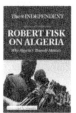

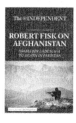

CPSIA information can be obtained at www.ICGtesting.com
Printed in the USA
BVOW06s1301070916

460927BV00005B/15/P